KETTLE'S YARD ART & ARTISTS

KETTLE'S YARD

ART & ARTISTS

Edited by Inga Fraser

Kettle's Yard, University of Cambridge

CONTENTS

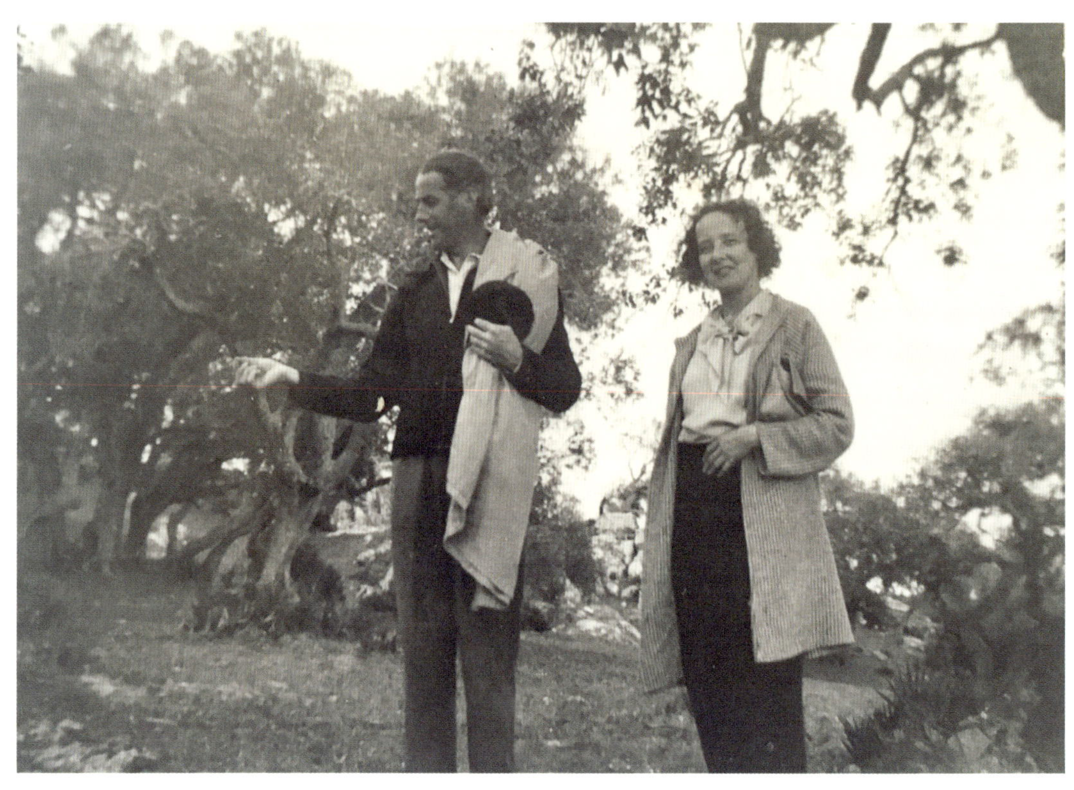

Jim and Helen Ede in Tangier, late 1930s

INTRODUCTION

INGA FRASER

Kettle's Yard Art & Artists is an anthology of writings on the artists whose works were collected by H.S. (known as 'Jim') Ede and displayed at Kettle's Yard, University of Cambridge. The majority of writing is drawn from Ede's letters to and from these artists, alongside a handful of excerpts from published or manuscript essays by Jim Ede, all held within the Papers of H.S. Ede in the Kettle's Yard Archive.

Jim Ede's earliest published work of art history was about artists of the Italian Renaissance. In a small book on Quattrocento Florentine drawings, Ede discussed the work of Fra Angelico, Sandro Botticelli, Masaccio, Leonardo da Vinci and others in a tone of interested familiarity. He found in their drawings the 'swift capture and light notation of a visual idea', and the 'subtleties of hesitation' that - to his mind - brought the viewer into 'immediate contact with the artist'.[1] But it was through sustained contact with artists of his own time - the twentieth century - that Ede found his purpose. The artists whose works now comprise the Kettle's Yard collection, and who feature as subjects in this anthology, are resolutely modern. Their work, their ideas - and sometimes the environment they created in their studios - prompted Jim Ede to become a collector and to discover the value of living with art. He promoted these artists' work in his writing and via his lectures in the UK and in the United States. Most prominently, his values were expressed through keeping 'open house' at the homes he shared with his wife Helen Ede (née Helene Schlapp) at 1 Elm Row in London (1925-1936), where their two children Elisabeth and Mary grew up, at Whitestone in Tangier (1936-1952) and at Kettle's Yard in Cambridge (1957-1973).

Jim Ede wrote and spoke about some artists in his collection more than others, and among his papers are numerous letters and other texts about the artists he was closest to: Ben and Winifred Nicholson, Christopher Wood and David Jones. Not every artist whose work is on display at Kettle's Yard is included in this book.

1 H.S. Ede, *Florentine Drawings of the Quattrocento* (London: Ernest Benn Ltd., 1926) p. 6.

Rather, it focuses on those the Edes knew, whose work they had the closest contact with and supported over many years. Some artists within, who are very well represented in the Kettle's Yard collection, Jim Ede never met, most notably Alfred Wallis and Henri Gaudier-Brzeska. Other artists who he greatly admired, sometimes met, and frequently cited, are not, as the Edes were never in a position to acquire their works. Pablo Picasso and Henri Rousseau can be counted in this category.

Throughout his writing on art and artists, Jim Ede remains sensitive to his personal encounter with and experience of particular artworks. He believed this brought him closest to artists' original ideas and intentions. This intimate dialogue defined Ede's way of life, and was something he wanted to help others experience. Ede gave and sold to public museums and galleries, lent works to students, and established bursaries to enable young people to travel, see art and meet artists as he had done. Above all, he welcomed visitors to his home and encouraged them to get to know his collection.

Kettle's Yard's engagement with art and artists did not stop when the Edes retired to Edinburgh in 1973, but broadened through the staging of temporary exhibitions, in gallery spaces that were first opened in 1970 and extended and remodelled several times over. The collection has also expanded since 1973 through gift and bequest, and such acquisitions have occasionally brought new artists into the Kettle's Yard house, and into dialogue with its visitors. As Ede himself recommended: 'We need to see things as they are and not as they used to be; our formed judgements of yesterday cannot possibly be our judgements of to-day. We ask ourselves what is happening in painting, and in doing so we ask what is happening in life.'[2]

2 Jim Ede, 'Foreword', *7th Exhibition of the Seven and Five Society*, (London: Beaux Arts Gallery, 1927) pp. 2-3.

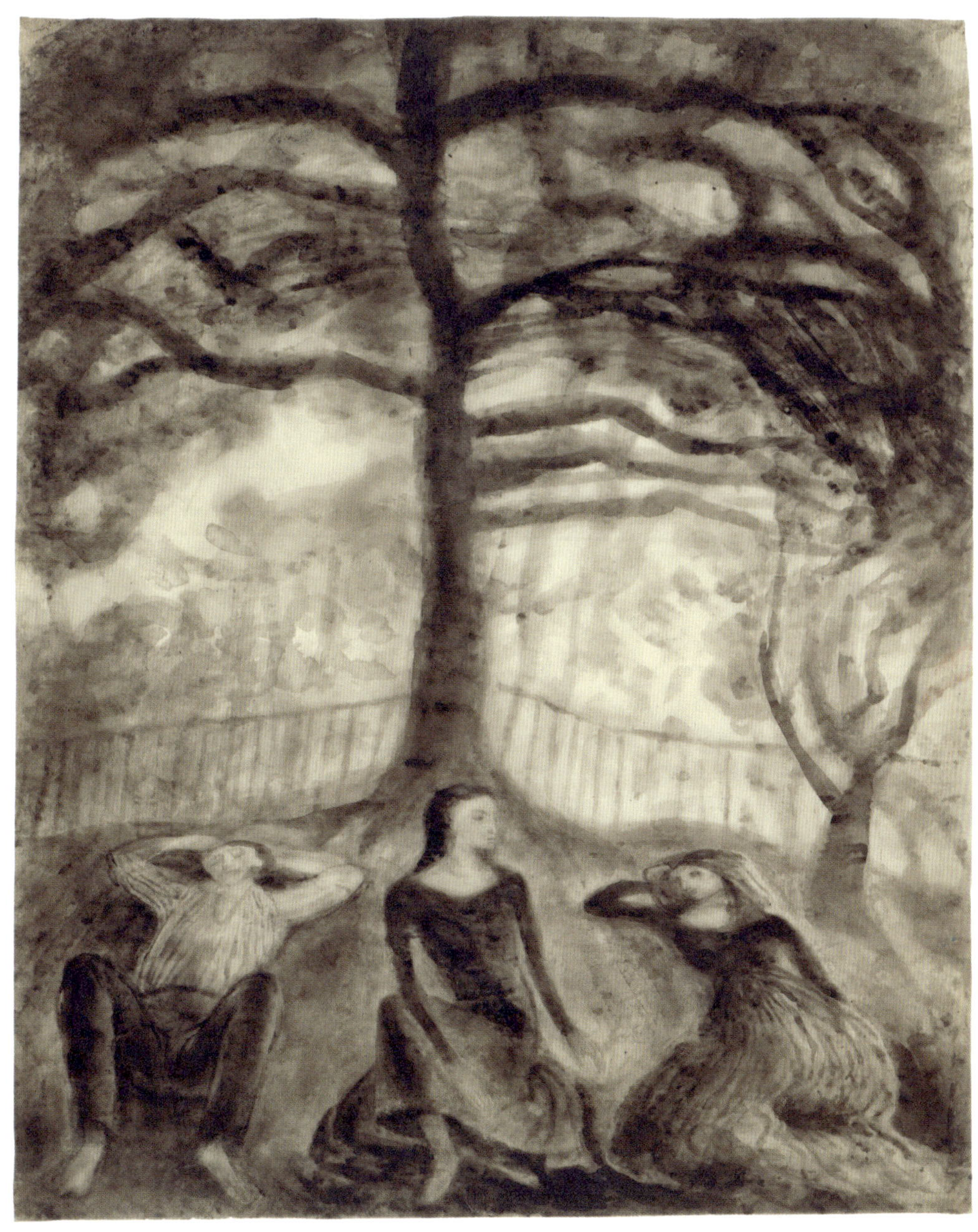

Elisabeth Vellacott, *Figures under a Tree*, 1951
Brush and ink on tracing paper, 60.2 × 49.6 cm
KY01324

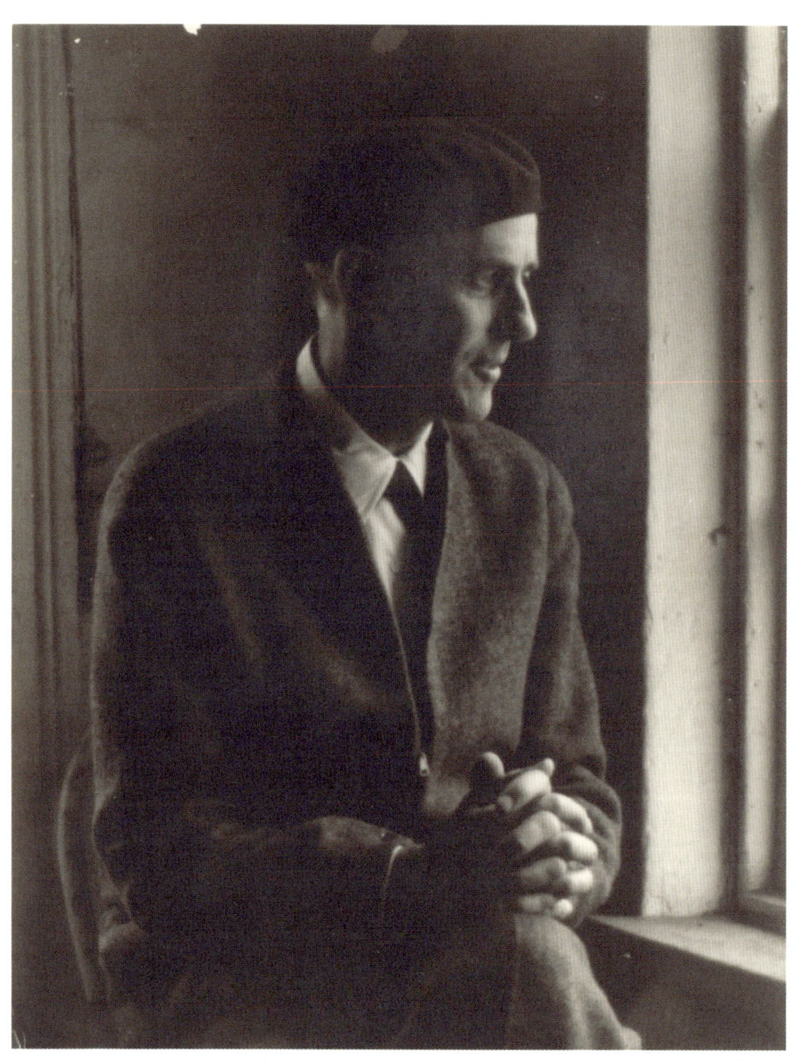

Richard Pousette-Dart, *Portrait of H.S. ('Jim') Ede*, c. 1944
Photograph, 32 × 24.5 cm
KY01395

WHAT ARE PICTURES?

JIM EDE

It is impossible to know what you will find in a picture, for it is a window opening onto life, a window opening onto mystery, a window opening onto God. The joy of seeing through these windows is so real, that it is worth a great effort to train the eyes to see.

[...] we have, I believe, a natural instinct to understand what we see in art, this instinct only needs sharpening. [...] We must always be looking at pictures and looking at nature, not in a spirit of antagonism but with a desire to learn, to see; and we will see.

[...] We are interested to read the lives of great people, to learn their reaction to usual daily events; how they coloured this or that thought; for in knowing the details of their lives, we can more fully appreciate that rich depth of texture from which their outward actions spring. [...]

To look into the details of pictures or of sculpture is often to approach, not only to a knowledge of what the artist was like, but to what the work itself conveys [...]

[...] the arts spring from a most specialised world; a world every bit as specialised as that of mathematics, astronomy, or science, and that familiarity with them will take the same amount of applied devotion. There is, however, a great difference, for I believe that in regard to the visual arts [...] we each one of us have a natural inclination [...]

— Extracts from Jim Ede [Unpublished lecture]
'What are pictures?', 1940s. Kettle's Yard Archive.
Papers of Harold Stanley 'Jim' Ede. KY/EDE/4/3/2.

MAKING FRIENDS WITH ARTISTS: A TIMELINE

1921 Jim Ede starts work at the National Gallery, London - initially as a photographic assistant, but later as an assistant at the National Gallery of British Art, known as the Tate Gallery.

1924 Jim and Helen meet Ben and Winifred Nicholson and through them, Christopher Wood. David Jones also becomes a close friend.

Jim Ede meets the artist Edward Wolfe at the home of the art historians Bernard and Mary Berenson, 'Villa I Tatti' in Florence, Italy.

1925 Jim Ede becomes assistant secretary for the Contemporary Art Society.

1926 The Edes regularly entertain guests at their Georgian townhouse at 1 Elm Row in Hampstead, London. They welcome artists, musicians, poets, collectors and actors including the Nicholsons, Henry Moore and Abani Roy.

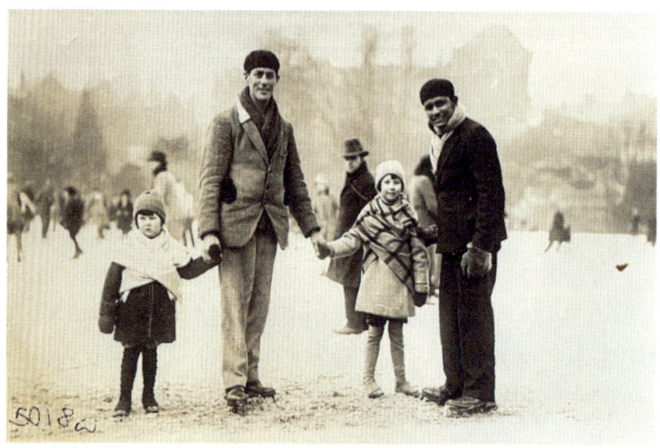

Mary, Jim and Elisabeth Ede with Abani Roy, late 1920s

During visits to Paris Jim Ede meets artists including Constantin Brâncuși, Georges Braque, Marc Chagall, Naum Gabo, Natalia Goncharova, Joan Miró, Antoine Pevsner and Pablo Picasso.

1927 Jim Ede writes a foreword in the catalogue of the 1927 Seven and Five Society exhibition in London, which includes works by Jessica Dismorr, Sophie Fedorovitch, Ivon Hitchens, Evi Hone, Sidney Hunt, Cedric Morris, Betty Muntz, Ben Nicholson, Winifred Nicholson, Lena Pillico, Colin Sealy, Edward Wolfe and Christopher Wood.

The Edes purchase the Estates of the French sculptor Henri Gaudier-Brzeska and his partner, the writer Sophie Gaudier-Brzeska via an intermediary.

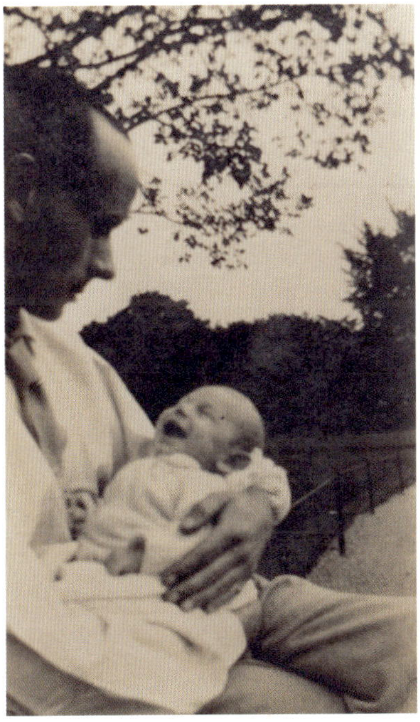

Ben Nicholson with his son Jake, 1934

1928 Jim Ede meets the potter William Staite Murray after writing a catalogue text for his exhibition with Ben and Winifred Nicholson at the Lefevre Gallery, London.

Sculptor Barbara Hepworth first visits the Edes at Elm Row with her then husband, John Skeaping.

1929 Jim Ede begins corresponding with Alfred Wallis and buying his paintings.

1930 The first edition of Jim Ede's biography of Henri Gaudier-Brzeska (later titled *Savage Messiah*) is published. Jim Ede meets the young artist Winston McQuoid.

1933 Faber publish H.S. Ede, *A Chart of British Artists 1560–1860*.

1936 Jim Ede resigns from the Tate Gallery and the Contemporary Art Society and moves with his family to Tangier, Morocco.

1937 The Edes travel to the United States where Jim Ede lectures on art at venues including The Frick Collection in New York and the Fogg Art Museum at Harvard, Massachusetts.

1940 Jim Ede meets artist Richard Pousette-Dart in New York.

1949 On a visit to Scotland with Helen during the summer, Jim Ede gets to know the work of Kate Nicholson, daughter of Winifred and Ben Nicholson.

1950 While on a lecture tour in the United States, Jim Ede meets the painter William Congdon.

1957 The Edes renovate the four small houses in Cambridge that become Kettle's Yard, opening their home to visiting University students every weekday afternoon during term.

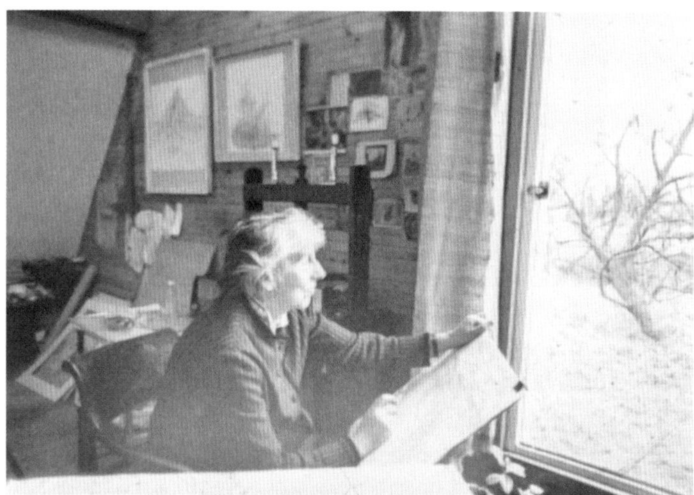

Elisabeth Vellacott in her studio, Hemingford Grey, undated

1958 Jim Ede befriends and acquires work by artists including Roger Hilton, George Kennethson and Elisabeth Vellacott.

1959 Jim Ede is awarded the French Légion d'Honneur following donations of works by Henri Gaudier-Brzeska to the Musée des Beaux-Arts in Orléans and the Musée National d'Art Moderne in Paris.

1962 The Edes meet a number of artists whose works they would begin to collect, including John Blackburn, Avinash Chandra, David Peace and Italo Valenti. Jim Ede also acquires a work by Simon Nicholson, son of Barbara Hepworth and Ben Nicholson.

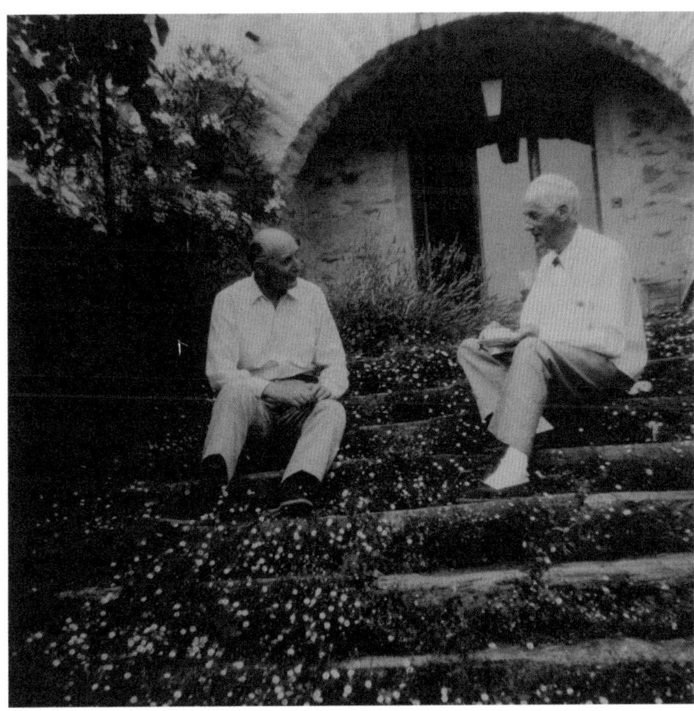

Italo Valenti and Jim Ede in Locarno, 1968, photographed by Anne de Montet

1964 Jim Ede donates manuscripts by Sophie and Henri Gaudier-Brzeska and paintings by Alfred Wallis and Christopher Wood to the University of Essex.

1965 The Edes purchase works by Gregorio Vardanega.

1966 Kettle's Yard is given to the University of Cambridge. The Edes remain in residence and Jim is given the role of 'honorary curator'.

A substantial gift of sculptures and drawings by Henri Gaudier-Brzeska is made to the Tate Gallery.

At the Edes' invitation, Bryan Pearce and his mother Mary Pearce come to stay in Cambridge where the artist makes a number of paintings of the city's architecture.

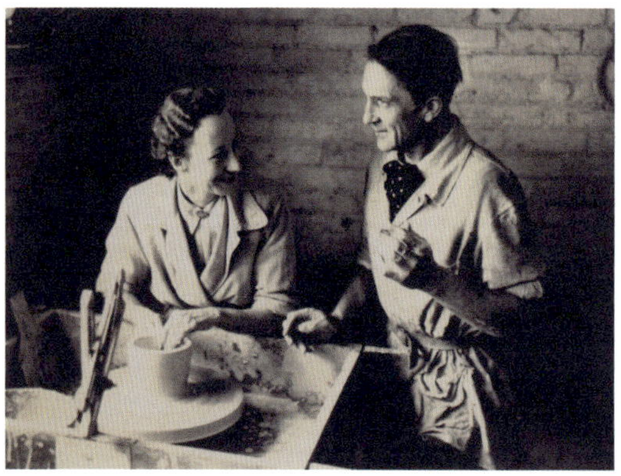

Zoë and Jan Ellison, c. 1940s

1967 Jim is promoted to Chevalier de la Légion d'Honneur after further gifts of works by Henri Gaudier-Brzeska to French museums.

Zoë Ellison brings her students from the Cambridge School of Art to visit Kettle's Yard.

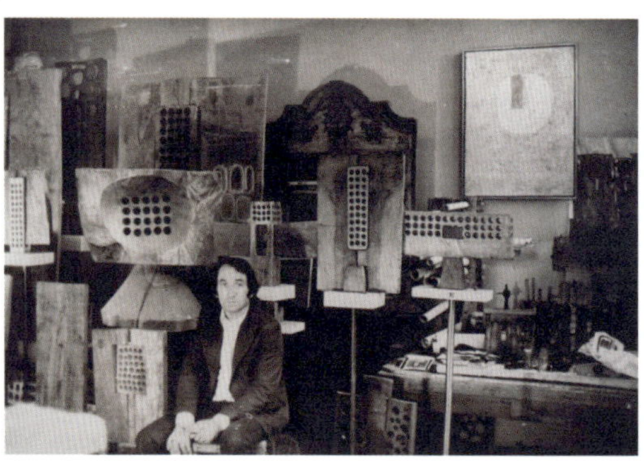

Ovidiu Maitec in his studio in Bucharest, 1973

1969 Jim Ede meets Ovidiu Maitec at the artist's Circle Gallery exhibition in London. Ede also acquires Ian Hamilton Finlay's *Poem/Print No. 11*, having known Finlay since 1964.

1970 On 5 May, an extension to Kettle's Yard designed by Sir Leslie Martin and David Owers, is opened by His Royal Highness The Prince of Wales with a performance by Daniel Barenboim and Jacqueline du Pré. The extension includes a gallery for temporary exhibitions of modern and contemporary art.

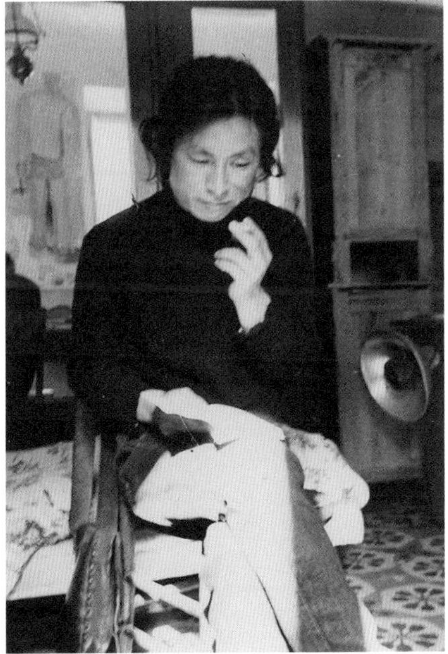

Kenji Umeda in Carrara, Italy, 1973

Artist Kenji Umeda visits Kettle's Yard while living in Cambridge, and begins helping Jim Ede with cleaning tasks in the house.

1971 Jim Ede discovers the work of Lucie Rie via a series of exhibitions staged at Kettle's Yard by Henry Rothschild.

1973 In June the Edes leave Cambridge for Edinburgh.

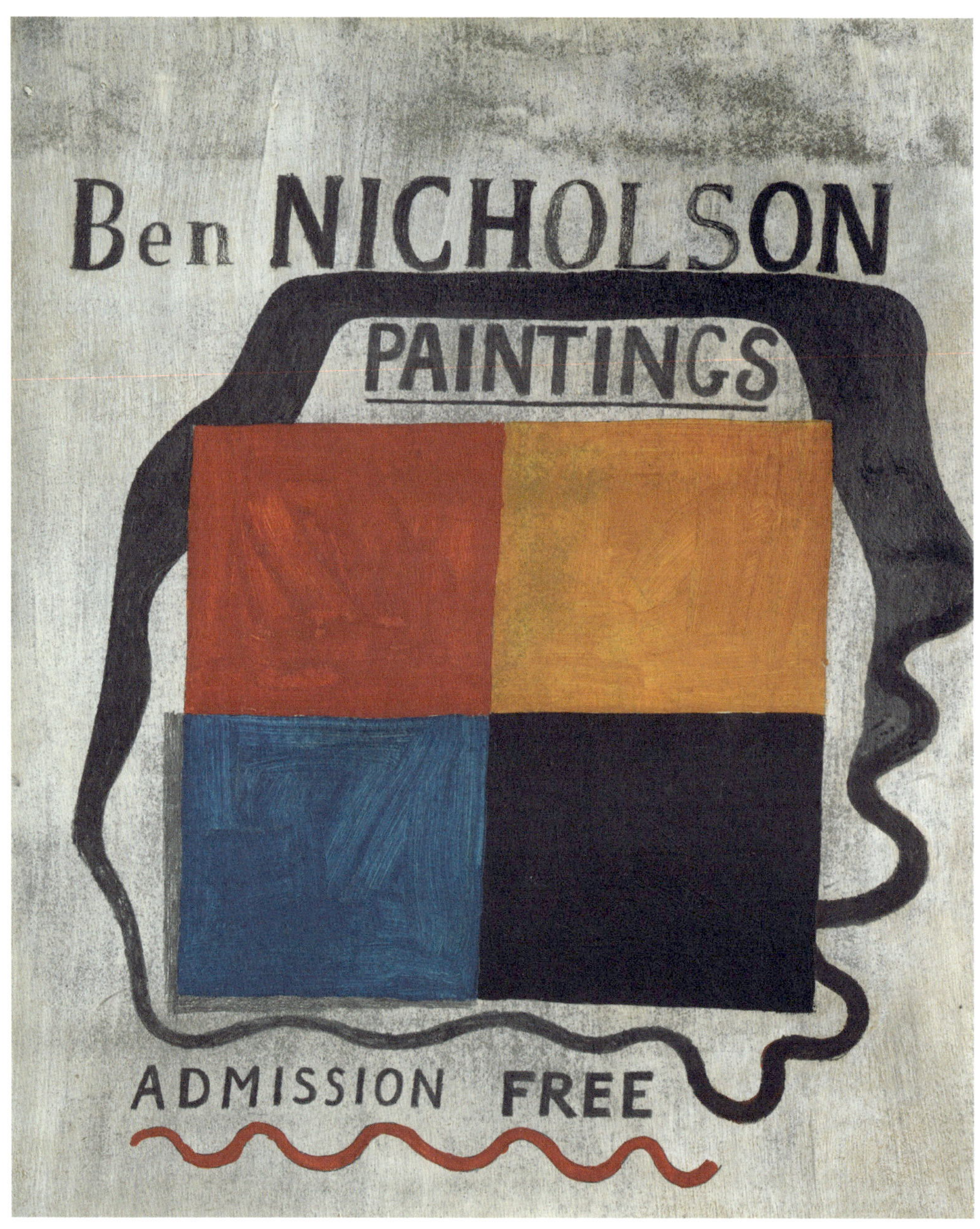

Ben Nicholson, *circa 1933 (exhibition sign)*, c. 1933
Oil paint on linoleum, 49.5 × 41 cm
KY00646.EH

ARTISTS A–Z

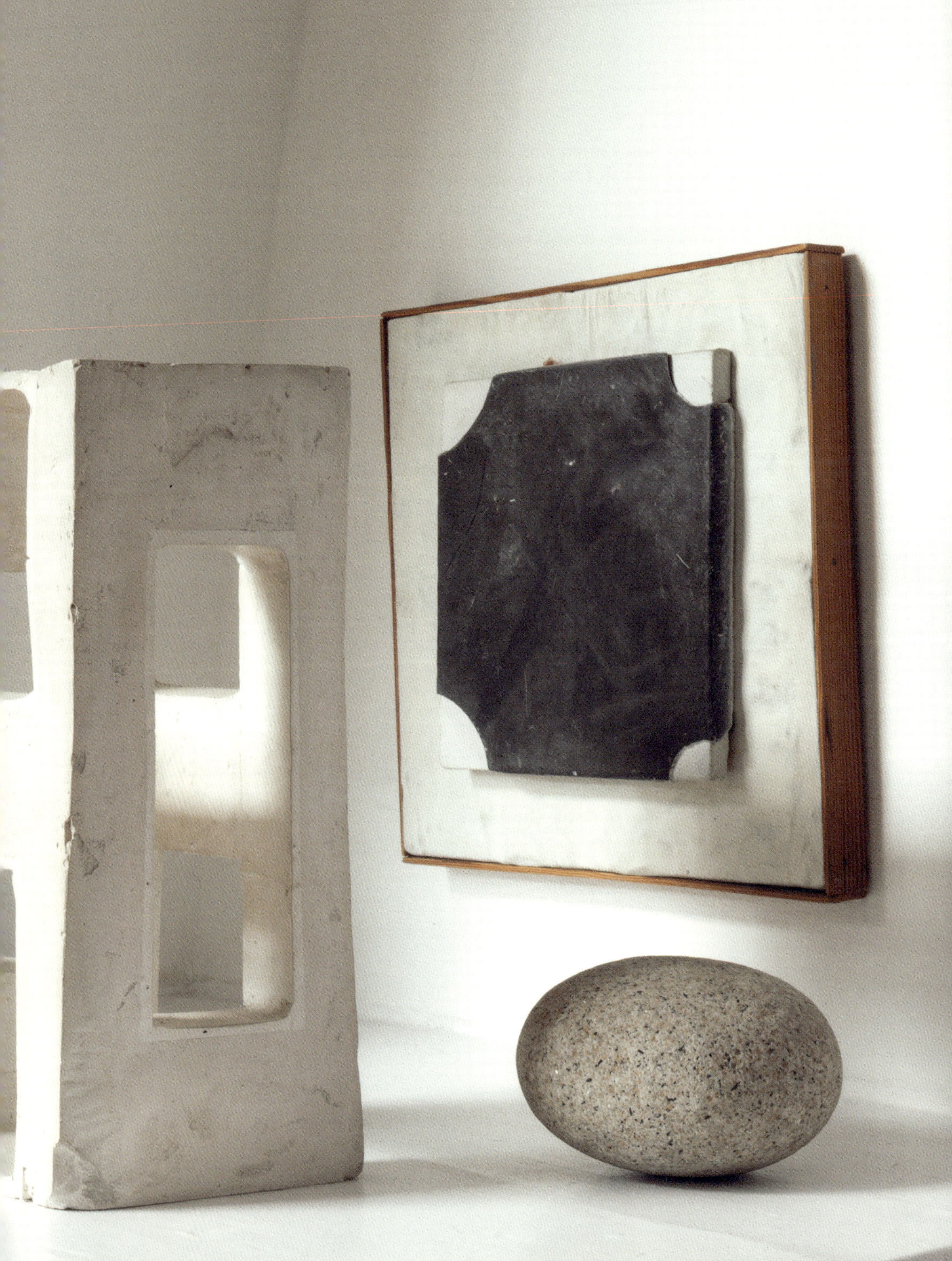

JOHN BLACKBURN

(1932–2022)

John Blackburn was born in Luton and studied at the Thanet School of Art in Margate, and later at the Maidenhead School of Art in Berkshire. Blackburn was conscripted to the Royal Air Force during the second world war, after which he spent seven years in New Zealand and the Pacific Islands. There, he met his wife, Maude McKinnon, and had three children. Blackburn was particularly interested in tachisme and abstract expressionism and developed a characteristic style using indigo blue and black forms set against a white background. Returning to England, he exhibited in the 1961 John Moores Painting Prize exhibition at the Walker Art Gallery in Liverpool and at the Woodstock Gallery in London, where Jim Ede encountered his work. They began to correspond, and the Edes acquired several of Blackburn's paintings for the Kettle's Yard collection, as well as encouraging his friends and contacts to purchase Blackburn's work.

Jim Ede, letter to John Blackburn, 14 April 1962
Courtesy of the Blackburn Estate

> I feel that I must send you a short note to say what pleasure I had in looking at some of your ptgs [paintings] at the Woodstock Gallery last Thursday. I was distressed that they were not selling - I suppose they are mostly too big - the only small one I did not feel quite got you or I would have made a bid. But what I did feel was an immense vigour & sensitivity to texture & colour & a joy in the doing of it - really Painting. I'm old now, & have no room to put anything - but it made me feel what fun it would be to be young, with a great barn & fill it. I did the best I could in the meantime & talked specially to two go ahead dealers - Gimpel & Waddington. I hope I will see more, & also yourself.

Lead relief, c.1963
Lead and oil on cotton (mounted on wood),
20 × 21 cm
KY00859.EH

with (left) Michael Pine
Construction, 1955
Plaster,
32.8 × 19.5 × 13.4 cm
KY00824.EH

Jim Ede, letter to John Blackburn, 31 May 1962

Courtesy of the Blackburn Estate

It is good of you to have written to me as you have - & thankyou for the photos - I never can get much from them - one wants the clear impact of the painting itself - its vibration which is so much its design [...] I shall look forward someday to seeing some more - this is a funny little house & chockablock with ptgs [paintings] [...] got from friends when we were all mighty poor together - David Jones, Ben Nicholson, Winifred Nicholson, Christopher Wood, Alfred Wallis, Gaudier Brzeska, Miro, & later Roger Hilton, William Scott & an American [William] Congdon. I've put them all up & have open house for undergraduates every afternoon in the hope of passing on the good work. Your ptgs were far too big for this confined space & I think I said, I did not feel the small one or ones had fully come off.

Yes you should get a few back, but it might be well to keep some in London until you settle elsewhere & in case someone could go to see them there. I'll write again to Gimpel but don't suppose it will have <u>any</u> effect. I'm glad to hear of your friend in N.Z. No - I'm not a painter - but my wife & I were both art students in our early days & thought <u>then</u> we were artists!!!! But I paint all day in my heart which is a great joy to me - & helps me quite a lot to appreciate others.

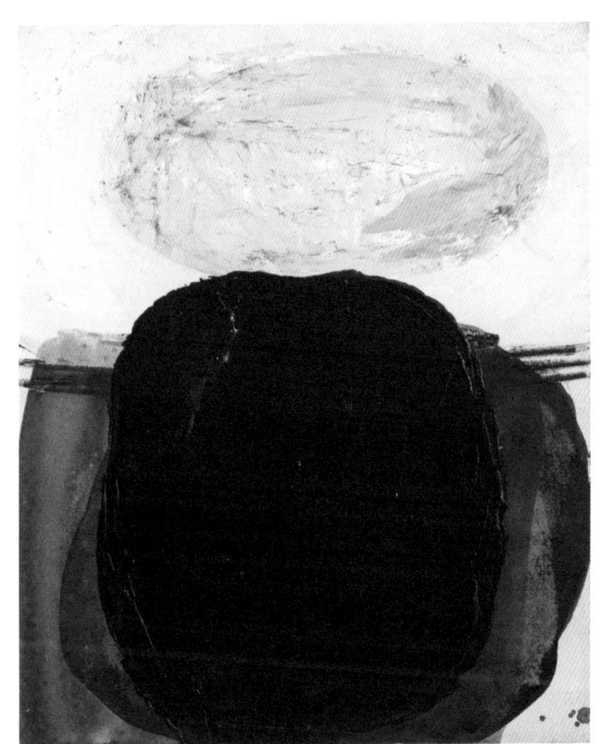

Design, 1964
Oil paint on card, 28.5 × 23.2 cm
KY00889.E

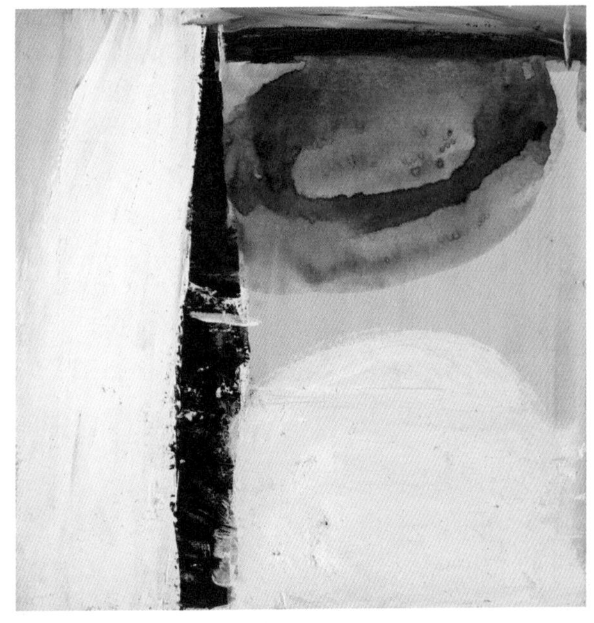

Design I, 1964
Oil paint on card, 26.5 × 25.5 cm
KY00883.E

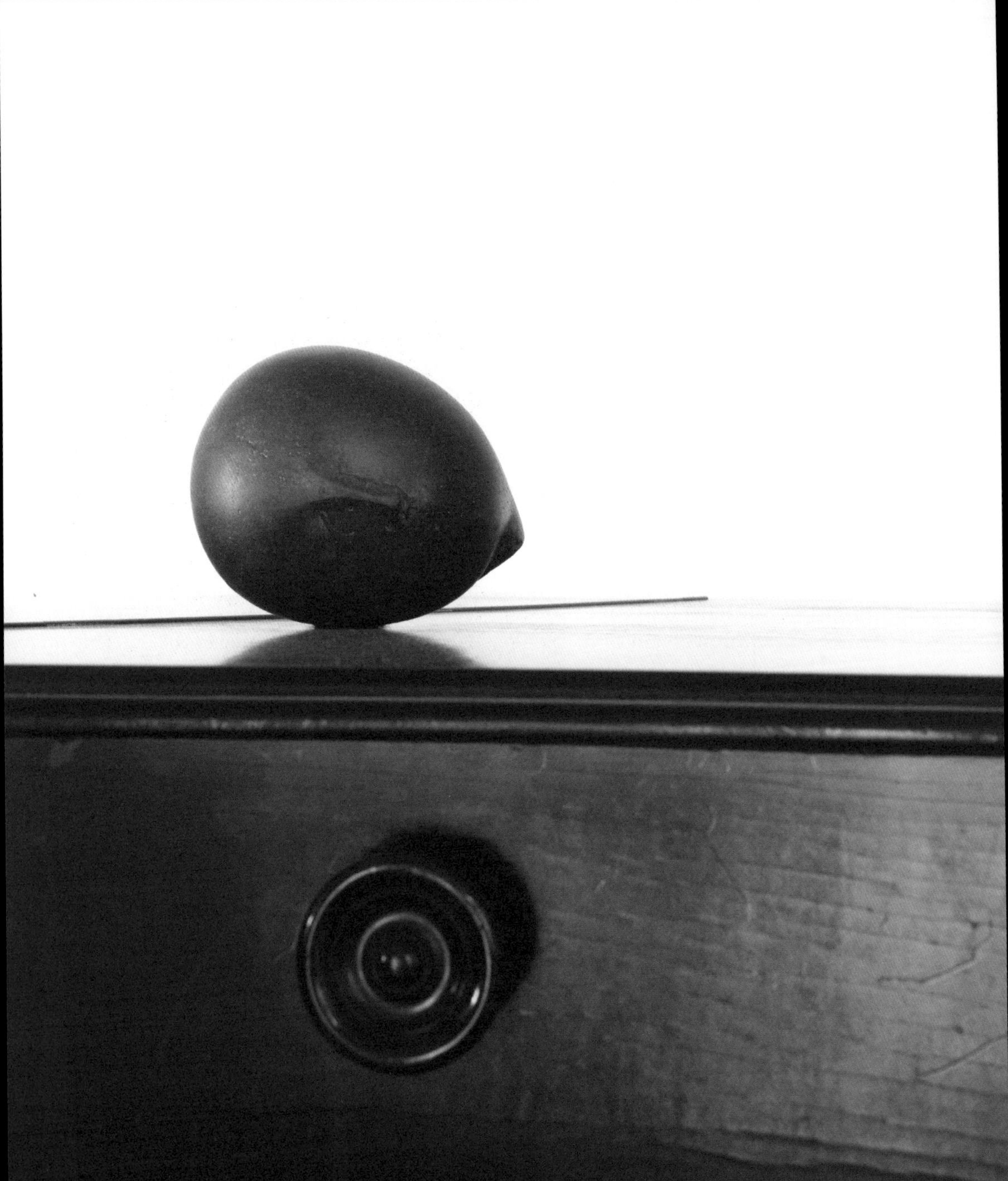

CONSTANTIN BRÂNCUȘI

(1876–1957)

Constantin Brâncuși was born in Hobița, Romania and studied in Bucharest before moving to Paris, France in 1904 to further his art education. He set up a studio in the city and lived there for the rest of his life. Ede purchased Brâncuși's *Fish* in 1927 for which Ede used the title *Golden Fish*. The year before, US custom officials had failed to recognise one of Brâncuși's abstract sculptures as art, classifying the imported work as a taxable item under the category 'Kitchen Utensils and Hospital Supplies'. The artist went to the US courts to defend his work as art. Similar incomprehension was encountered in London, where Jim Ede's enthusiasm for Brâncuși's work was not reflected in the Tate Gallery's collecting policy of the time.

Jim Ede regularly visited Brâncuși in Paris before he and Helen moved to Morocco. The sculptor's studio left an enormous impression that, for Ede, reinforced the significance of the context where a work of art was encountered. In March 1957, Brâncuși died, bequeathing the entire contents of his studio to the French government care of the Musée National d'Art Moderne, on the condition that it was reconstituted as a studio, containing his works, sketches, easels, tools and furniture. In the same year, Jim Ede sold Brâncuși's *Fish* to the Museum of Fine Arts in Boston, USA, using the funds to create student travel bursaries and to repair the roof of St Peter's Church, next-door to Kettle's Yard. In the 1960s he purchased Brâncuși's *Prometheus* from the pianist Vera Moore, and in 1973 acquired a replica of *Fish*, made from the sculpture he originally owned.

Prometheus, 1912
Cast stone, 13.7 × 17.8 × 13.6 cm
KY00980.EH

Jim Ede, [unpublished notes on Constantin Brâncuși], written in response to an enquiry from Constantin Roman, 24 November 1969

Kettle's Yard Archive. Papers of Harold Stanley 'Jim' Ede
KY/Ede/Artists/Brancusi/Correspondence 1928-1973

> When I went to Paris in 1924, as a young man of 29, I had already formed a special liking for the works of Brâncuși, Picasso and Braque [...] I was then working at the Tate Gallery where such people had not yet registered and it was much to my own surprise, and probably through the influence of Ben Nicholson, that I found myself reaching forward into the exciting world of art then to be found in Paris. I was a ready pupil and soon became friends with most of the great artists then living there, but chiefly with Brâncuși [...] His work has become a touchstone of perfection to all lovers of sculpture [...] by his extraordinary and penetrating simplification he has helped the world to see the inherent quality of balance in form, in the elimination of unnecessary local shapes, so that the way lay open to 'streamlining' - but no one yet has reached his perfection.

Jim Ede, *A way of life: Kettle's Yard*
(Cambridge University Press, 1984) pp. 199-200
(Text on Brâncuși first written c. 1927)

> When I first went to see Brâncuși I felt that all the elements were there collected in his studio, almost as though it were nature's workshop, there air (& forms) and light, poise and (the) rhythm of his carvings. It was really a collection of studios in a little courtyard; I pulled a string outside the door and a hammer hit upon a disk of brass within, making a lovely echoing sound. When Brâncuși opened the door it was still vibrating. 'People bring me music while they wait,' he said. The only dark thing in all that world was Brâncuși's eyes, they were like wet pebbles on the sand, everything else was finely powdered over, his grey hair and beard, his face, his clothes, the tall columns of eternal movement, the *Nouveaux nés*, the *Tête de Nègre*, the white cloths covering the polished brilliance of the *Fish*, the *Bird in Flight* and

Mademoiselle Pogani [sic]. Through the dim roof-glass the sky was blue and there was a gentle movement of trees.

It was the first of many visits and I never lost the sense of living energy it was to be there. Brâncuși seemed to talk more with his eyes than with his mouth, and he kept watching my enjoyment. He would lift the covers from those shining brasses, the *Fish* would start revolving on its plate of clear reflection; the *Bird*, full treated, hung poised like a star, the great grey *Fish* of marble swam in limitless waters, and Brâncuși was clearing a large slab of stone and laying white paper on it, glasses, knives, butter and fresh radishes, a long French loaf; and all the time some new object would come upon my wonder; forms of carved wood lying at hazard, or seemingly so, for nothing was at hazard in that studio, since all was part of one vision; or the remnants of some little bouquet. Brâncuși's flowers seemed never to wilt, but to become immobilised, perhaps they thrived on the powdered air; and in that air I now heard, so softly that it did not break my thought, the distant sound of xylophones, the quick beat of Balinese and Javanese music; and Brâncuși was coming in with a bucket of ice, in which stood bottles of wine, looking themselves like statues by Brâncuși. He laughed when I asked him where the music came from and said that a record should be played at a little distance, as a background to company, and with it he brought the most marvellous cooked chops I have ever tasted, and *haricots verts*. The salt took on a special whiteness on that white paper and the carvings all about became one and I was in that unity.

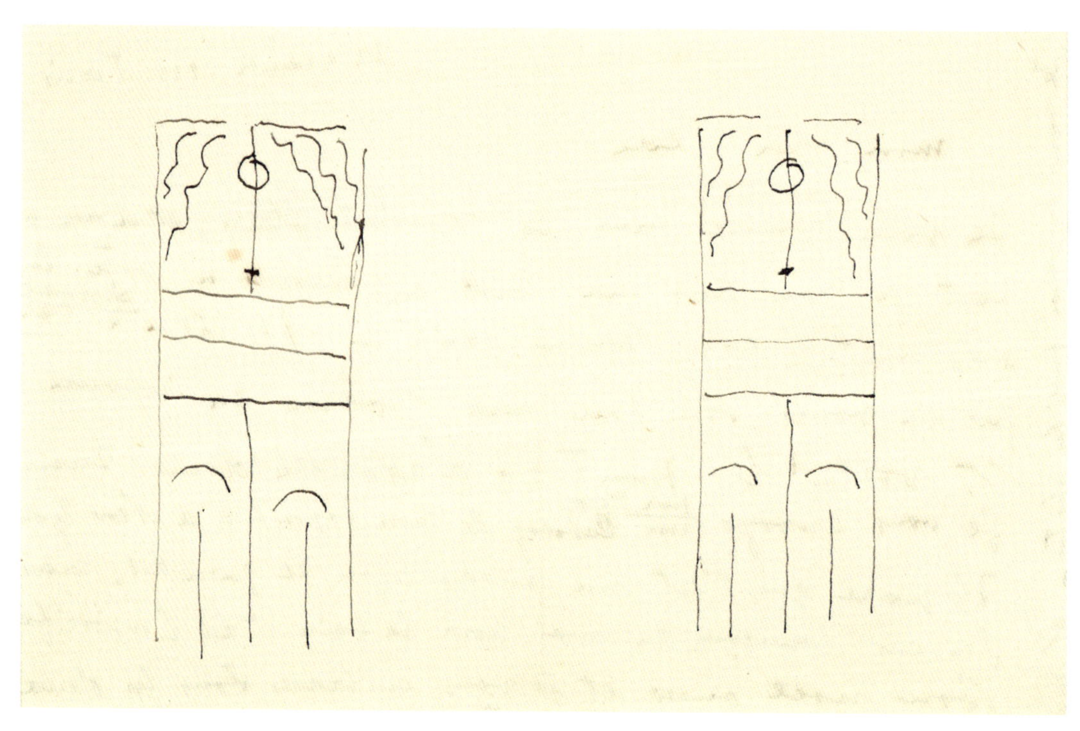

Letter with sketches of 'The Kiss', 1933
Ink on paper, 12.5 × 19.5 cm
KY00696.E

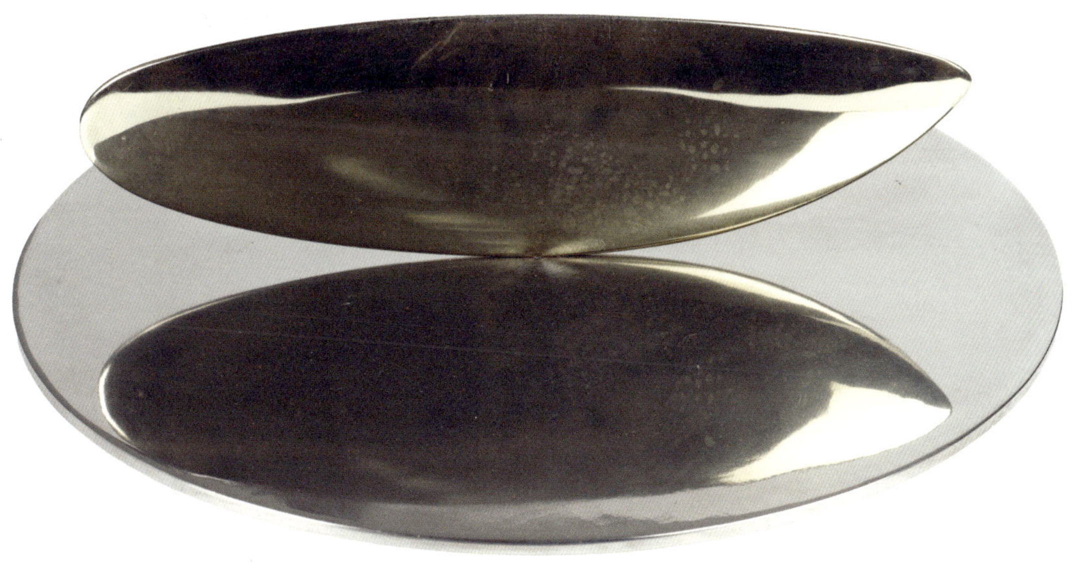

Fish, 1924 (cast 1973)
Brass and steel, 13 × 50 cm
KY01151.EH

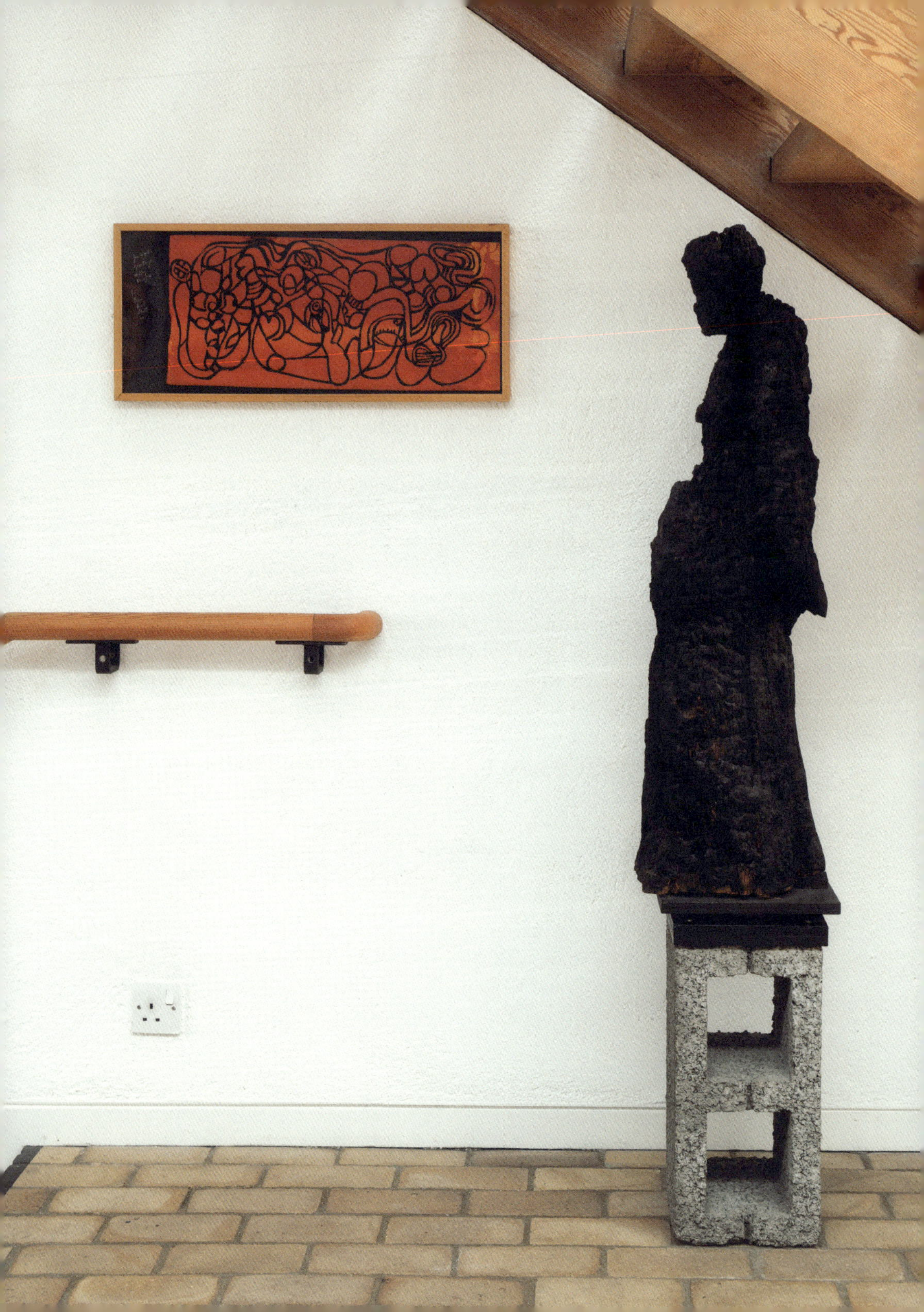

AVINASH CHANDRA

(1931–1991)

Avinash Chandra was born in Shimla, India. He studied painting at the Delhi Polytechnic Art School (1947-52) where he also taught between 1953 and 1956. Chandra was a member of the artists' collective Delhi Silpi Chakra and in 1954 was awarded first prize in the *First National Exhibition of Art* in New Delhi. Chandra was married to the artist Prem Lata Chhabra (1931-1975) and together they moved to London after she was offered a scholarship at St. Martin's School of Art in 1956. In the UK, Avinash Chandra's work was exhibited extensively, including at the Imperial Institute (1957) and Gallery One (1958) in London, and the Arnolfini Gallery in Bristol (1961). His work was collected by the Victoria and Albert Museum, the Belfast Municipal Museum and Art Gallery and the Musée d'Art Moderne in Paris, France. Chandra received the Prix Européen in 1962 and was the first Indian artist to be exhibited in *Documenta*, Kassel in Germany (1964). He received a John D. Rockefeller scholarship in 1965 and moved to New York in 1966, living in the United States until 1973. Chandra met the Edes in the early 1960s and Jim Ede acquired several of the artist's works during this decade. Chandra's paintings were among those originally on display in the cottages when the first catalogue of the Kettle's Yard collection was published in 1968.

Avinash Chandra, letter to Jim Ede, 14 May 1962
Kettle's Yard Archive, Papers of Harold Stanley 'Jim' Ede. KY/EDE/1/1

> It was a very great pleasure to have met you again and your charming wife. We enjoyed every minute in your beautiful home, and looking at your collection. I am indeed, very pleased to have 2 of my works in your house.

Untitled, 1964
Screenprint on card,
27.5 × 66 cm
KY00868.EH

with (right) John Catto
St Edmund
Charred willow wood,
102 × 28 × 27 cm
KY01110.EH

Avinash Chandra, letter to Jim Ede, 13 February 1963
Kettle's Yard Archive, Papers of Harold Stanley 'Jim' Ede. KY/EDE/1/1

> I have been thinking a lot since I got back, I was so happy to see both of you - and it is kind of you to buy another drawing for yourself:
>
> The set of drawings which you have kept now - makes a lot of sense altogether - I shall be greatful [sic] if you decide to keep them all for your collection. I shall consider it an honour, and will also be so well represented in your beautiful collection.
>
> You can pay me whatever you like, and when ever you can. You have been a great friend and it is difficult to find either a friend or a home like yours.

Avinash Chandra, letter to Jim Ede, 21 December 1965
Kettle's Yard Archive, Papers of Harold Stanley 'Jim' Ede. KY/EDE/1/1

> We came to New York about four months ago [...] My painting has been going well, I have now painted more than 100 pictures [...] This also meant we did not go out much! I have not yet started showing my work or selling it - I have a feeling that, important and valuable though this American interlude may be - I will only feel properly organised again when we are back in London. It will be good, however, if I can fix up a thoroughly good and efficient gallery for my work in New York.

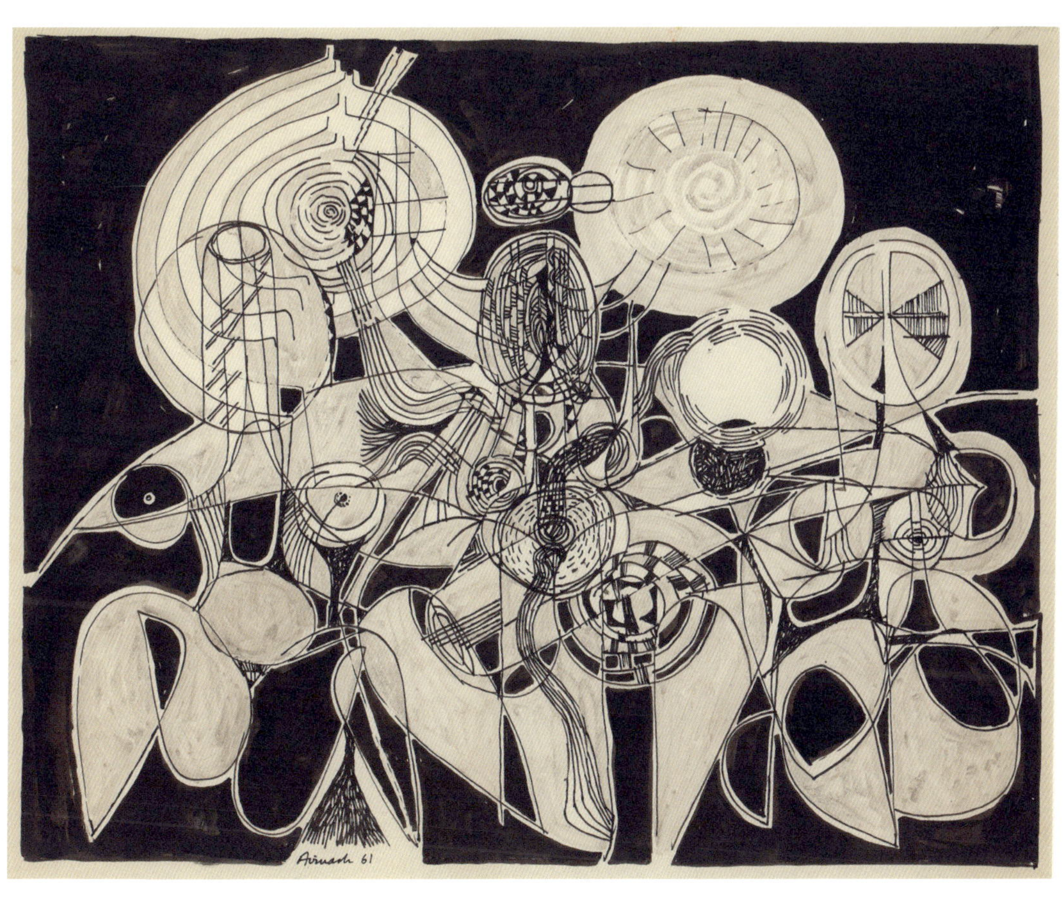

Design, 1961
Print and gouache on paper, 49.5 × 62 cm
KY00792.E

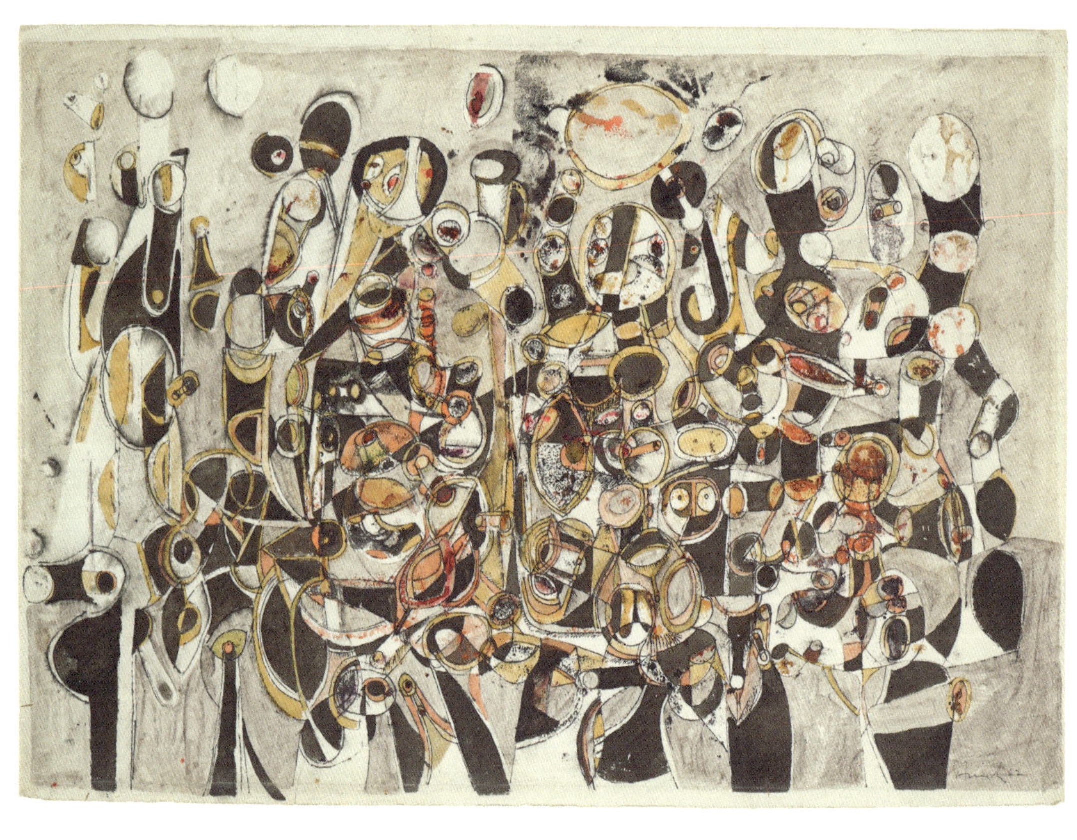

Black Feast, 1962
Ink and watercolour on paper, 56 × 78 cm
KY00793.EH

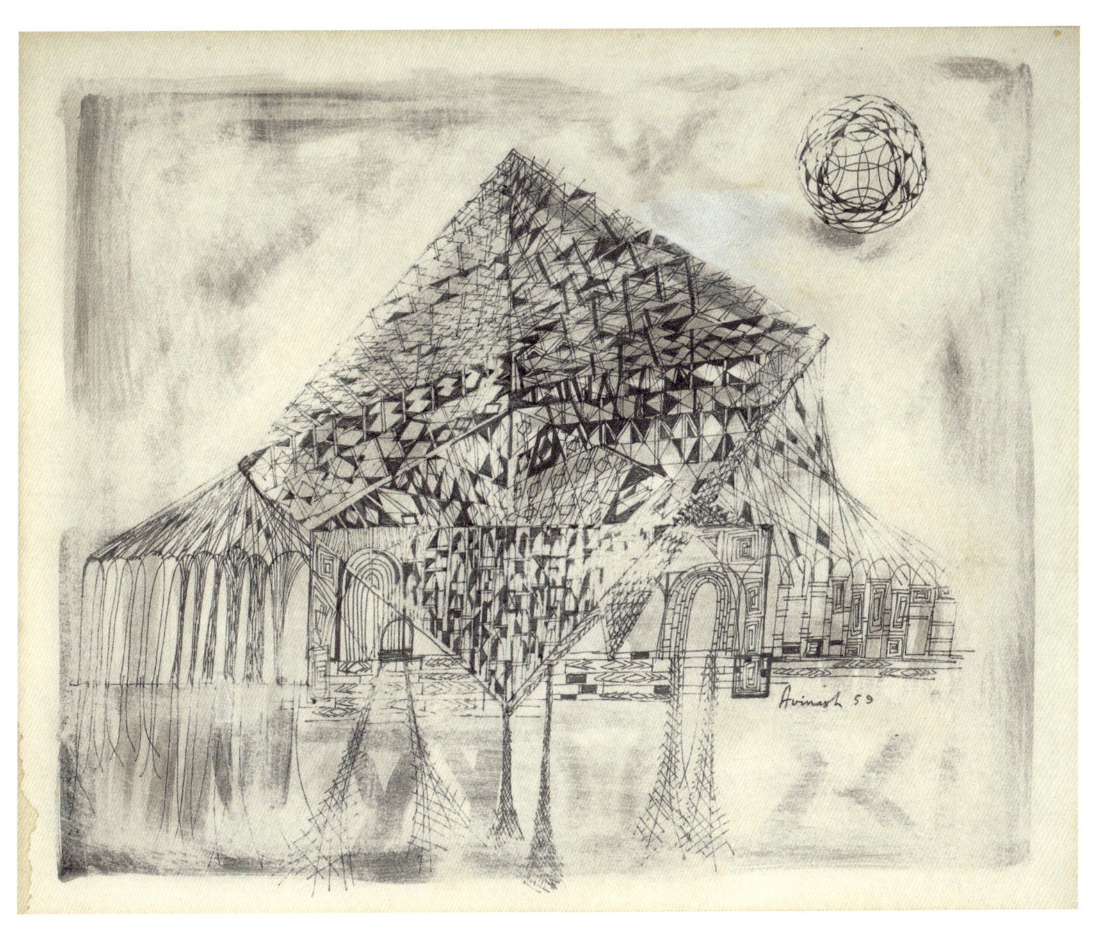

Temple, 1959
Ink and wash paint on card, 51.5 × 63 cm
KY00794.E

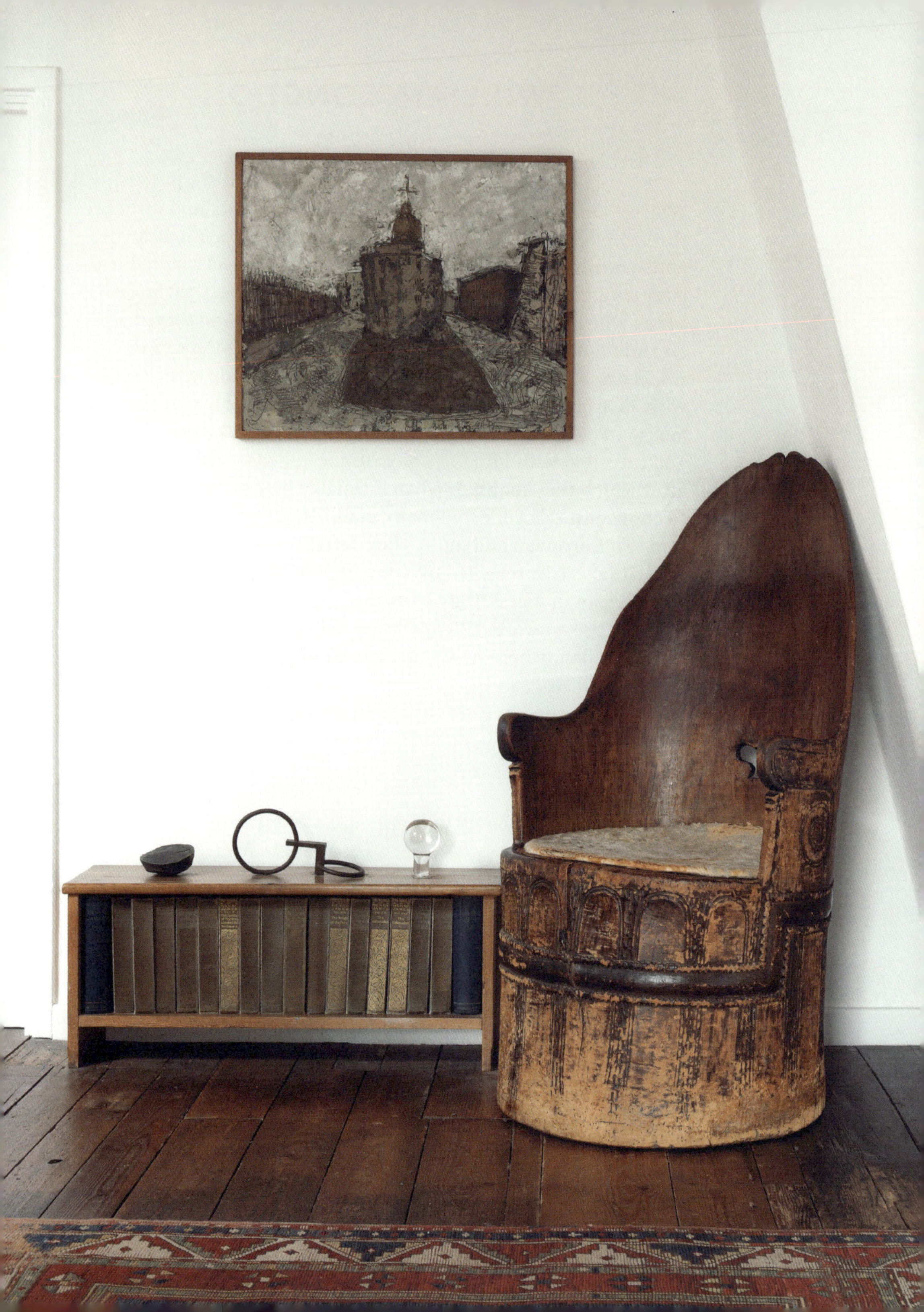

WILLIAM CONGDON

(1912–1998)

William Congdon was born in Providence, Rhode Island in the United States. He began to paint while studying English and Spanish literature at Yale University in Connecticut and later studied at the Pennsylvania Academy of Fine Arts. In the 1930s, Congdon travelled extensively in Europe, and served as an ambulance driver in Africa and Europe during the second world war. Upon returning to New York, he became associated with abstract expressionism, exhibiting alongside artists such as Jackson Pollock and Willem de Kooning. In 1950, he met Jim Ede, and travelled with him to Venice, Rome and elsewhere in Italy, after which they maintained an intimate correspondance for years to come. Jim Ede collected many of Congdon's works, introducing him to a European audience. Their letters saw the painter through a spiritual crisis, resolved by Congdon's conversion to Roman Catholicism in Assisi, Italy in 1958. Congdon spent his last years living in the annex to a Benedictine monastery in Buccinasco, outside Milan, where he set up the Foundation for Improving Understanding of the Arts. Buccinasco is today home to the William G. Congdon Foundation, which holds many of his works and his archive.

William Congdon, letter/ notes to Jim Ede, February 1954
Kettle's Yard Archive, Papers of Harold Stanley 'Jim' Ede. KY/EDE/1/3

> A painter must loathe his medium - nothing more boring than the physicals of painting to overcome, to arrive at, a pure image. There is no getting around the love for the idea (image) - all the knowledge, passion, etc. counts for nothing. If you can't lose yourself and be possessed, if you haven't the courage to suffer, to be possessed by an image - don't paint. Any section of a painting that is 'worked on' rather than inspired cannot be alive; there is no working a painting, only breathing it. If you have a battle, it is because the object intervened. Don't look at a painting (after doing it) unless you are in a painting mood, otherwise you'll see only trivia

Naples - Church, 1950
Oil paint on hardboard,
54.2 × 67.2 cm
KY00775.EH

with (below)
Tam MacPhail
Construction, c. 1968
Iron, 27 × 13 × 13 cm
KY00937.EH

[...] A painter's studio walls should be empty. He should aspire to people them but, not succeeding, is constantly driven onward. If there are old hats on the wall, you can only be working in submissive terms of those hats. Not even a print of 'Mona Lisa' or by Picasso. They have nothing to do with you. They are past products only valid of another art, another moment of history. You must create your own moment, and know that even that will have left you by the moment of its creation, so that you cannot even put one of your own on the wall. Let your heart be your only wall, and people it with visions and, if you're lucky, paintings [...] As soon as you cease to discover new of yourself in them, take them down, for by now others are crowding your heart.

Must never approach painting, nor think of painting, unless equipped with an image or passion. Any other motive is a waste of time. There is zero to learn, to talk about. Painters are not colleagues, except in the sense of being human beings. Painting is not a thing to be conscious of or about until after it is done. Intelligence enters into it only to know [your] self enough not to be deluded into nursing false images. To know that your image is life is not easy, especially in these times. But if it is life, others will know.

Use a knife - never a brush which only compromises. A knife constructs! - without tricks. Don't presume to pick, mix, chose your colors, but toss a sea and fish for gold in it. It comes with courage and freedom. Don't mix colors - mix ideas, feelings.

It is not important that you see in terms of a painting - but enough in terms of the subject, so that, however diverse seeming a painting results [it] bears the inner life of that subject. Let it surprise you - enjoy yourself. Don't insist on the subject (idea). That the painting lives is more than the subject. And it will live if you loved the idea, no matter how much the image that results diverges (seems to diverge) from your original idea.

William Congdon, letter to Jim Ede, 7 December 1950.
Kettle's Yard Archive, Papers of Harold Stanley 'Jim' Ede. KY/EDE/1/3

> It is always the most paintable place in the world. It is too fantastic to paint just a painted portrait of it. I know well that before-night drama when the sun from a streak in the West sets fire to S. Giorgio & to the tip of S. Marco's campanile – I used to rush at that moment over to S. Marco from the Giudecca to see it from within the piazza, but by the time the motoscafo came & I arrived, it was too late. Oh yes – I've seen a White Venice – & in the pearly early winter morning too when the sun, in order to manifest itself through the mist, had to turn a deep red. Yes. I'd thought often how thick S M's [S. Marco's] campanile is. But there's the miracle – because physically it is thick so to fill the space, & yet what an illusion of soaring it gives – the light itself catches the upper half & lifts it trembling & dimensionless high above the city.

11 Sept. '50.

Dear Jim –
Found for you an excellent large spacious apt. $40 for December
2 bedrooms, large dining (salon) room with door window balcony, bath & kitchen – but it is on the Giudecca.

Piazza
San Marco
Grand Canal
Salute
San Giorgio
your house
to Lido
Giudecca
3 minute motorboat service to San Marco.

I'd take it – . Write confirmation with I suppose some sort of deposit to Adele de Maria
43 Giudecca
Venice –
I'm still not sure about myself – Love, Bill.

William Congdon, letter to Jim Ede, 11 September 1950
Kettle's Yard Archive, Papers of Harold Stanley 'Jim' Ede. KY/EDE/1/3

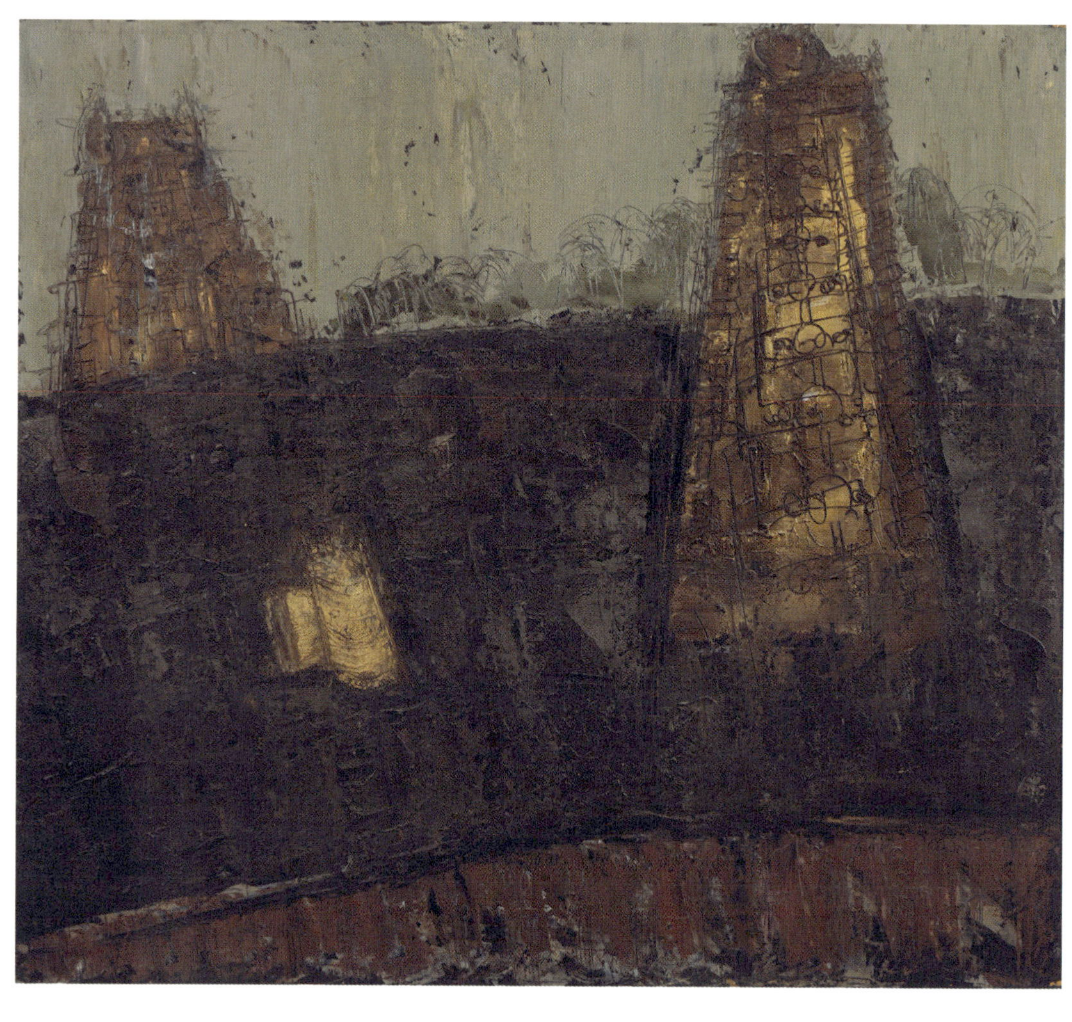

India Temples no. 1 (Sri Ranganathaswamy Temple, Tiruchirapalli), 1954 (February)
Oil paint, gold paint and enamel on hardboard, 125 × 140 cm
KY00785.EH

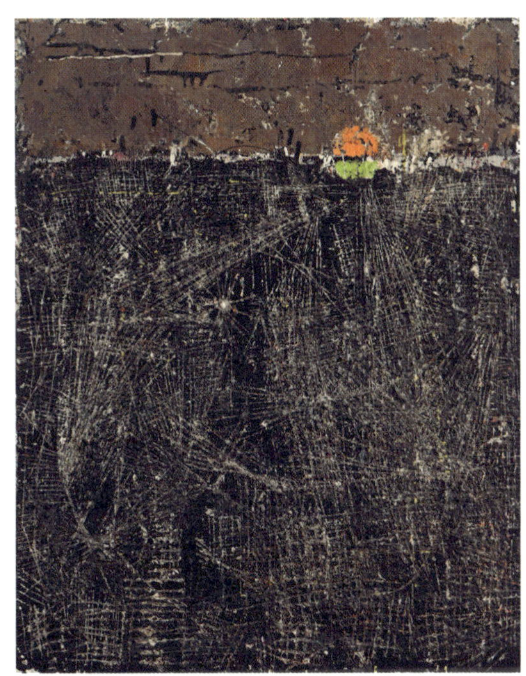

The Black City I (New York), 1949
Oil paint, enamel and ink on hardboard, 76 × 61 cm
KY00989.EH

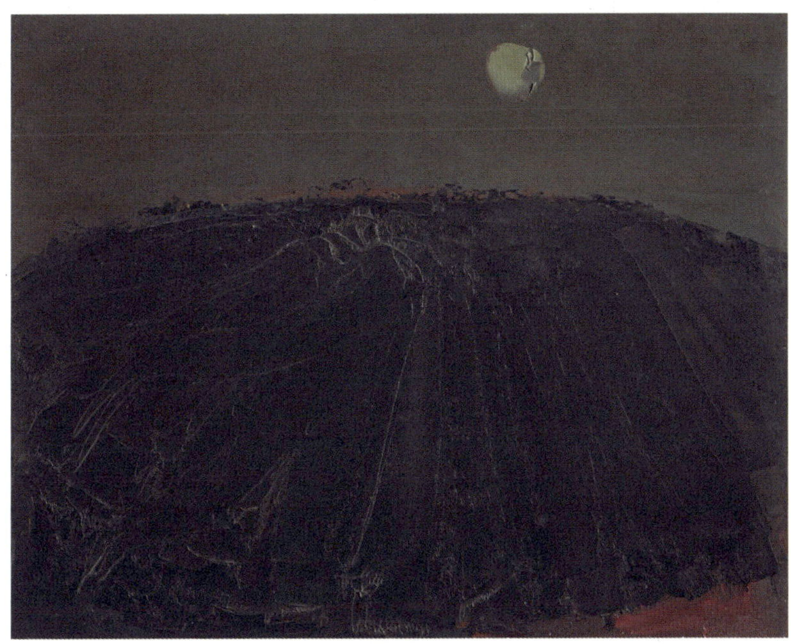

Luna 7, Subiaco,
1967 (26 July)
Oil paint on hardboard,
69.4 × 89.3 cm
KY00830.EH

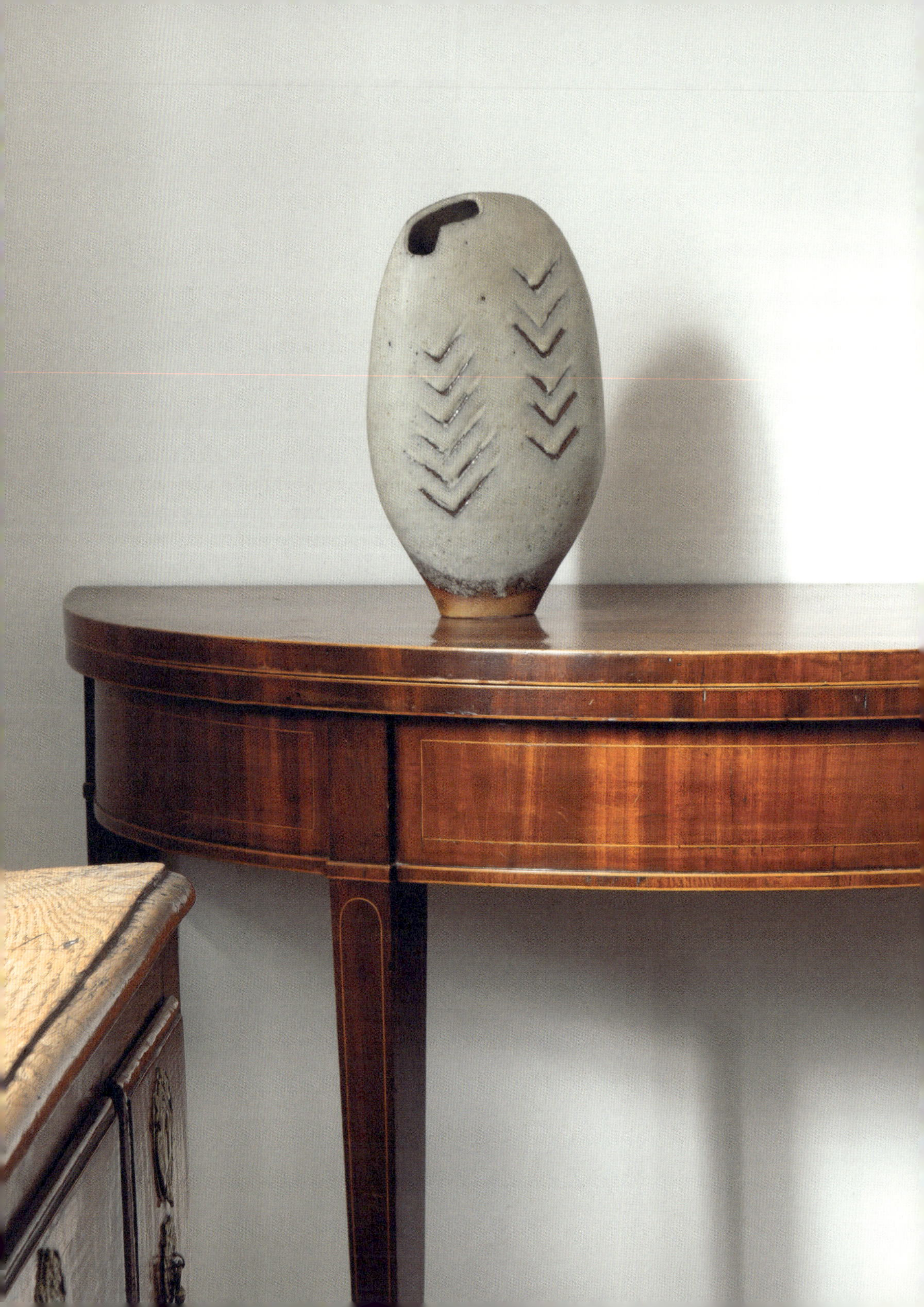

ZOË ELLISON

(1916–1986)

Zoë Thelma Wilson-Hewetson was born in Zimbabwe and came to England in 1948. She studied at the Ewenny Pottery, Bridgend (then in Glamorgan) and at the Camberwell College of Art, London. In 1951, with her husband Jan Ellison, also a potter, she established the Crosskeys Pottery in Swaffham Bulbeck, Cambridgeshire, which operated until 1960. Working with earthenware and stoneware clays, Zoë Ellison experimented with techniques such as spattered glazes and sawdust firing. Her work ranges from glossy domestic wares to earthy sculptural vessels. In the 1960s she taught at the Cambridge School of Art where her students included Elspeth Owen and Magdalene Odundo, who credits Ellison with introducing her to ceramics. Zoë Ellison was a frequent visitor to Kettle's Yard, and in 1977, she and her husband donated a number of works to the Kettle's Yard collection, including their own and those of Katherine Pleydell-Bouverie and David Harvey.

Sebastian Blackie (student at the Cambridge School of Art 1966-68), Interview with Naomi Polonsky, 2024
Kettle's Yard Archive, House and Gallery Records

> I was taught by Zoë from September 1966 to June 1968. I remember her as serious, intelligent, economic but clear in her directions [...] she arranged for us to visit Kettle's Yard and discussed Jim's collection [...] Zoë seemed to know everyone in Cambridge who was artistic: [Henry] Rothschild, Ede, painters etc., but she did not name drop. [...] she would speak knowledgably about the better known modern British potters suggesting she knew them personally. [...] It was clear she was in touch with the wider ceramic community including Lucie Rie who had given her a bowl as a wedding present [...]

Grey flattened vase, c. 1959
Stoneware (glazed), 28 × 16 × 7 cm
KY01206

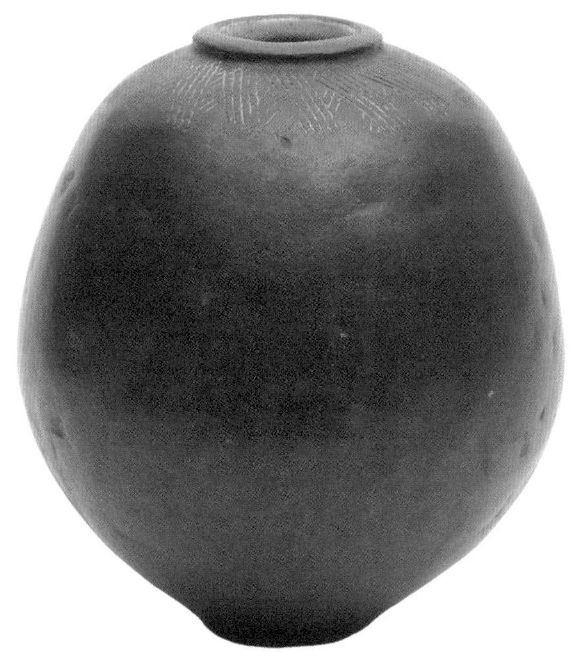

Vase, c. 1955
Glazed stoneware, 17.5 × 15 cm
KY01199

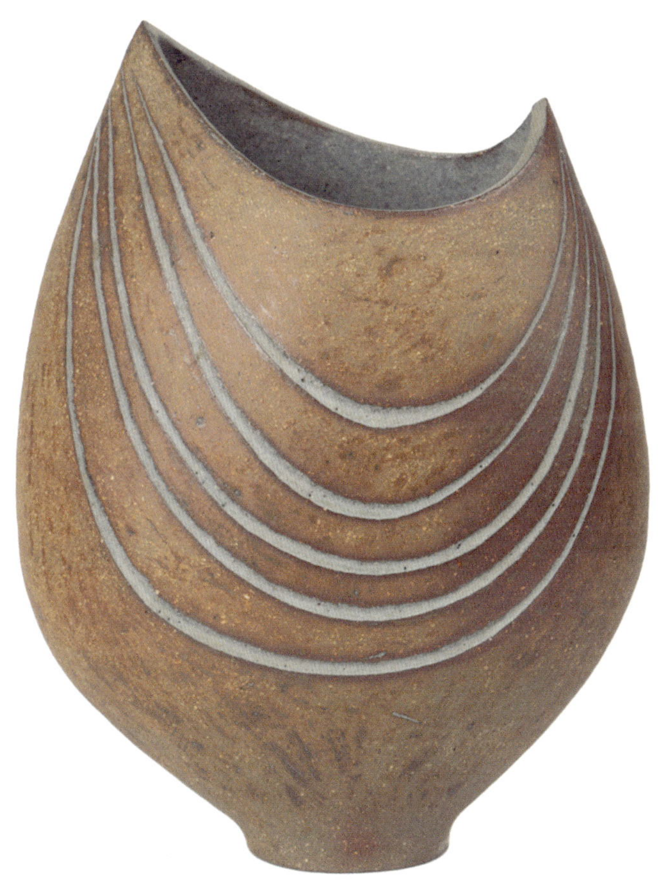

Vase, c.1959
Glazed earthenware, 35 × 26 × 14 cm
KY01204

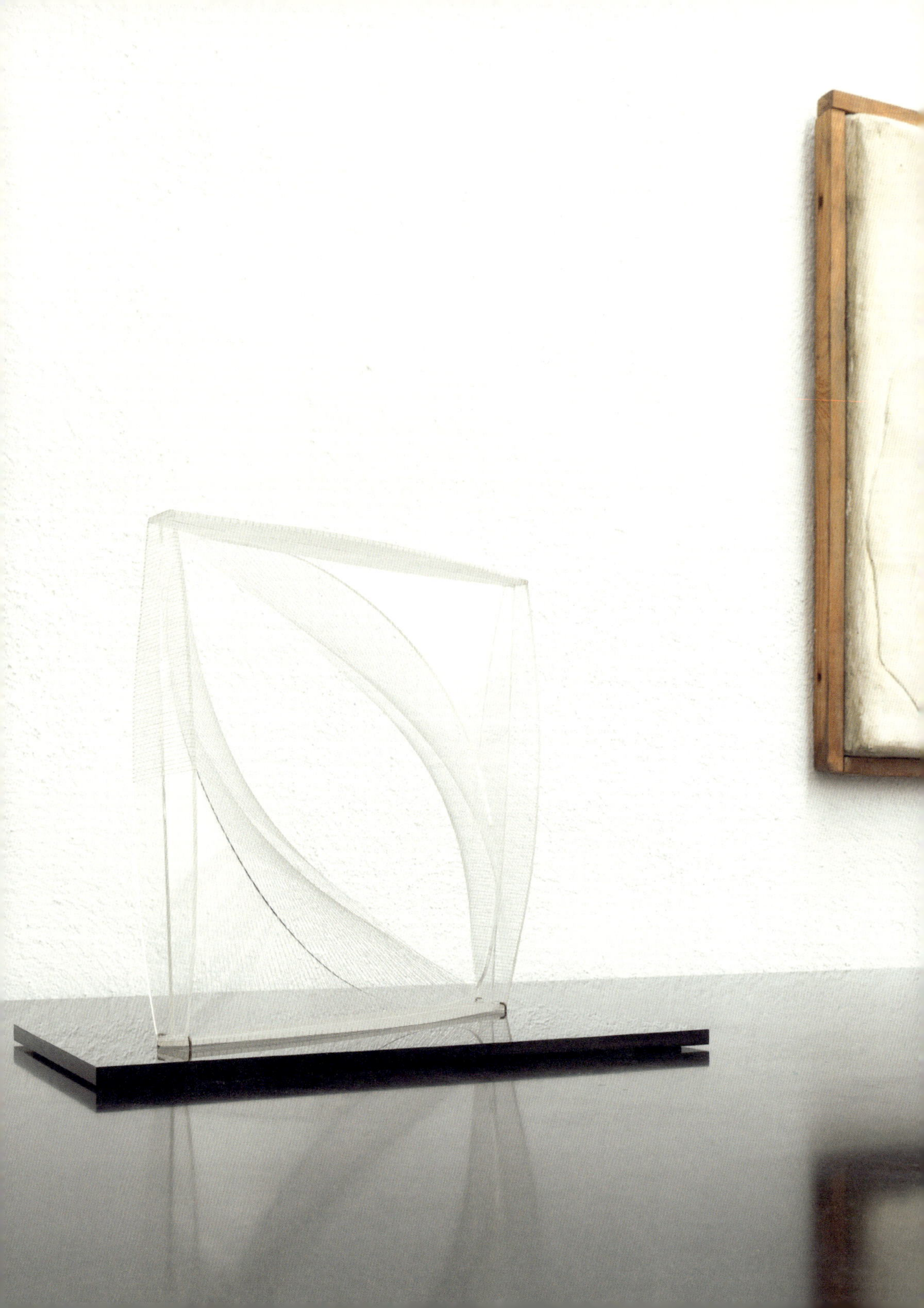

NAUM GABO

(1890–1977)

Naum Gabo was born in Bryansk, Russia and worked alongside artists Wassily Kandinsky, Vladimir Tatlin and Kazimir Malevich in Moscow until 1921, when he moved to Berlin, Germany. There he and his brother, Antoine Pevsner, became leading exponents of constructivism. They jointly authored a key manifesto of 1920 asserting the relationship between art, science and modern life, in which they declared that art, 'should attend us everywhere that life flows and acts'. Gabo's sculpture prioritised light, space and the kinetic, and the artist often made use of new materials, including plastics. In 1927, he and Pevsner designed striking, modernist sets and costumes for Sergei Diaghilev's Ballets Russes production of *La Chatte*, which opened in Paris and toured Europe.

In Paris, Gabo met British artists Ben Nicholson and Barbara Hepworth through the Abstraction-Création group, and he moved to England in spring 1936. Gabo lived in Hampstead, London where his neighbours included Leslie Martin, Herbert Read and Margaret Gardiner. His work was included in Nicolete Gray's *Abstract and Concrete* exhibition which opened in February 1936. With Nicholson, Martin, Hepworth and Sadie Speight, Gabo contributed to and co-edited the publication *Circle: An International Survey of Constructive Art* published by Faber in 1937. Following the outbreak of the second world war he moved with his wife Miriam to Carbis Bay, near St. Ives in Cornwall, where Ben Nicholson and Barbara Hepworth also lived. In 1946, they emigrated to the United States, where Gabo was able to work on a larger scale, taking on numerous high-profile commissions. Gabo gave a monoprint *Opus 5* to Jim Ede in 1952. His *Linear Construction in Space No. 1* was later given to Kettle's Yard by Joy Finzi in memory of Frank and Vera Swanson. Nina Williams (Gabo's daughter) and her husband Graham gifted further works, including *Construction in Space: Suspended*, 1962.

Linear Construction in Space No.1, 1944–45
Perspex and nylon thread,
30.8 × 31 × 6.3 cm
KY00988.EH

with (right) Henri Gaudier-Brzeska
Wrestlers relief, 1913 (cast 1965)
Herculite,
72.5 × 91.5 × 7 cm
KY00896.EH

Naum Gabo, letter to Jim Ede, 23 May 1969

Kettle's Yard Archive, Papers of Harold Stanley 'Jim' Ede. KY/EDE/1/1

> Much as it is painful for me to disappoint you, I have to be frank and tell you that I cannot now respond to your wish to have a work of mine, for the following reasons. In 1970 I am going to be 80. On that occasion there are comprehensive exhibitions being planned [...] both in Europe and here. As you know, I think, I am not a prolific artist and the amount of work in my possession is very limited. I will hope to collect all that is left and try to avoid any borrowing of works [...] Apart from that, I don't want to frighten you, but it will give you a picture of the prices of my work when I tell you that there is not a single piece in my studio that is not priced much above the sum you mentioned. This scale is for works of medium size [...] I hope you will understand my difficulties.

Jim Ede, *A way of life: Kettle's Yard*

(Cambridge University Press, 1984) p. 177

> I had become friends with Naum Gabo and his brother [Antoine] Pevsner in Paris around 1923 or 1924. I had found them in a garret almost in the sky - they were making a model for a construction perhaps 40 cm high which they hoped to have placed in the Champs Elysées, but then it would be 100 metres high. It would be in perpetual movement. I don't think that this was ever made.

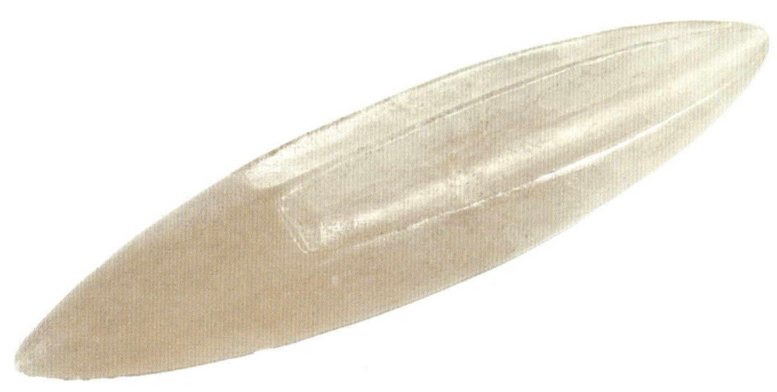

Alabaster Carving (aka The Bobbin), 1938
Alabaster, 16 × 4.5 × 2.5 cm
KY01351

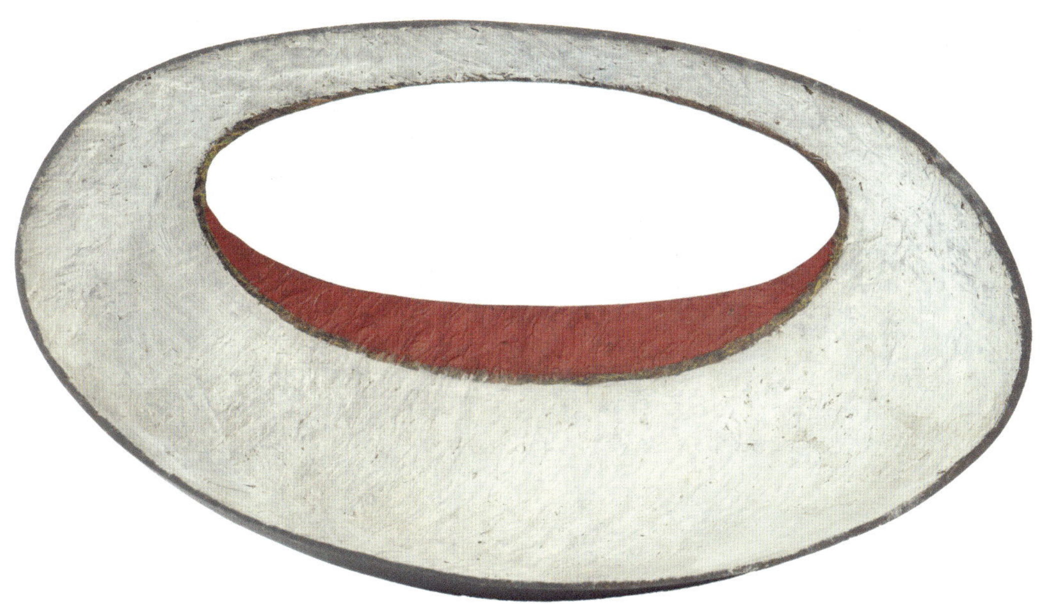

Negative Volume, 1940
Coco de mer and oil paint, 14.5 × 22.8 × 7 cm
KY01357

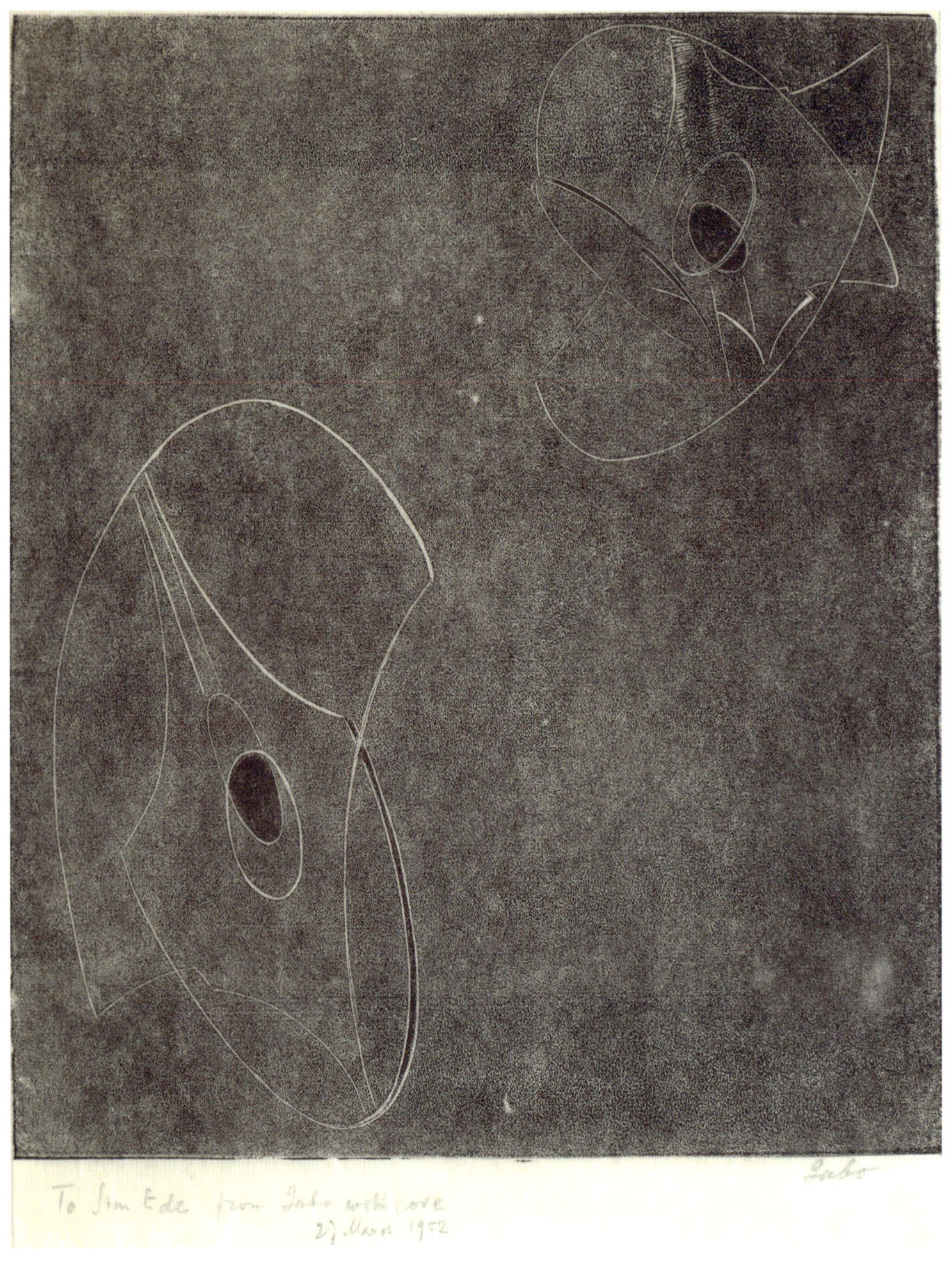

Opus 5 (aka The Constellations), 1950
Wood engraving (monoprint) on paper, 27 × 22 cm
KY00777.EH

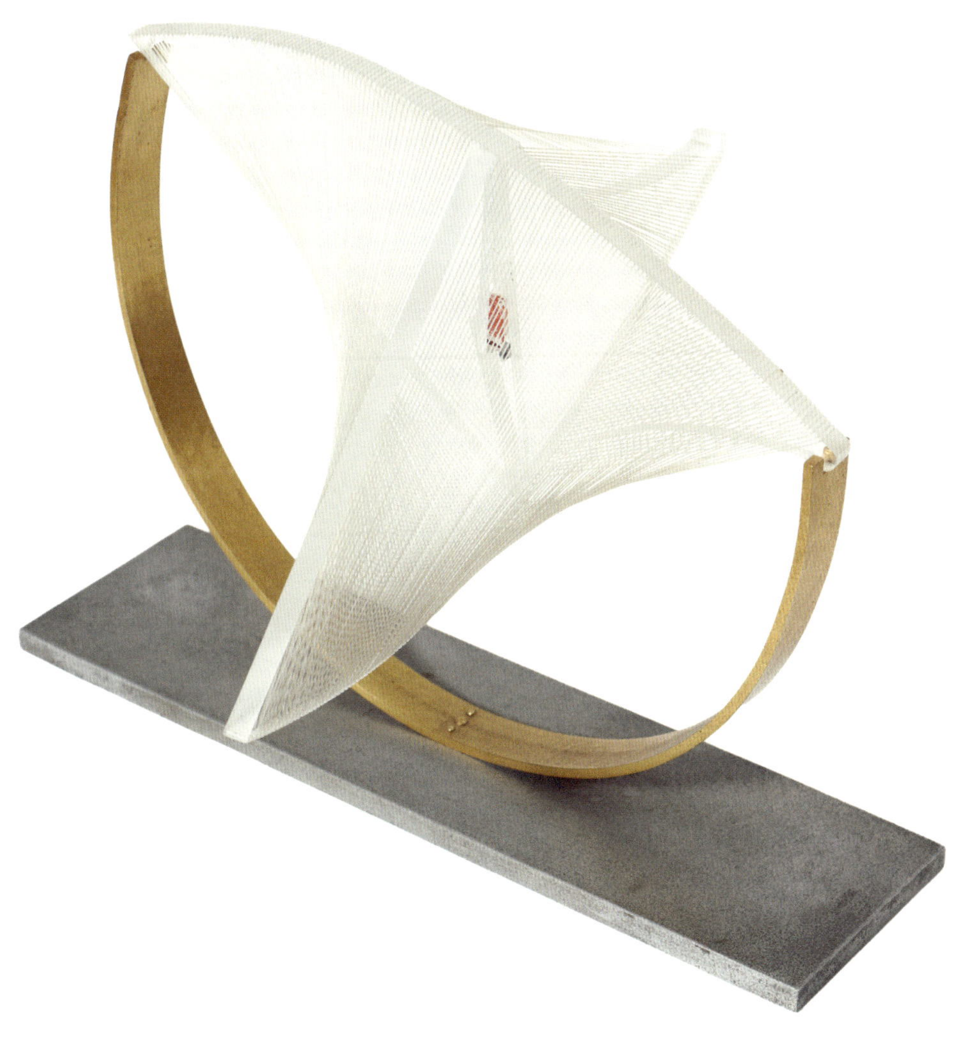

Construction in Space: Suspended, 1962
Perspex, nylon thread, acrylic paint and steel, 30.5 × 28 × 28 cm
KY01350

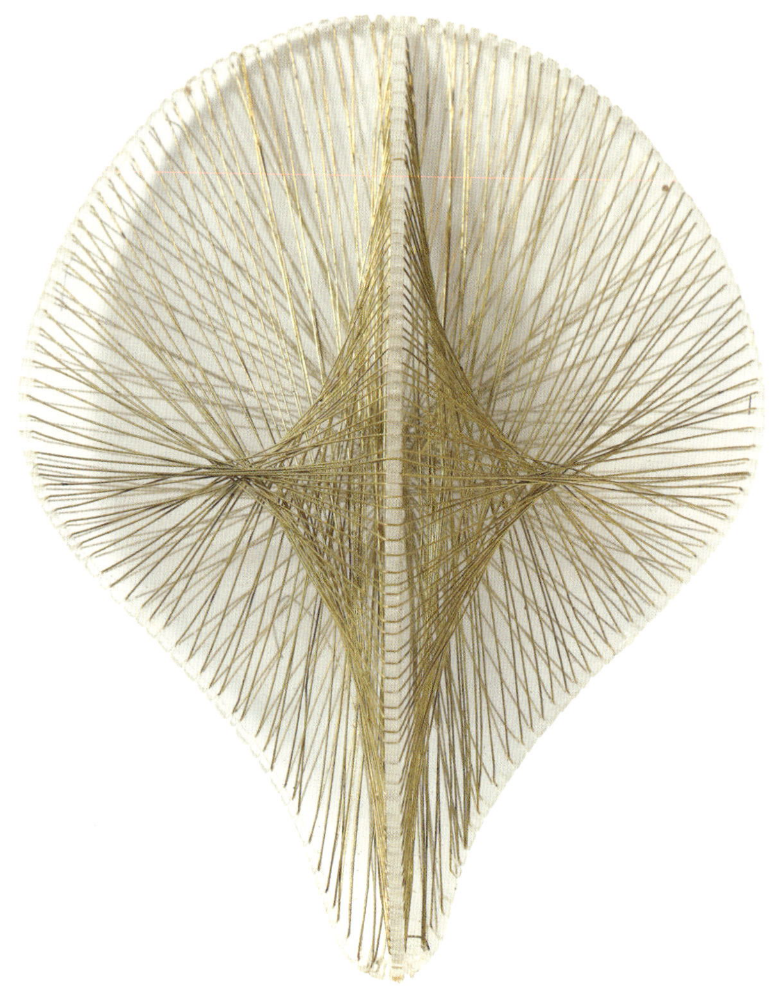

Linear Bas-Relief, 1954
Plastic with rolled gold wire, 7.5 cm
KY01389

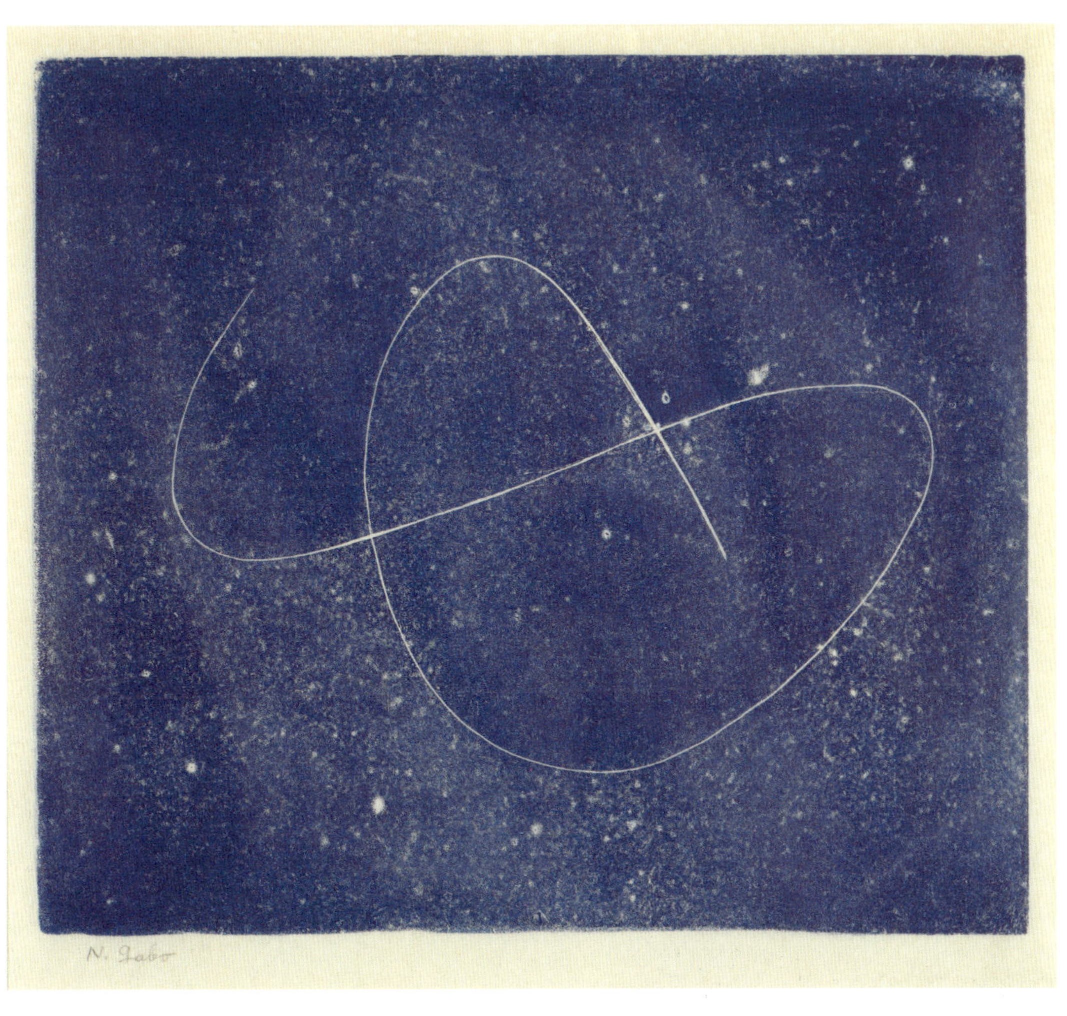

Opus 9 (W/E 57), c.1957
Wood engraving (monoprint) on paper, 26 × 29.5 cm
KY01269

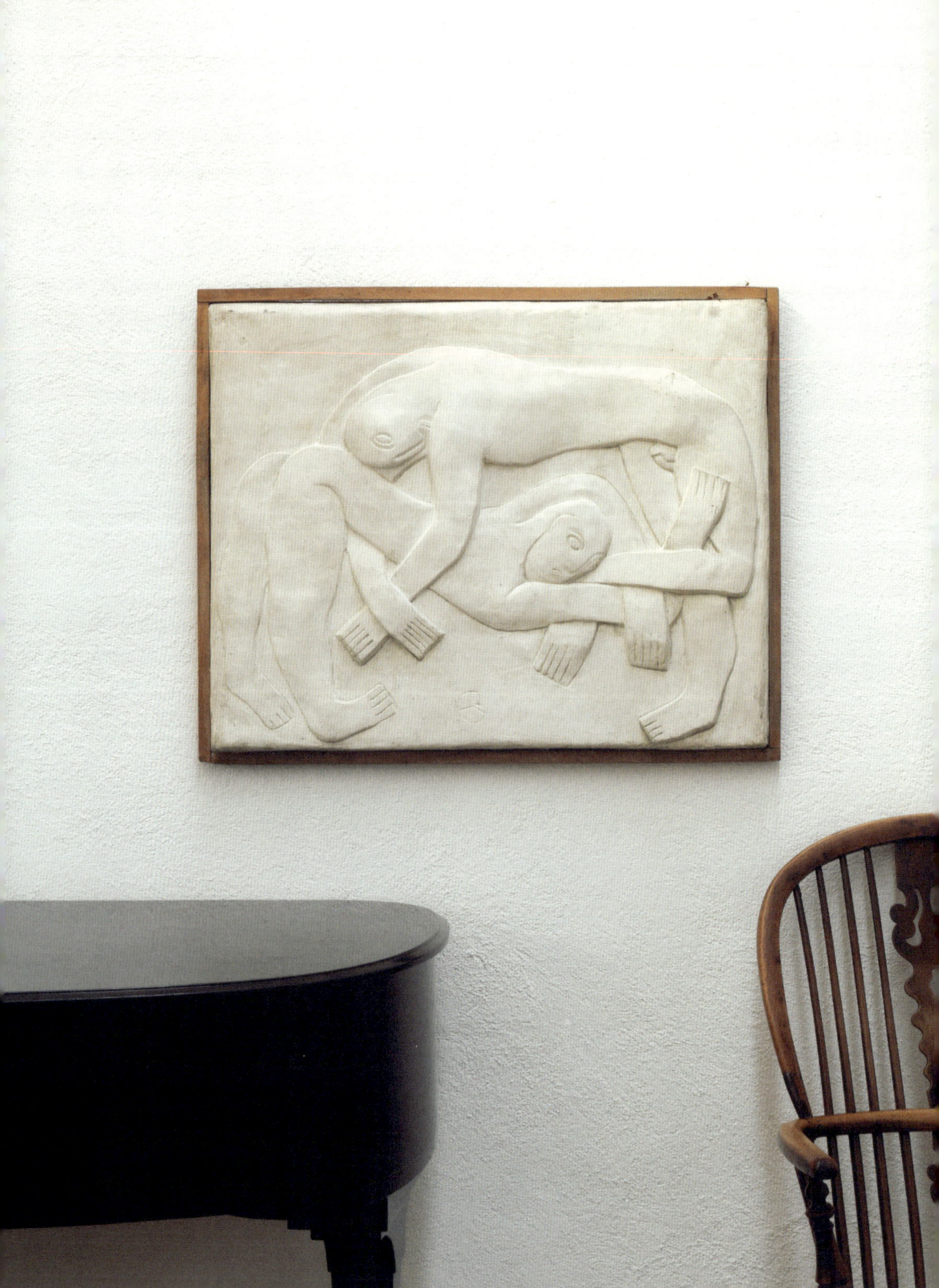

HENRI GAUDIER-BRZESKA

(1891–1915)

Henri Gaudier was born in Saint Jean de Braye, France. He aspired to be an artist, and both admired and sought to surpass the influence of Auguste Rodin in sculpture. In 1910, Gaudier met the Polish-born writer Sophie Brzeska at Sainte-Geneviève Library in Paris and moved with her to London in early 1911. Gaudier and Brzeska were partners and combined their surnames, although Brzeska - twenty years senior - sometimes pretended to be the artist's sister. In London, Henri Gaudier-Brzeska met Jacob Epstein, and allied himself to the vorticist circle around Ezra Pound and Wyndham Lewis. In this short time, Henri Gaudier-Brzeska's work underwent a rapid transformation from naturalism to almost abstract forms. In 1914, he volunteered for the French army and was killed in the trenches the following year. A memorial exhibition was held in London in 1918 at Sophie Gaudier-Brzeska's instigation. She died in 1925 without leaving a will, and Jim Ede purchased the majority of the couple's estates through an intermediary in 1927. He used the couple's letters as the basis for his biography of Henri Gaudier-Brzeska, *Savage Messiah*, and advocated for his significance as an artist, selling or gifting works to public collections in the UK and France.

Henri Gaudier-Brzeska, letter to Dr Uhlemayr, 5 March 1910
Published in H.S. Ede, *Savage Messiah* (London: William Heinemann Ltd., 1931) pp. 23-24

> When I face the beauty of nature, I am no longer sensitive to art, but in the town I appreciate the myriad benefits - the more I go into the woods and the fields the more distrustful I become of art and wish all civilisation to the devil; the more I wander about amidst filth and sweat the better I understand art and love it; the desire for it becomes my crying need [...]

Wrestlers relief, 1913 (cast 1965)
Herculite, 72.5 × 91.5 cm
KY00896.EH

Henri Gaudier-Brzeska, letter to Sophie Gaudier-Brzeska, May 1911

Published in H.S. Ede, *Savage Messiah; A Biography of the Sculptor Henri Gaudier-Brzeska* (London: Heinemann, 1931), pp. 81-82

> Line is nothing but a decoy - it does not exist, and although the Greeks are praised for having put it to so good a use, I [...] am sure that it has nothing essentially to do with beauty. There are a few things so detestable as the Venus of Milo - and exactly because she is no more than a line enjoyed by pigs - an enormous stomach if you like, without lumps, without holes, without hardness, without angles, without mystery, and without force - a flabby thing made of wool, which goes in if you lean against it, and, what's worse, makes a fellow hot [...] I loathe Praxiteles, for he, better than any other, has rounded the angles and levelled the depressions: stumps of marble very polished, very sweet, Mr. Praxiteles, Sir Scopas idem. But these are not men, only well-oiled corpses which one has set up; and they give pleasure because they are corpses, they are not forms which can give a local rhythm, do not evoke the base or the sublime, have no vibrating life-force; and that is why all the Greeks, with the exception of Phidias, Polycletus and Lysippus, are nothing but vulgar hewers of marble.

Henri Gaudier-Brzeska, letter to Sophie Gaudier-Brzeska, 28 October 1912

Published in H.S. Ede, *Savage Messiah; A Biography of the Sculptor Henri Gaudier-Brzeska* (London: Heinemann, 1931), pp. 169-171

> Bergson expressly demonstrates that the world is positive, real; and that it is pernicious and useless to rack your brains to find out if the world was created by a God or not. He emphasizes intuition as more valuable than reason - for reason is scientific and leads to the absurd... [...] As to my ideas about art, I'm perpetually modifying them, and I am very glad I do. If I stuck to some fixed idea, I should grow mannered, and so spoil the whole of my development. As far as I can see at this moment, I believe that art is the interpretation of emotions, and consequently of the idea.

For this emotion I recognize as necessary only the discipline of technique, and at this moment I think the idea comes better the more the technique is simple and limited; on the other hand, I fully recognize that the more you limit your technique, the greater danger you run of falling into mannerism, which is the negation of all the emotion which we experience in front of nature.

Henri Gaudier-Brzeska, letter to Sophie Gaudier-Brzeska, 6 December 1912

Published in H.S. Ede, *Savage Messiah; A Biography of the Sculptor Henri Gaudier-Brzeska* (London: Heinemann, 1931), pp. 217-218

Last night I went to see the wrestlers – God! I have seldom seen anything so lovely – two athletic types, large shoulders, taut, big necks like bulls, small in the build with firm thighs and slender ankles, feet sensitive as hands, and not tall. They fought with amazing vivacity and spirit, turning in the air, falling back on their heads, and in a flash were up again on the other side, utterly incomprehensible. They have reached such a state of perfection that one can take the other by a foot and, without exaggeration, can whirl him five times round and round himself, and then let go so that the other flies off like a ball and falls on his head – but he is up in a moment and back again more ferocious than ever to the fight – and Pik [Henri himself] who thought he would be smashed to bits! I stayed and drew for two hours and am going to begin the statuettes on Sunday.

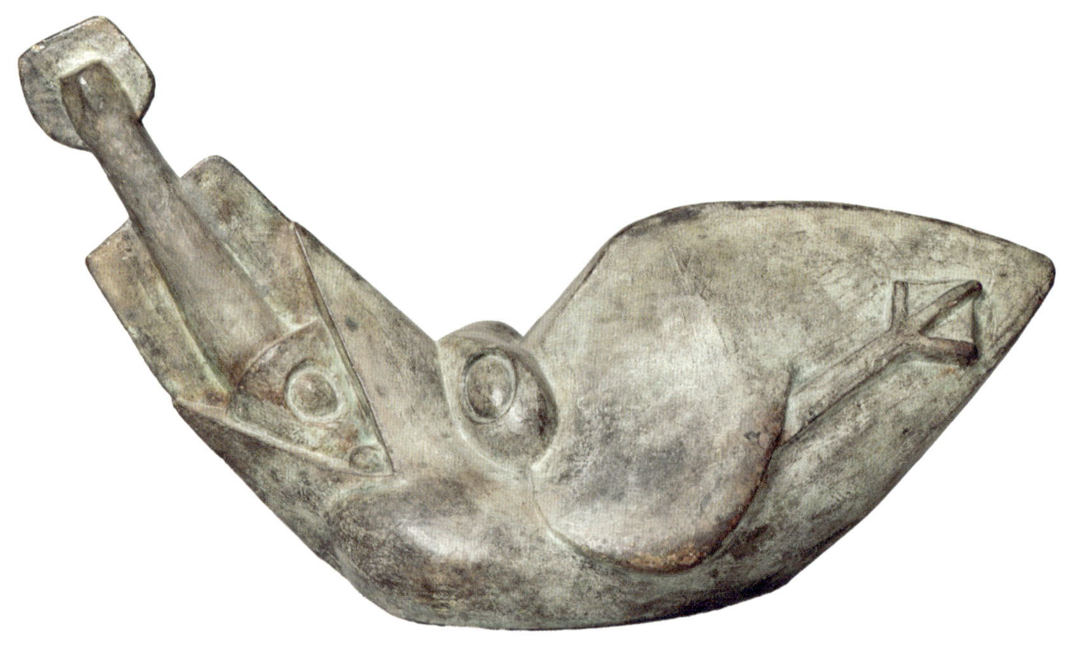

Bird Swallowing a Fish, 1914
Plaster and green paint, 33 × 58 × 27 cm
KY00493.EH

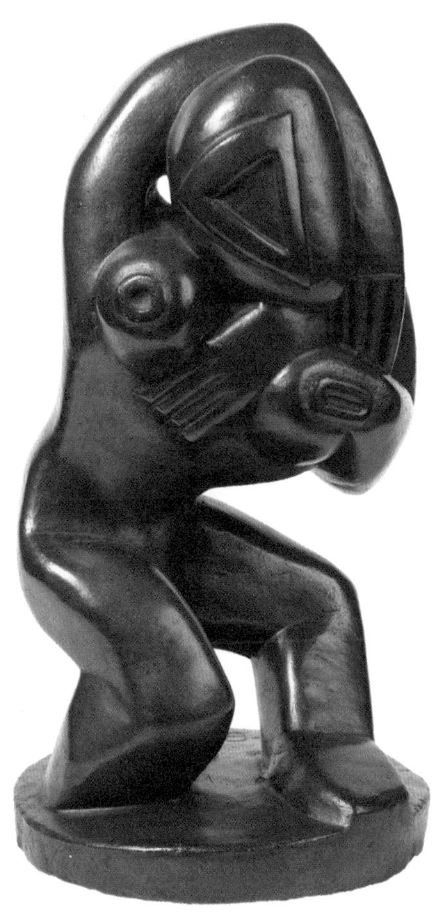

Red Stone Dancer, 1913-14 (cast 1969)
Bronze, 42.6 × 23 × 22.4 cm
KY00984.EH

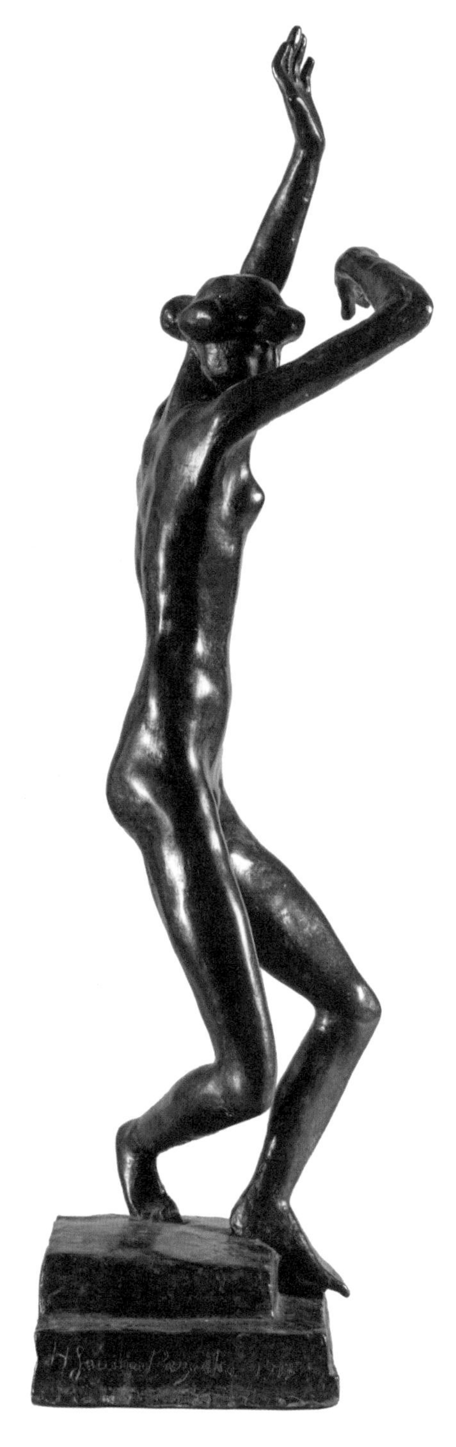

Dancer, 1913 (cast 1967)
Bronze, 76.5 × 22 × 21 cm
KY00818.EH

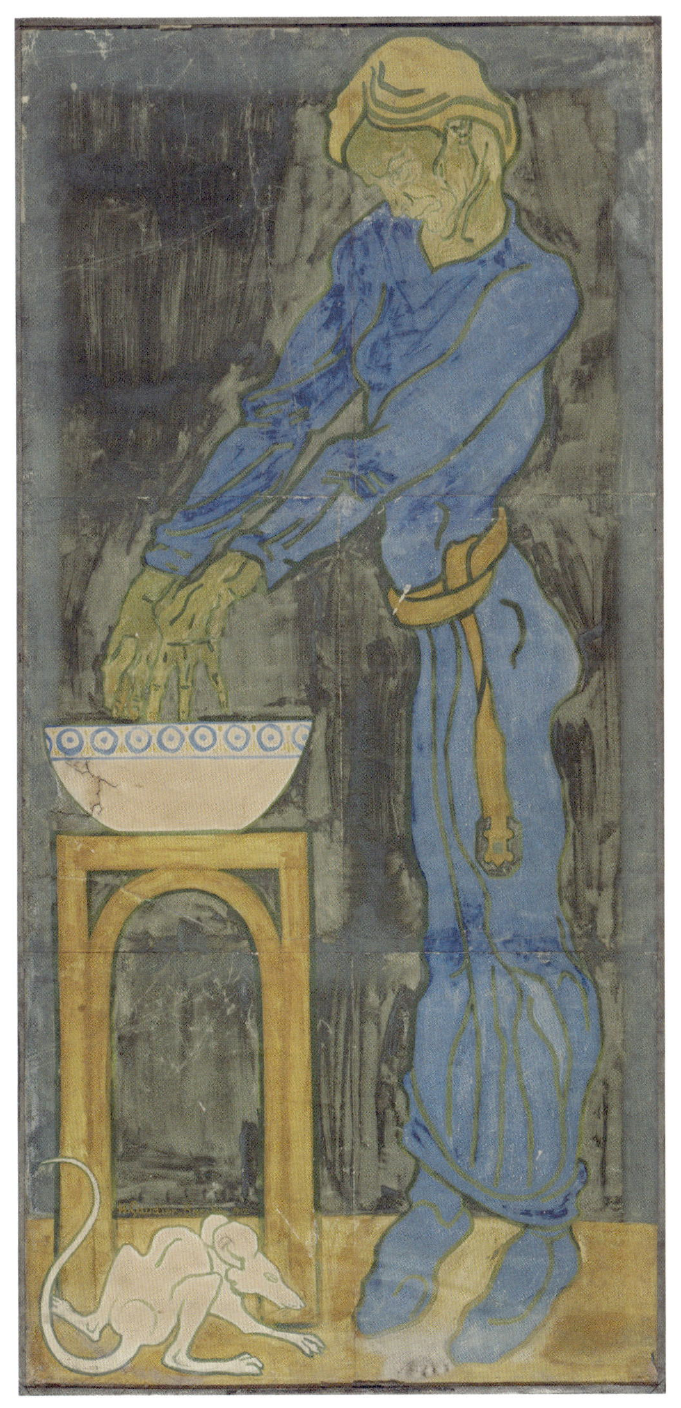

Lady Macbeth poster, 1912
Gouache on paper, laid on canvas,
229 × 109 cm
KY00497.EH

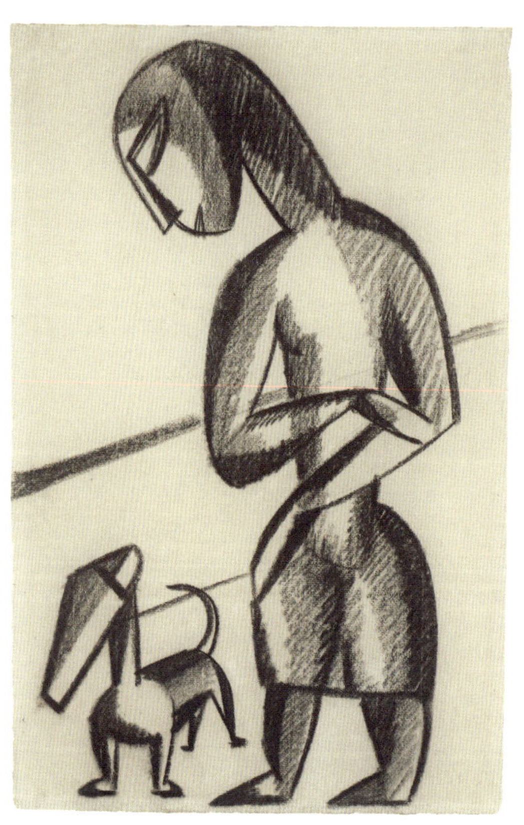

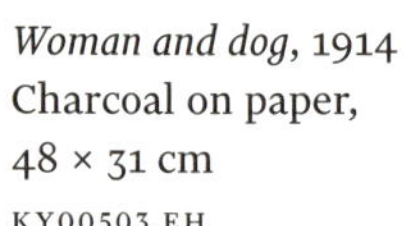

Woman and dog, 1914
Charcoal on paper,
48 × 31 cm
KY00503.EH

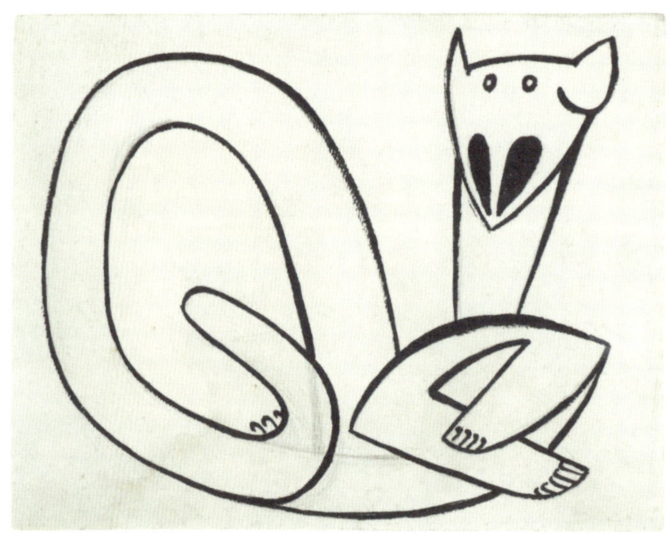

Cat, c. 1913
Ink on paper,
22.2 × 29 cm
KY00534.EH

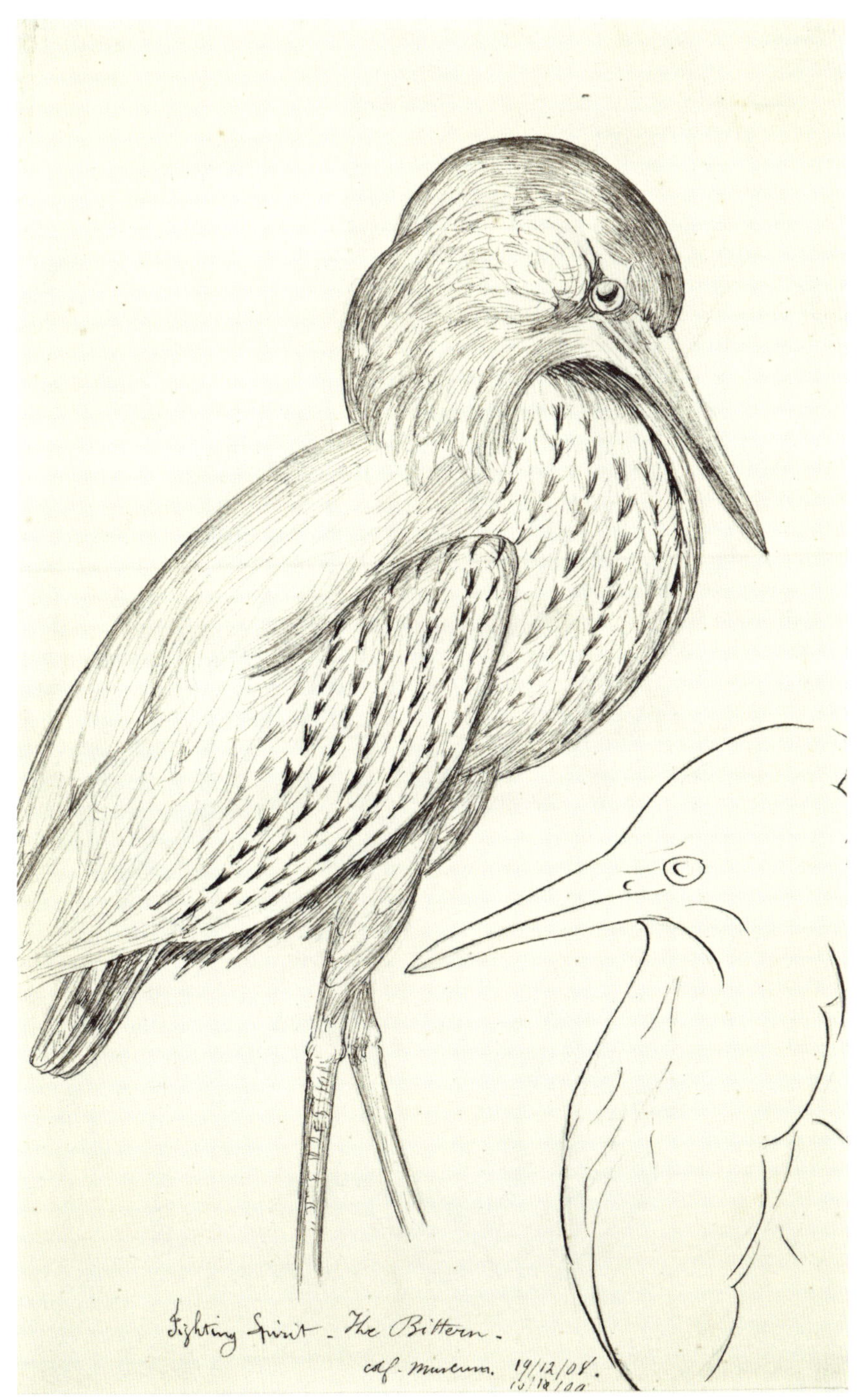

Studies (The Bittern),
1908-9
Ink on paper,
22 × 14 cm
KY00544.EH

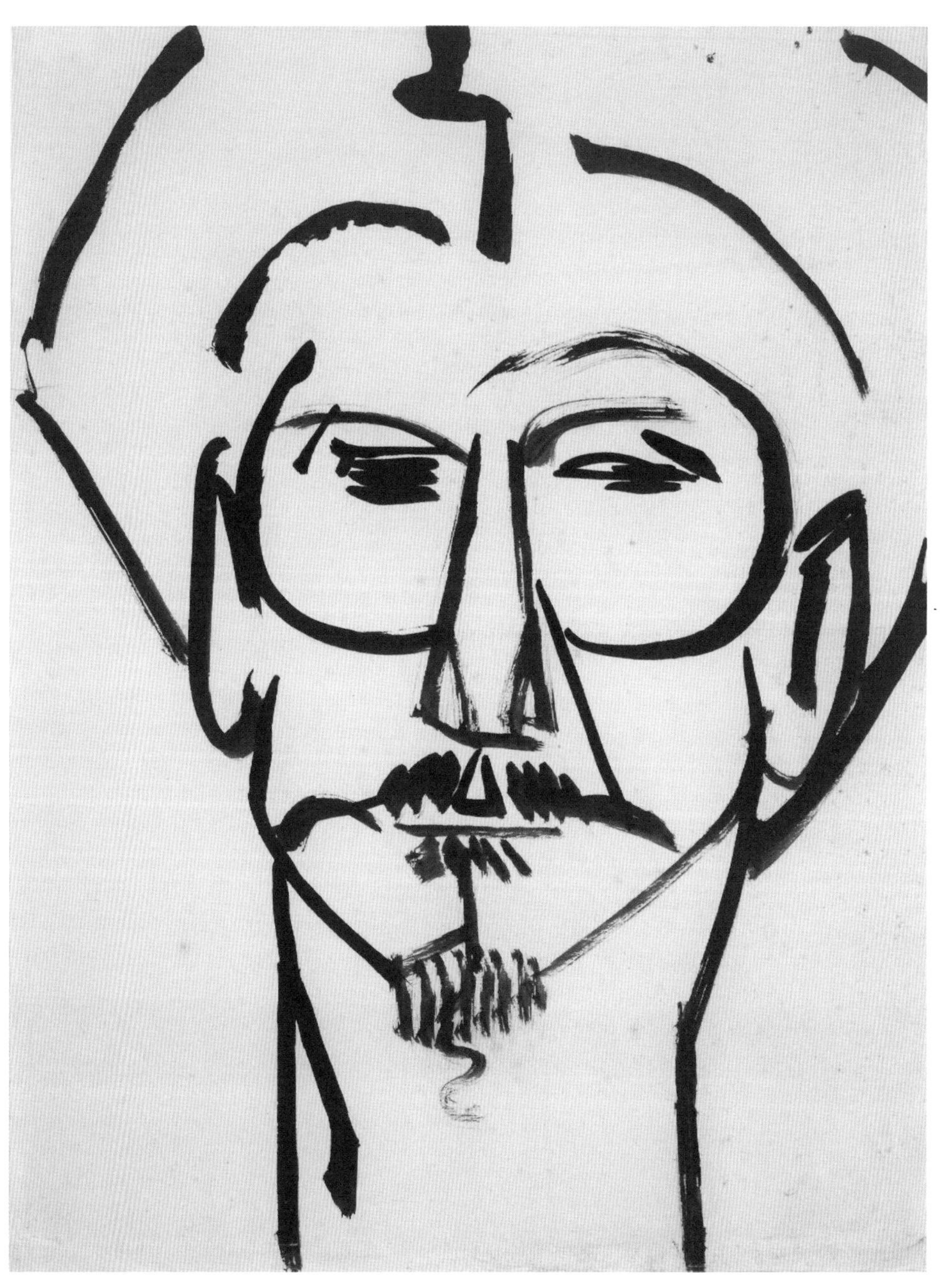

Ezra Pound, 1914
Ink on paper, 50 × 38 cm
KY00504.EH

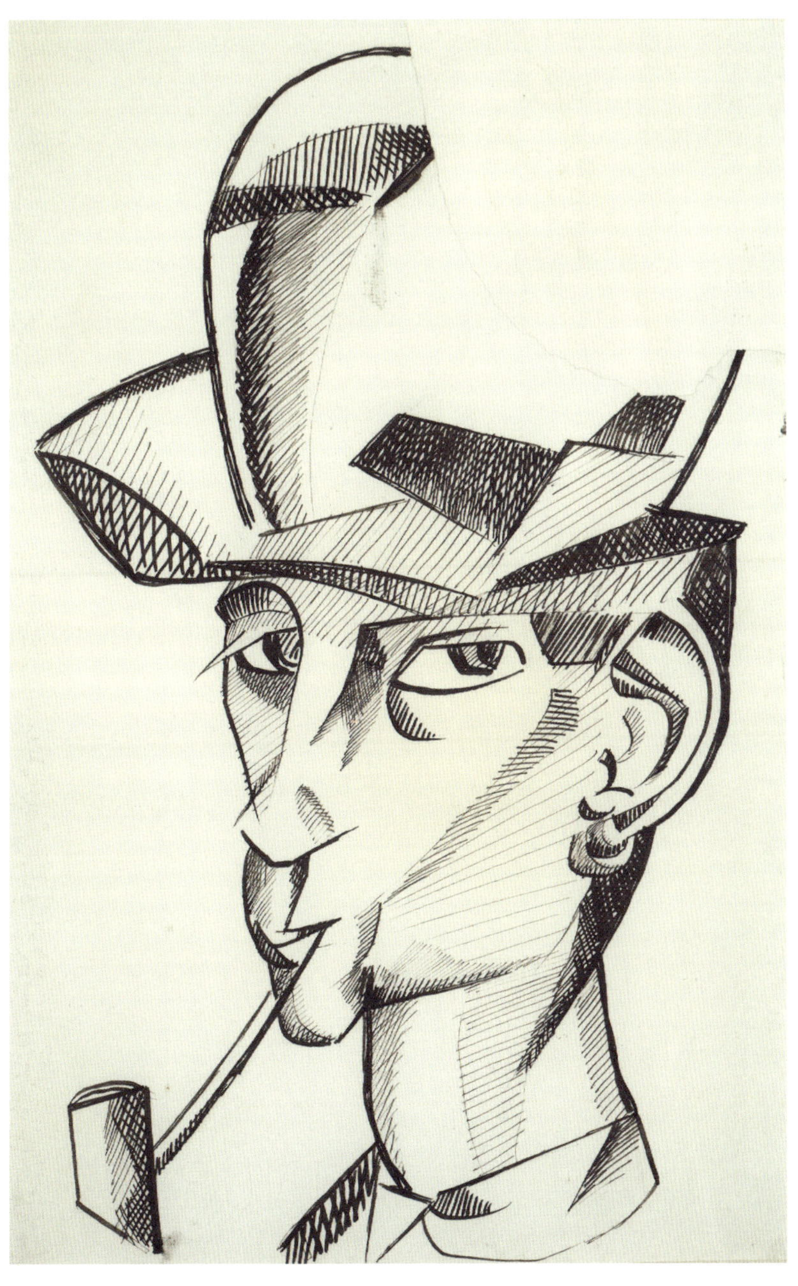

Self-portrait with a pipe (2), 1913
Ink on paper, 47 × 30.5 cm
KY00567.EH

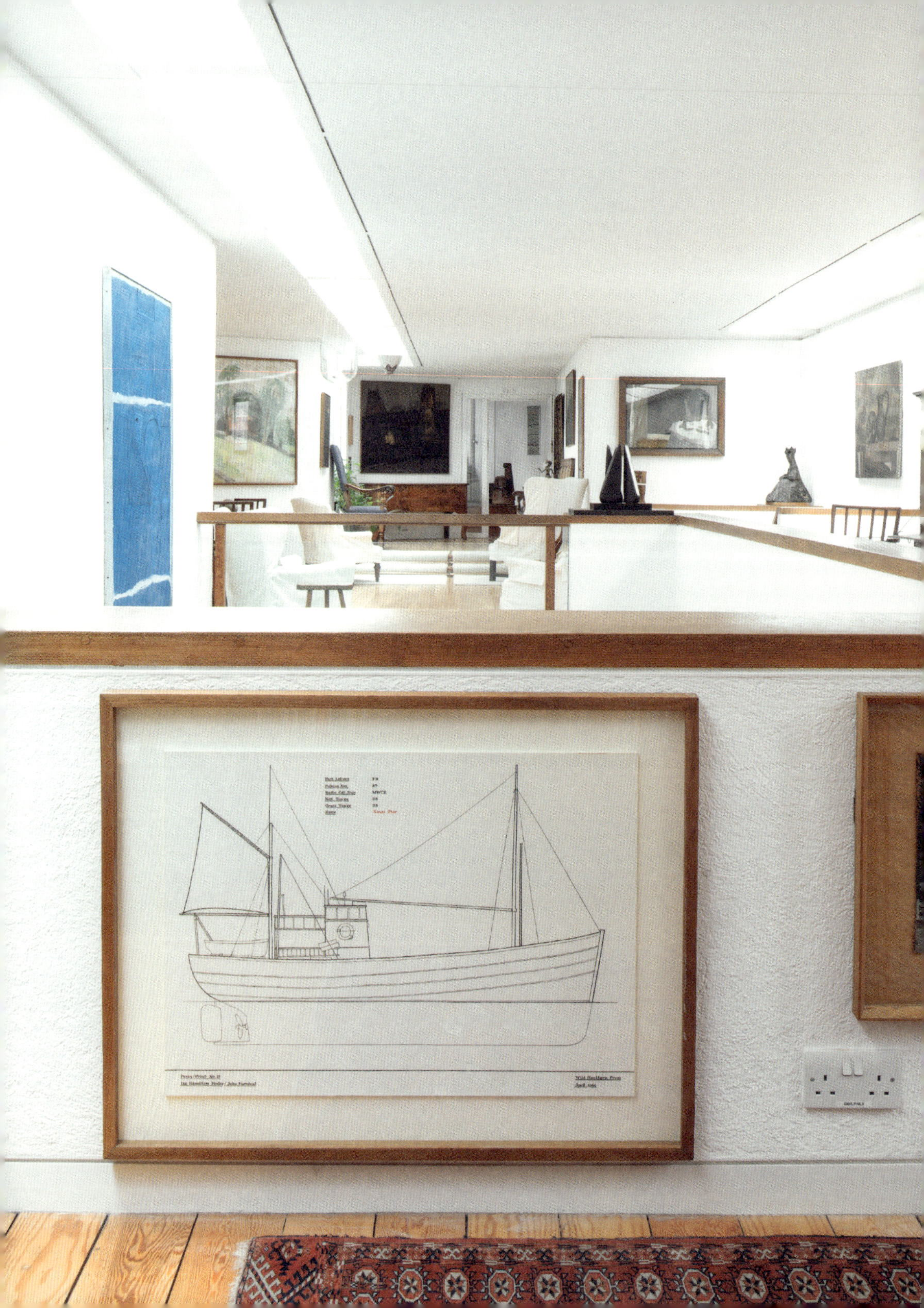

IAN HAMILTON FINLAY

(1925–2006)

Ian Hamilton Finlay was born in Nassau in The Bahamas and attended the Glasgow School of Art. He served with the Royal Army Service Corps during the second world war, resulting in a longstanding and sometimes controversial interest in military iconography. Alongside agricultural work after the war, Finlay began to write fiction, drama and poetry. He started the Wild Hawthorn Press with Jessie McGuffie, publishing his visual poetry magazine *Poor. Old. Tired. Horse. (POTH)*, copies of which he sent to Jim Ede at Kettle's Yard. At his home in Lanarkshire, Finlay built a classical garden which he called 'Little Sparta', filled with sculptural, poetic and landscape work on maritime themes and those relating to classical antiquity, the French Revolution, and the second world war. He first met Jim Ede in Scotland, in 1964.

Ian Hamilton Finlay, letter to Jim Ede, 27 October 1964
Kettle's Yard Archive, Papers of Harold Stanley 'Jim' Ede. KY/EDE/1/5

> I have an idea, of starting a series of Wild Hawthorn poem-prints - that is, single concrete poems, printed quite large, and in colours, sold to be framed like pictures, for the wall. It seems a nice idea, and perhaps economically more feasible than the smaller books, because there is no longer - though there was still a year ago - such a thing as cheap printing... I have had this idea for some time, but it has all at once become more real to me, and I hope we can go ahead [...]

Poem/Print no.11, 1969
Silkscreen print on paper, 51 × 71.5 cm
KY00999.EH

Also pictured are paintings by William Scott, Winifred Nicholson, William Congdon and Ben Nicholson, and sculptures by Barbara Hepworth and Henri Gaudier-Brzeska.

Ian Hamilton Finlay, letter to Jim Ede, 15 February 1965

Kettle's Yard Archive, Papers of Harold Stanley 'Jim' Ede. KY/EDE/1/5

> I have been working poems: literally making the 2 wee standing poems, which you'll see, with cut paper ... and typing other poems ... and puzzling as usual about what's right in them, and what's wrong. [...]
>
> I am very fond of boats at present. Especially fishing trawlers. I made a nice poem out of just the names of some: I mean their actual names, not names I made up... I have a list of about 100 names in my notebook. I also love their numbers on their barrels: so lovely, just like the words in a picture by Gris... I made a poem of them, too...

Ian Hamilton Finlay, letter to Jim Ede, 1965

Kettle's Yard Archive, Papers of Harold Stanley 'Jim' Ede. KY/EDE/1/5

> I have written only a few new poems since I came, but have a new booklet/ poem ready - *Cythera* - which you'll be getting one of these days when we get down to addressing envelopes... I like it a lot, it's very <u>cool</u> and leafy and <u>pure</u>. But I'm not sure how to <u>go on</u> from it at all...

Ian Hamilton Finlay, letter to Jim Ede, 25 January 1966

Kettle's Yard Archive, Papers of Harold Stanley 'Jim' Ede. KY/EDE/1/5

> Your present arrived today. It is a wonderful surprise for us. [...] Please understand we are very deeply and sincerely grateful: thank you so much. Part of it will be used to buy a pram - something that I don't feel able to make... Prams have a sort of super-platonic being: no pram can depart <u>far</u> from <u>all</u> prams, or essence-of-pram... and a <u>contemporary</u> pram is not to be imagined... contemporary chair, yes... or even cradle... but a pram is a pram is a pram, quite obdurately and for all time...

Ian Hamilton Finlay, letter to Jim Ede, 17 October c. 1966

Kettle's Yard Archive, Papers of Harold Stanley 'Jim' Ede. KY/EDE/1/5

We had a very nice visit from Stephen Bann, and he was telling me about your collection of paintings, and that you have Christopher Woods... How wonderful! I like his paintings very much indeed. At one time I had a big book of them, but that was long ago. However, I still think of them quite often, and of course, as you know, I am very fond of fishing boats.

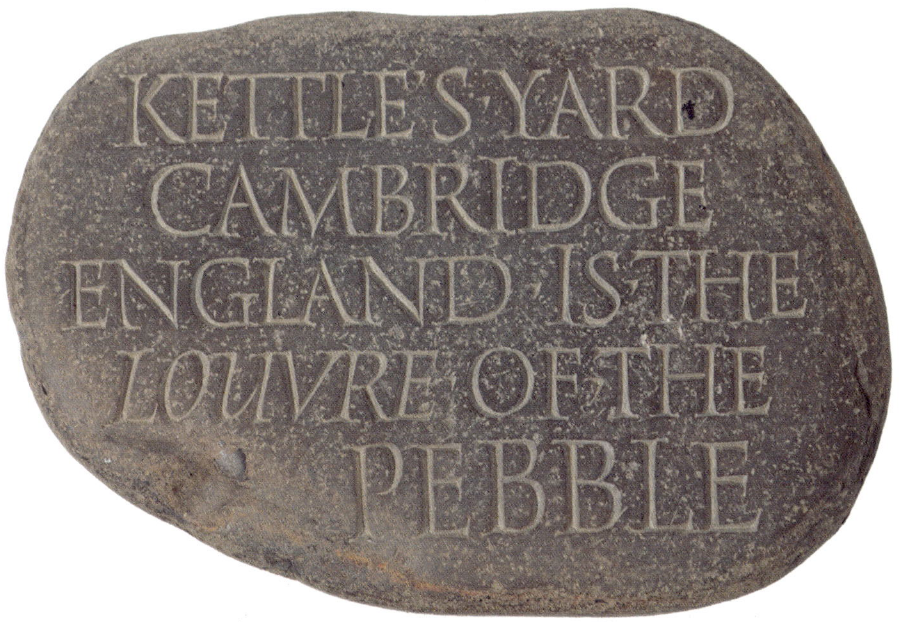

KETTLE'S YARD / CAMBRIDGE / ENGLAND IS THE / LOUVRE OF THE PEBBLE, 1995
Inscribed stone, 9.7 × 14.5 × 1.4 cm
KY01360

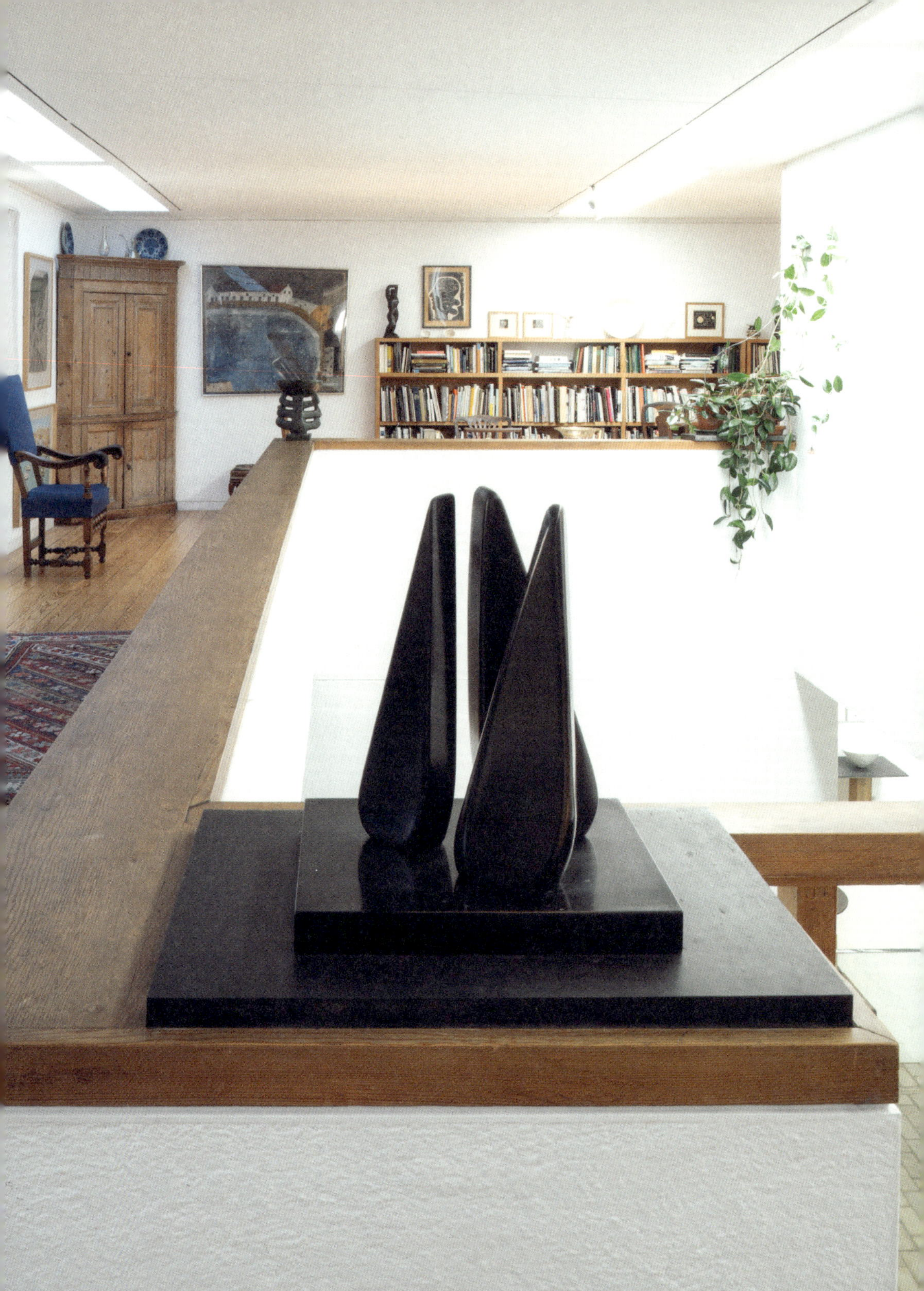

BARBARA HEPWORTH

(1903–1975)

Barbara Hepworth was born in Wakefield, Yorkshire. She studied at the Leeds School of Art and at the Royal College of Art in London, where she was one of several students carving directly in stone and wood. In 1924, she won a scholarship which enabled her to travel to Florence and study art and architecture in Italy. She married fellow sculptor John Skeaping the following year and they exhibited together in London in 1927 and 1928. In 1931, Hepworth met the painter Ben Nicholson, who shortly afterwards moved into her studio in Hampstead, London. Their circle at that time included the artist Henry Moore and the critic Herbert Read. In the 1930s, she and Nicholson both produced designs for fabrics, examples of which are among the Kettle's Yard collection.

In spring 1933, Hepworth and Nicholson travelled through France together, visiting Sophie Taeuber-Arp, Constantin Brâncuși, Pablo Picasso and others. Hepworth became part of an international community of artists, and images of her work were published in key modernist art periodicals *Axis* and *Abstraction-Création*. As artists such as László Moholy-Nagy, Naum Gabo and Piet Mondrian migrated to London, international exchange accelerated. In 1937, this community was celebrated in *Circle: International Survey of Constructivist Art*, a single-issue journal produced by Hepworth with Nicholson, Gabo, Sadie Speight and Leslie Martin (one of the architects responsible for the 1970 extension to Kettle's Yard).

At the outbreak of the second world war in 1939, Hepworth and Nicholson moved to Cornwall, near to critic Adrian Stokes and artist Margaret Mellis and were soon joined by Naum and Miriam Gabo. During the war, now a parent to four young children, Hepworth lacked the space, time and materials to carve, and turned to drawing, which she retained as part of her practice. In 1949, Hepworth moved into Trewyn Studios in St Ives, where she lived until the end of her life. Jim Ede was late to acquire a sculpture by Hepworth for his collection, finally purchasing *Three Personages* (1965) in 1969.

Three Personages, 1965
Slate on black lacquered wood base, 39.7 × 35.5 × 27.8 cm
KY00979.EH

Also pictured are a painting by James Dixon, sculptures by Henri Gaudier Brzeska, and works on paper by Ben Nicholson.

Letter from Barbara Hepworth to Jim Ede, 14 April 1968

Kettle's Yard Archive, Papers of Harold Stanley 'Jim' Ede. KY/EDE/1/7

When Ben brought me to your beautiful house to share those wonderful evenings with you and Helen, nobody was more aware than I of your generosity and love and inspiration in face of lack of money and yet with the exquisite presentation of real beauty for all to share. In fact I tried hard to learn from you and Helen and to emulate – and I was ever deeply grateful. But in my heart I longed to have a work of mine in your house and in the lovely company of paintings by BN [Ben Nicholson], Winifred [Nicholson], Kit [Christopher Wood], [Alfred] Wallis and so on. I longed to give you something; but to do so without seeing your face light up, as it did with Ben [Nicholson]'s, seemed like buying myself a place. I just waited hopefully. I gave as many works away then as I do now to those whose face lights up and those who have no money and I still want to when I can. If you read my letter carefully you will see that I promised one as soon as possible to you and your wonderful collection so generously given to the generations to come [...]

Letter from Jim Ede to Barbara Hepworth, 24 May 1969

Tate Archive. Papers of Barbara Hepworth. TGA 20132/1/48/20

Dearest Barbara, I have at long last got a little money of my own over and above what is needed for the building of our two extensions – & I want if it isn't long ago too late to buy a Barbara Hepworth and so at least in a small way redeem my inability in the past. [...]

Turning Form, 1957
Ink on paper, 36 × 25 cm
KY01252

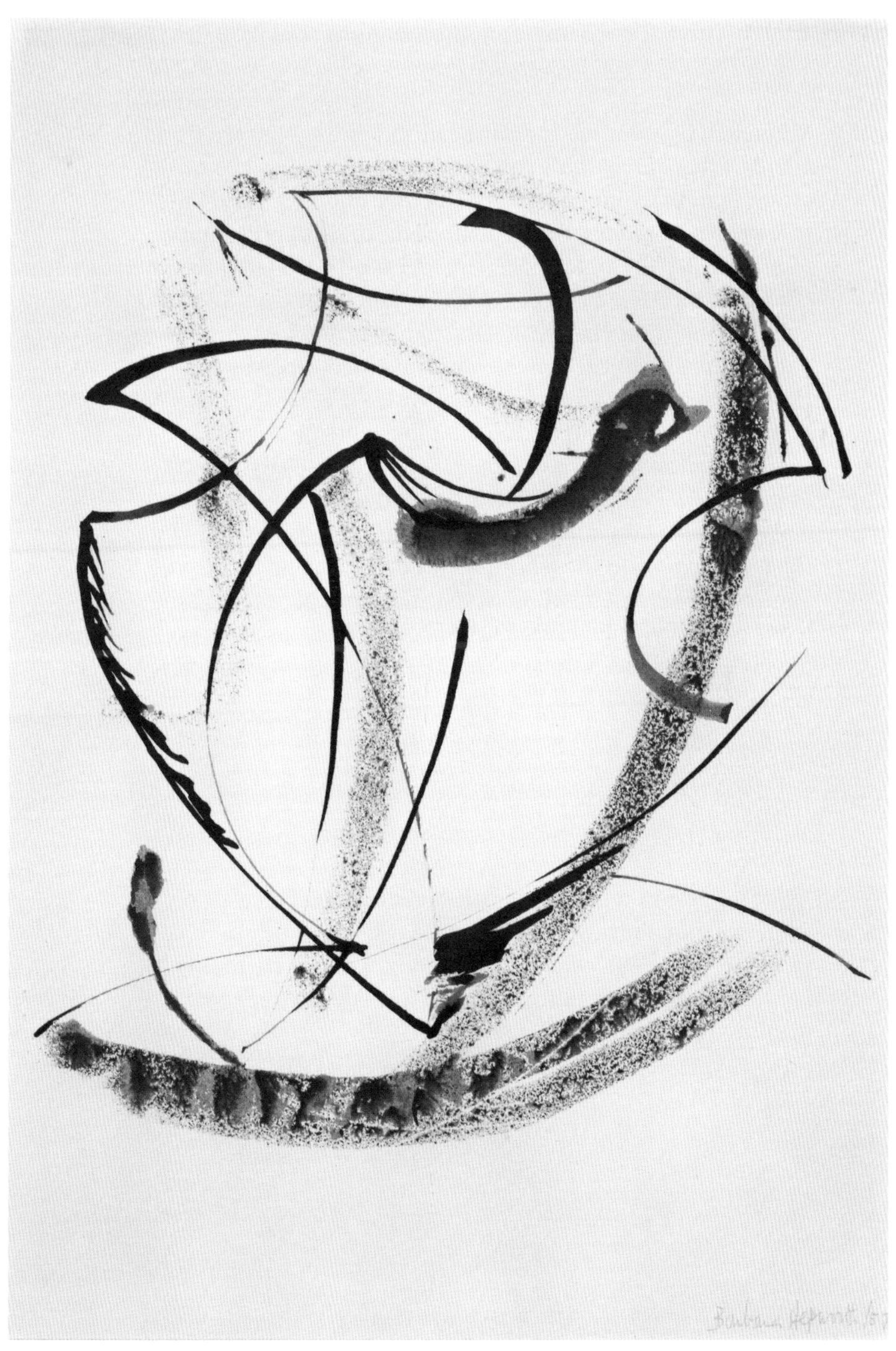
Barbara Hepworth

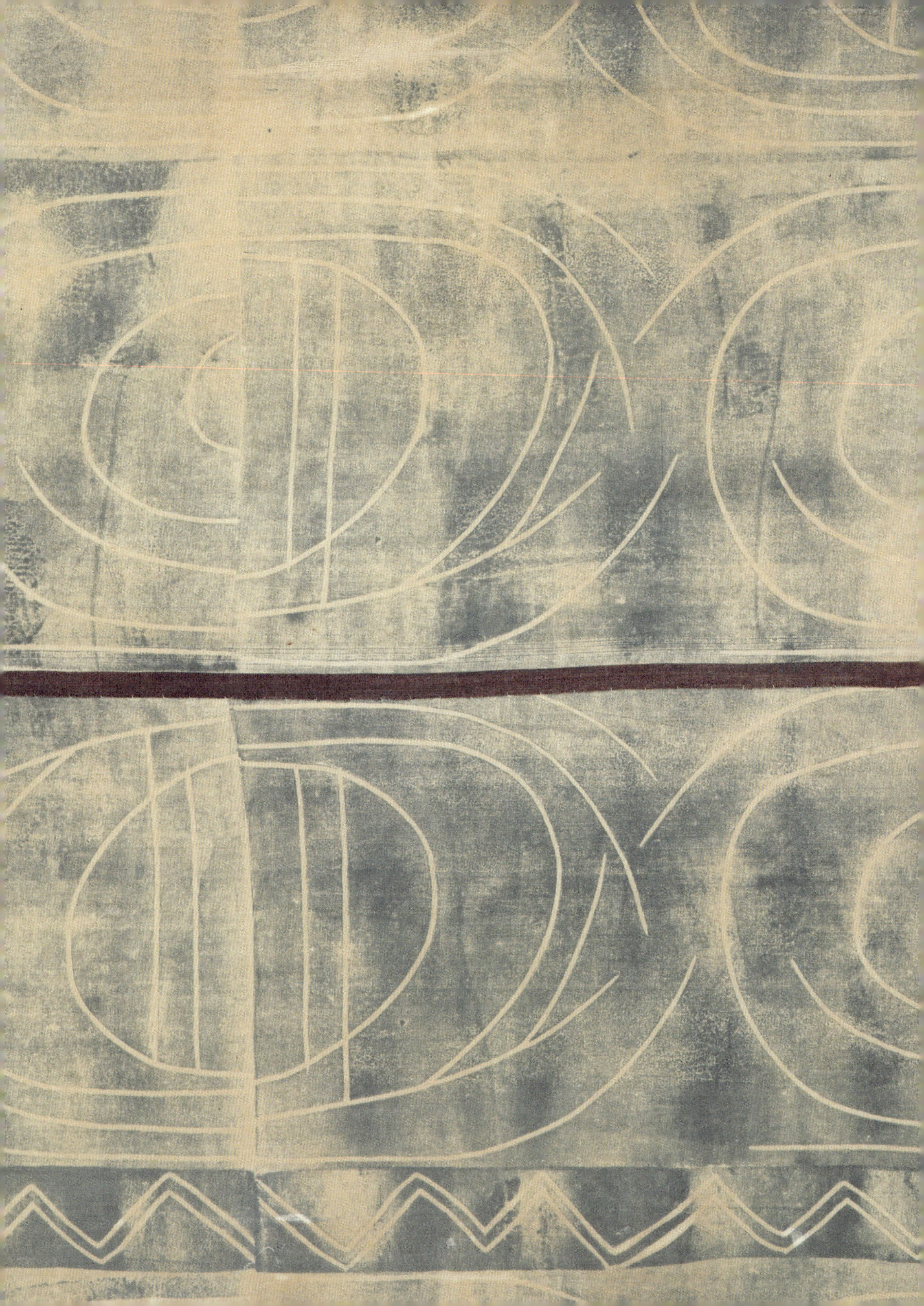

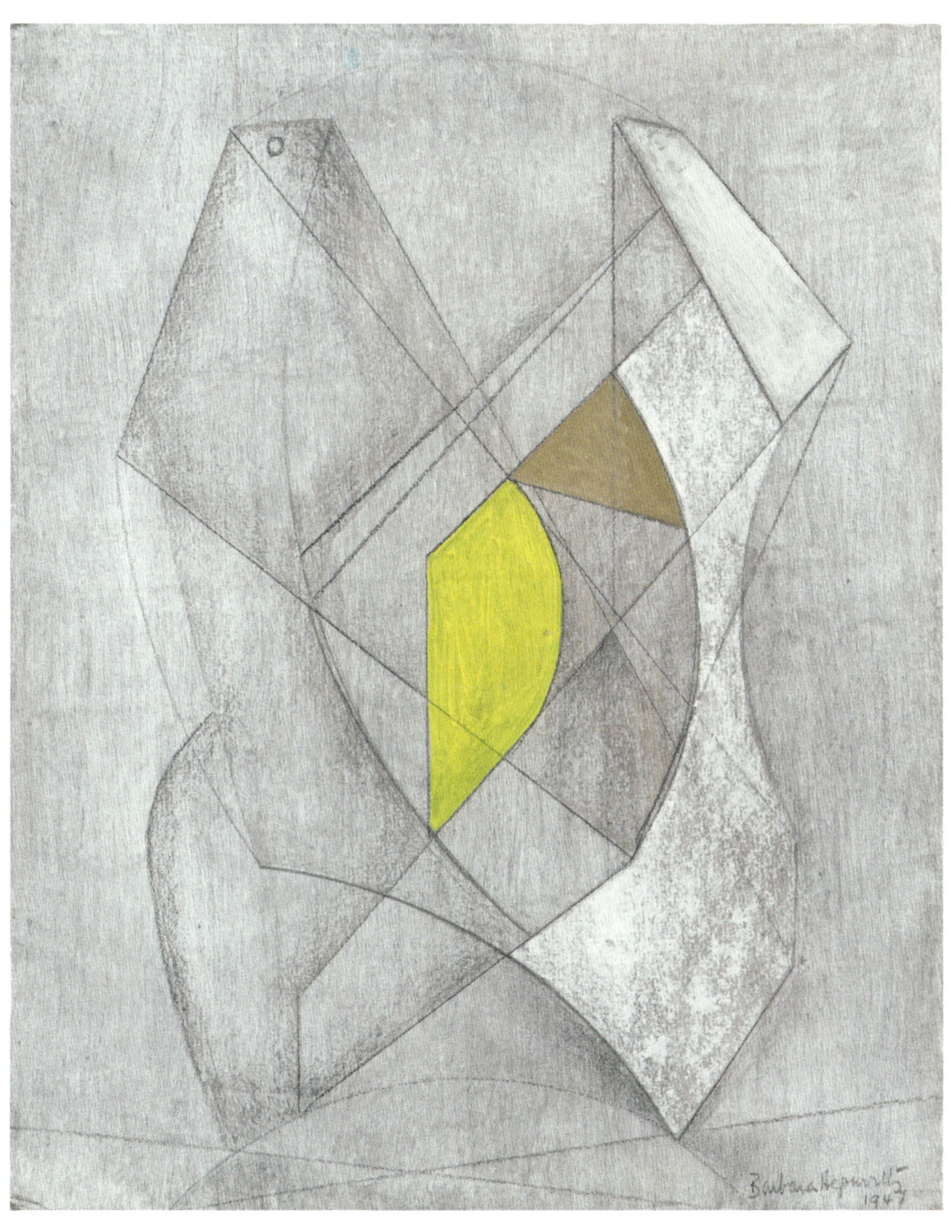

Design, c. 1933
Print on cotton, 48 × 39 cm
KY00700.EH

Group for sculpture (contrapuntal forms), 1947
Oil paint and graphite on card mounted on hardboard, 29 × 23.5 cm
KY01251

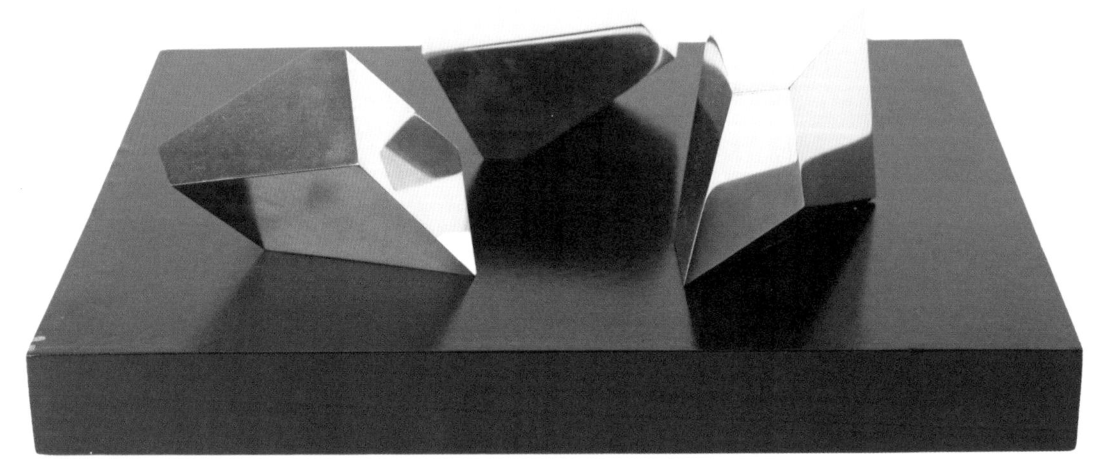

Group of Three Magic Stones, 1973
Silver on black lacquered wood base, 12 × 37 × 31.6 cm
KY01253

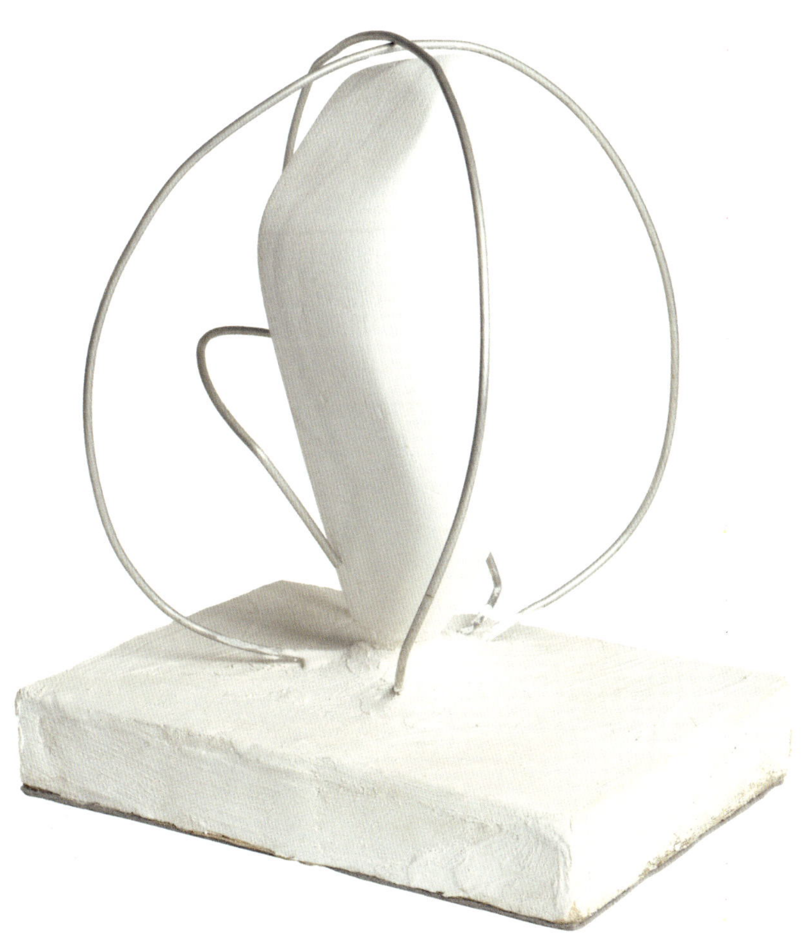

Maquette for Garden Sculpture, 1951
Plaster and lead wire, 26 × 22 × 18 cm
KY01254

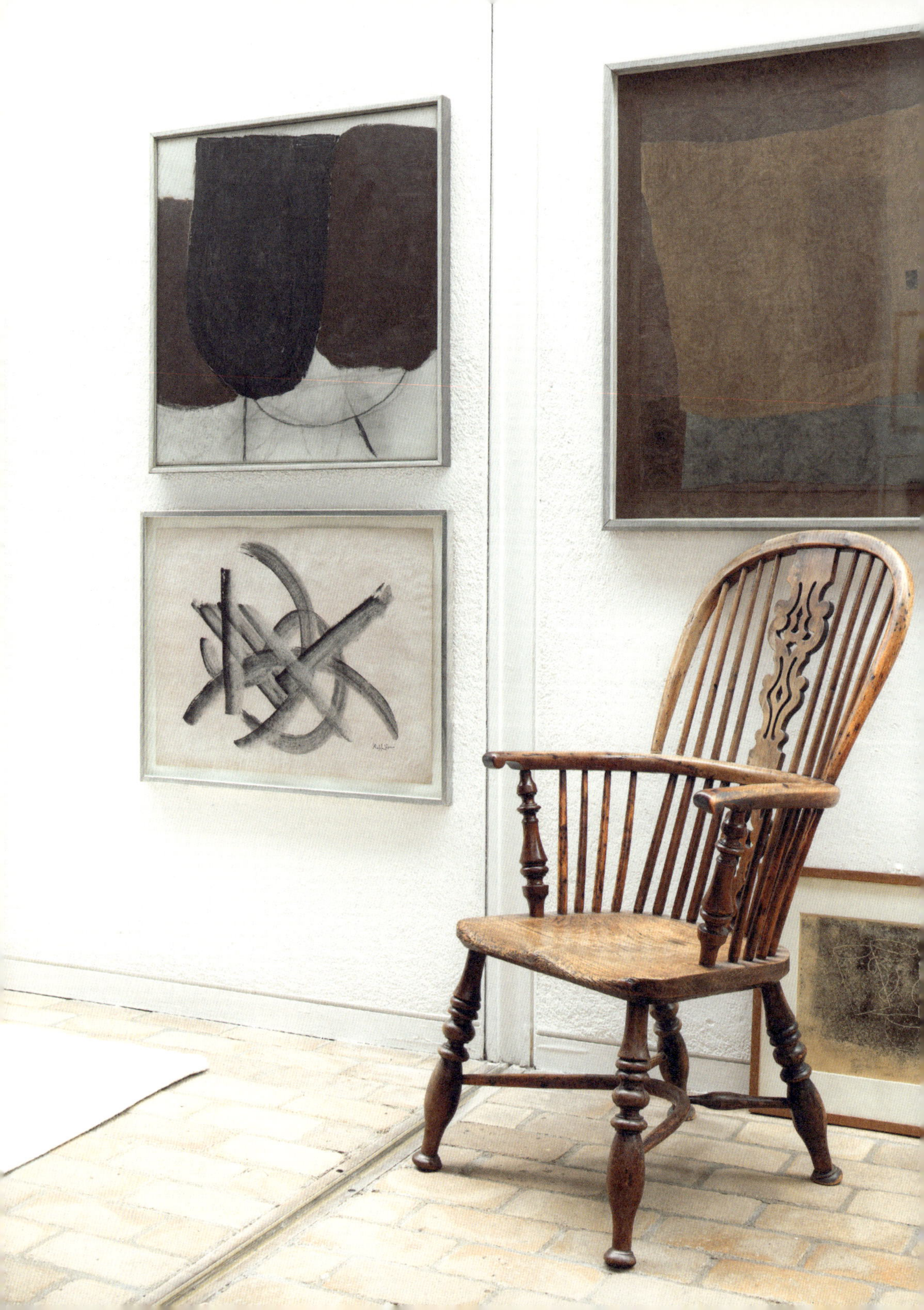

ROGER HILTON

(1911–1975)

Roger Hilton was born in Northwood, Middlesex. His mother had trained as a painter at the Slade School of Art in London, where Hilton also studied 1929–31 and 1935–36. In 1937, Hilton moved to Paris, where he received further training with Roger Bissière at the Académie Ranson. Hilton served in the British Army during the second world war, and was a prisoner of war 1942–45. Afterwards, he enrolled at the Central School of Art in London, and in 1950 visited Cornwall for the first time. Hilton began painting abstract compositions, which became increasingly simplified following a meeting with the Dutch artist Constant Nieuwenhuys in 1953. Hilton taught at London's Central School 1954–56. He won the John Moore's Painting Prize in 1959 and 1963 and the UNESCO prize at the 1964 Venice Biennale. In 1965 Hilton moved to Cornwall, where he lived and worked for the rest of his life.

January 1961 (Black and Brown on White), 1961
Oil paint on canvas,
66 × 66 cm
KY00855.EH

with (below)
Edmond Xavier Kapp
Design, 1965
Wash paint on paper,
48 × 65 cm
KY00806.EH

and (right) Italo Valenti
Veneti, 1964
Paper collage on board,
80 × 110 cm
KY00918.EH

and (bottom right)
Ben Nicholson
1928 (three mugs and a bowl), 1928
Linocut print on paper,
26 × 33 cm

Roger Hilton, letter to Jim Ede, c. 1957
Kettle's Yard Archive, Papers of Harold Stanley 'Jim' Ede. KY/EDE/1/1

> I very much enjoyed my time in Cornwall. Have come back for a bit of peace and quiet and hope to get some work done in my new studio during the summer.

Roger Hilton, letter to Jim Ede, c. 1963
Kettle's Yard Archive, Papers of Harold Stanley 'Jim' Ede. KY/EDE/1/1

> I think that picture will go very nicely with the other one you have. You chose well both times. Victor Pasmore told me he liked the one you bought the best in the show. If I'm ever in Cambridge I'd like to come and call if I may.

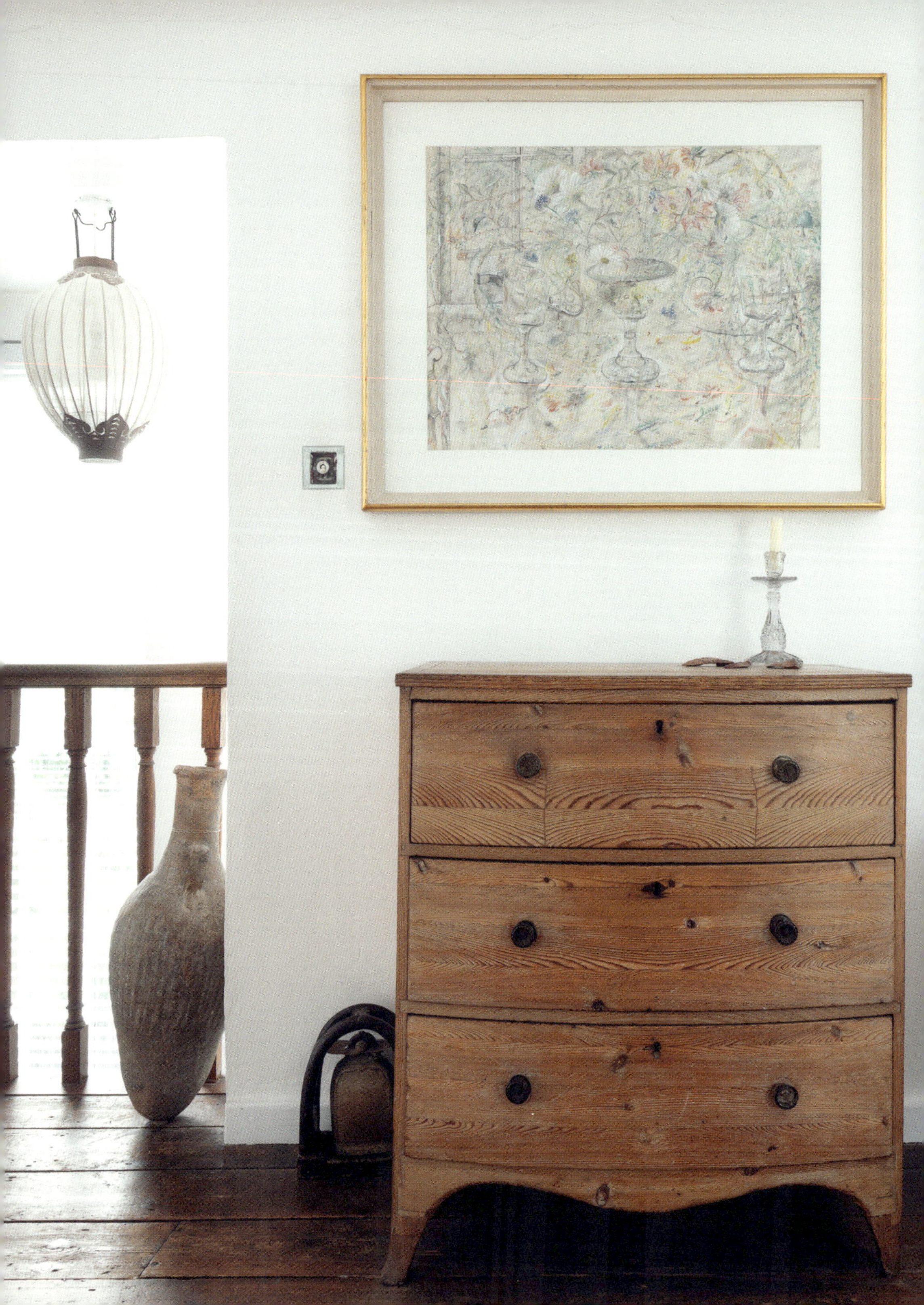

DAVID JONES

(1895–1974)

David Jones was born in Brockley, south London (then part of Kent). In 1921, after his experience of fighting in the trenches during the first world war, he converted to Roman Catholicism. Jones learned engraving with Eric Gill and illustrated the Golden Cockerell Press's *The Chester Play of the Deluge* (1927) as well as the Douglas Cleverdon edition of Samuel Coleridge's *The Rime of the Ancient Mariner* (1929). Jones met the Edes in 1924 and became one of the most regular visitors to their Hampstead home.

In the early 1930s Jones experienced a period of illness which caused his eyesight to deteriorate, necessitating a change to watercolour. Jim Ede organised for a group of friends to support Jones through his convalescence. During this time, the artist drew upon his wartime experience to write *In Parenthesis* (1937), which was followed by *The Anathemata* (1952). In the late 1940s, Jones moved to Harrow, near London, and resumed painting, using techniques and imagery as complex as his writing style. Two major works acquired by Ede from this period include *Vexilla Regis* (1947-48) and *Flora in Calix Light* (1950).

David Jones, letter to Jim Ede, 18 January 1934
Kettle's Yard Archive, Papers of Harold Stanley 'Jim' Ede. KY/EDE/1/8

> I've only just tried to call to mind the bits of things that seem to me the high spots of what I feel characteristic in the arts of this complex island - it's to me always a loving 'handled' 'textured' free-flowing affair with a bit of-thunder-storm-behind-an-apple-tree - linear - tentative - not large - packed with life a bit of a joke - speckled - like a large thrush's breast & spear points in a garden. All this again is obviously futile but yet you would not, I think, be able to make this list fit say German - French - Italian Art - would you?
>
> It's the work of a motley race with Kent gardens & Capel-y-Ffin darknesses within a day's walk perhaps - it's a patch-work quilt, in a way, on the bed of a princess with a dead dog

Flora in Calix Light, 1950
Graphite and watercolour on paper, 57 × 76.8 cm
KY00765.EH

on the mat [...] but I can't for the life of me think of a painter or draughtsman who I would rise from my bed to look at with any certainty of reward since Blake – bad business, I only just realise how bad [...] PS. Take it all with a large pinch of salt.

David Jones, letter to Jim and Helen Ede, 25 November 1936
Kettle's Yard Archive, Papers of Harold Stanley 'Jim' Ede. KY/EDE/1/8

I do wish I had proper sets of my things & proper series of engravings & a lot of paintings – because you tell the world I am a good artist & then when you look round for a picture or two there aren't any ... I send you and Helen a great lot of love – & shall think about you in Africa. I do so often look back on the days I used to come so frequently to Hampstead & laugh with you round the fire. I do not think I could have stood those years without coming. It's odd this life I spend now. I hope when my writing is really done I shall be able to paint again & that the condition of the world will allow it.

David Jones, letter to Mildred Ede (Jim Ede's mother) about his painting *Vexilla Regis*, 28 August 1949
Kettle's Yard Archive, Papers of Harold Stanley 'Jim' Ede. KY/EDE/1/8

[...] the main jumping off ground was, I think, a Latin hymn we sing as part of the Good Friday Liturgy in the Roman rite. Two hymns in fact, one starting 'Vexilla Regis prodeunt', 'Forth come the standards of the King', a very ancient processional hymn, in which are many allusions to the tree and the Cross, and to the Cross as a tree etc. and the other starting: 'Crux fidelis inter omnes, arbor una nobis' ['The faithful cross among all, one tree for us'] [...] The general idea of the picture was also associated, in my mind, with the collapse of the Roman world. The three trees as it were left standing on Calvary – the various bits and pieces of classical ruins dotting the landscape – also older things, such as the Stonehenge or 'druidic' circle a little to the right of the right hand tree in the distance and then the Welsh hills more to the right again, the rushing ponies are, more or less, the horses of the Roman cavalry, turned to grass and gone wild and off to the hills. (This idea, probably in turn, comes from something in Malory's 'Morte D'Arthur' when right at the end, after the death of Guenevere and the break-up of the Round Table, Lancelot and other knights let their armed horses go free to roam where they will [...]) The leopard's pelt and the trumpet in the left hand bottom corner are supposed to be the instrument and insignia of a Roman buccinator or trumpeter, as though the owner of them had been part of the guard on Calvary – that sort of idea. The tree on the left of the main tree is, as it were, the tree of the 'good thief', it grows firmly in the ground and the pelican has made her nest and feeds her young in its branches – Our Lord is likened to a pelican in her piety in one of the Latin hymns of Thomas Aquinas. The tree on the right is that of the other thief, it is partly tree and partly triumphal column and partly imperial standard – a power symbol, it is not rooted in the ground but is part supported by wedges. St. Augustine's remark that 'empire is great robbery' influenced me here. It is not meant to be bad in itself but in some senses proud and self-sufficient. Nevertheless it is shadowed by the spreading central Tree and the dove, in fact, hovers over this tree of the truculent robber for somehow he is 'redeemed' too! ... The nails with their ribbons were suggested by the Paschal Candle which, in Catholic Churches, is lit during the Easter season. It is a very large candle and always decorated with flowers etc, and in the middle of it are inserted five separate grains of incense usually in little gilt containers, arranged in diamond formation and although the actual history of this custom is very obscure, they are now taken to signify the Five Wounds of our Lord [...]

P.S. Also of course the Yggdrasil of Northern Mythology, the great tree with its roots far in the earth and its flowering in heaven no doubt comes into the picture – for all these things are one thing in some sense.

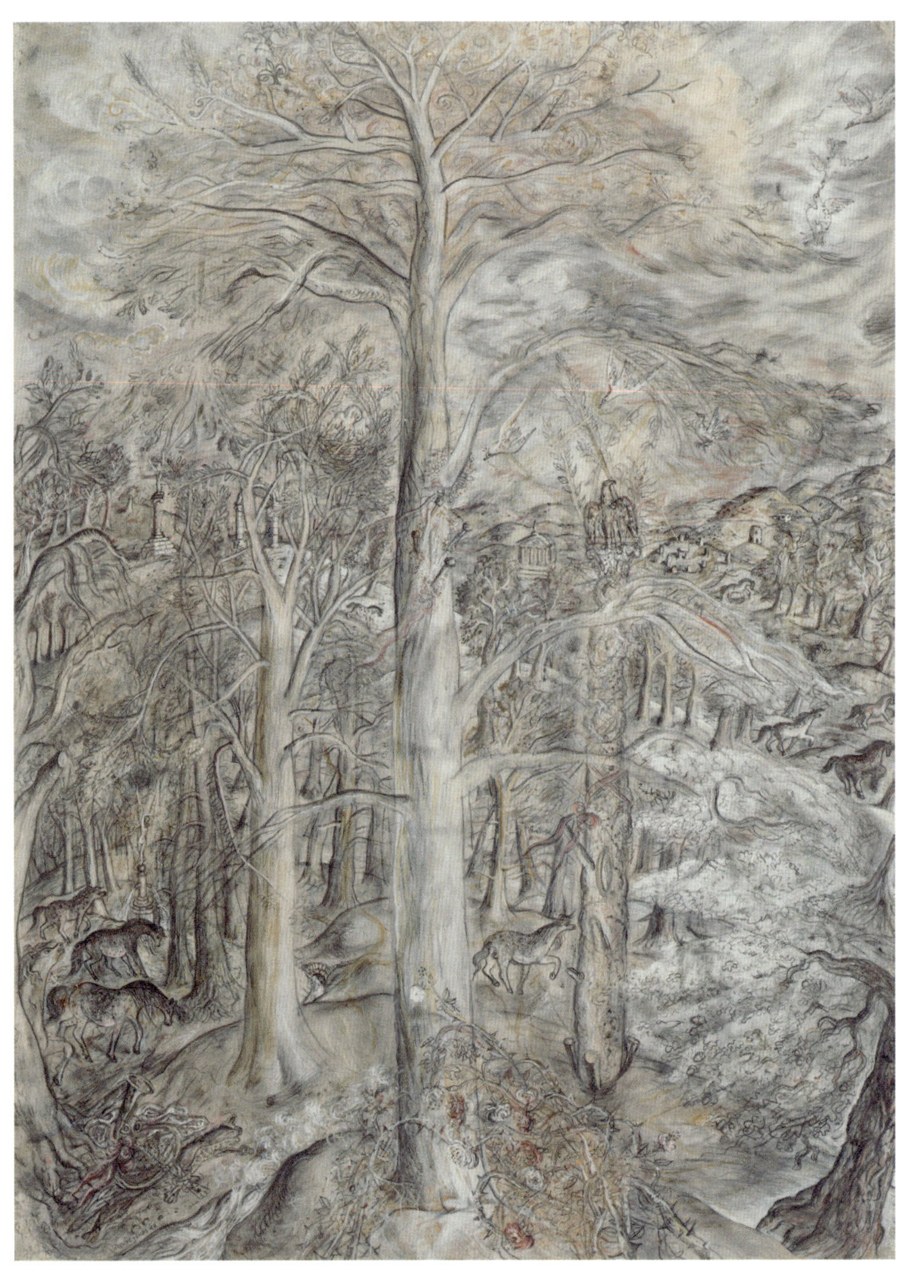

Vexilla Regis, 1948
Graphite and watercolour on paper, 75 × 55.2 cm
KY00757.EH

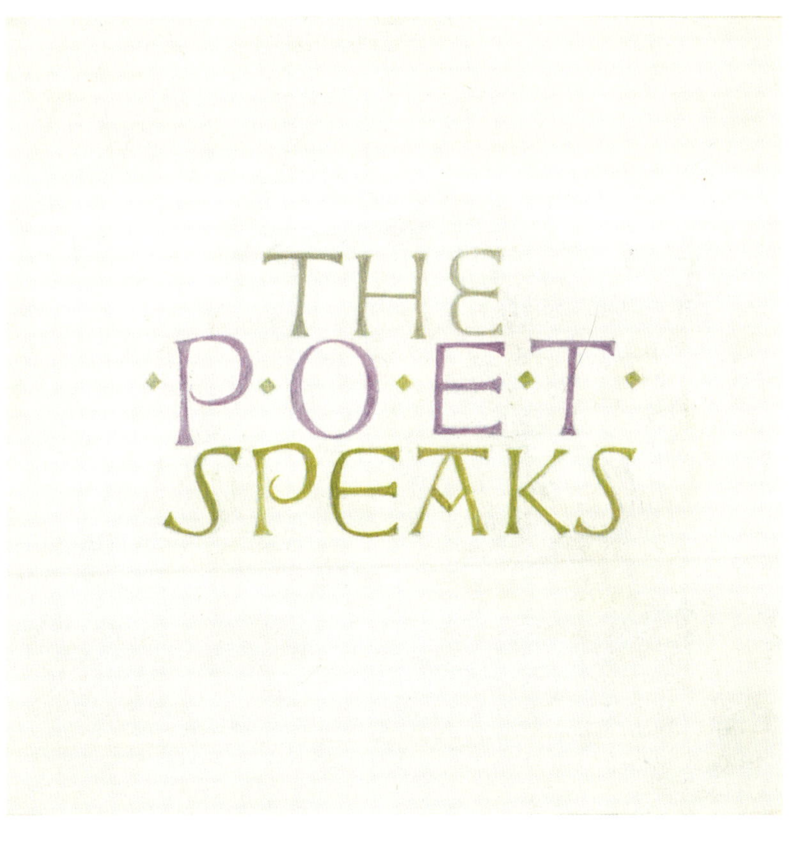

The Poet Speaks, c. 1965
Design for the cover of a Gramophone album of poetry readings
Watercolour on paper
KY01361

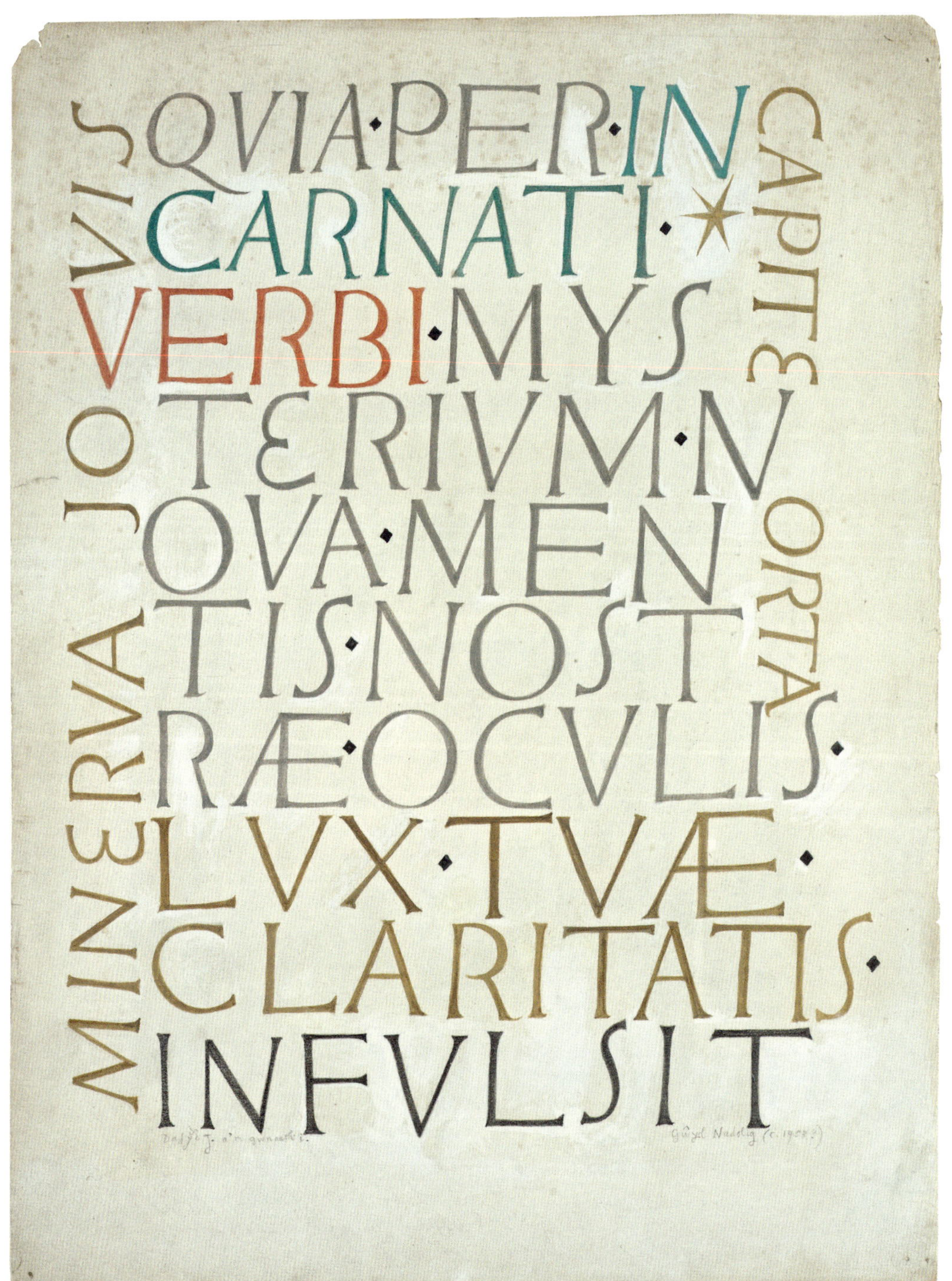
QVIA·PER·IN
CARNATI·
VERBI·MYS
TERIVM·N
OVA·MEN
TIS·NOST
RÆ·OCVLIS·
LVX·TVÆ·
CLARITATIS·
INFVLSIT
MINERVA JOVIS
CAPITE ORTA

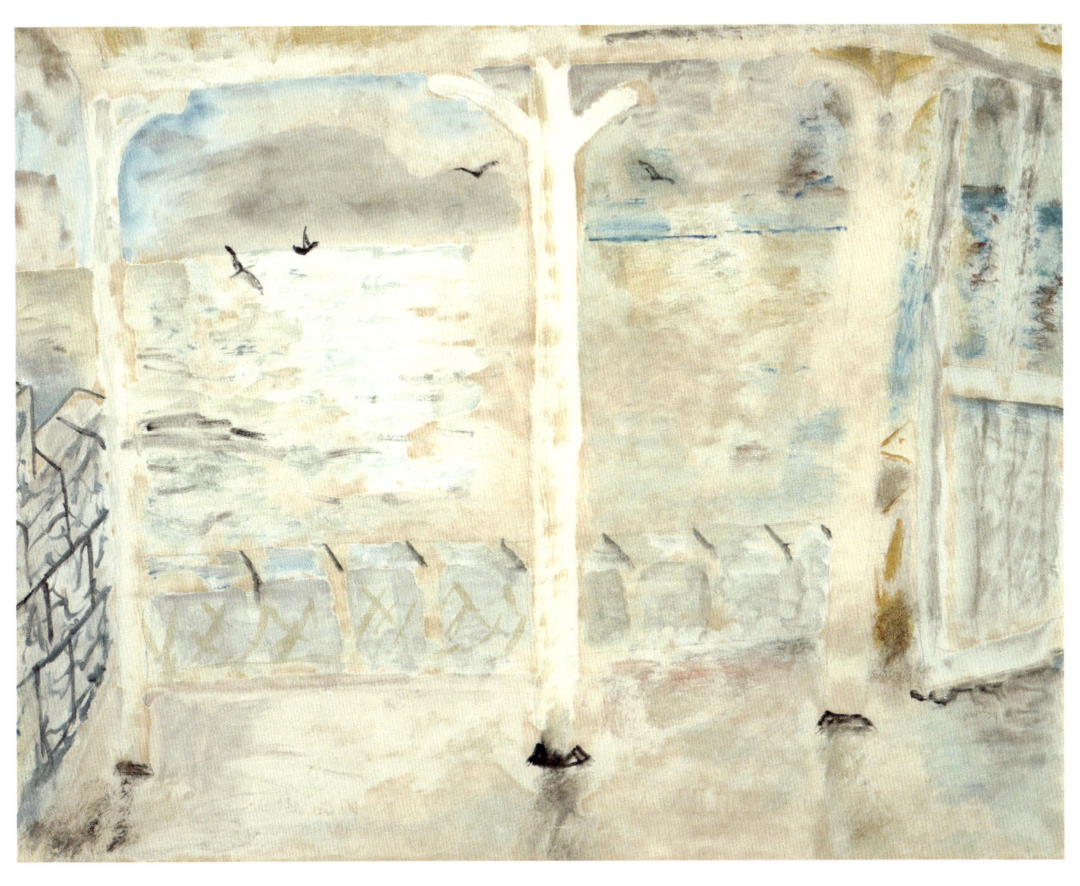

Quia per Incarnati, c. 1953
Watercolour and graphite on paper, 50 × 38 cm
KY00766.EH

Seascape from a Terrace, 1929
Watercolour on paper, 49 × 63 cm
KY00345.EH

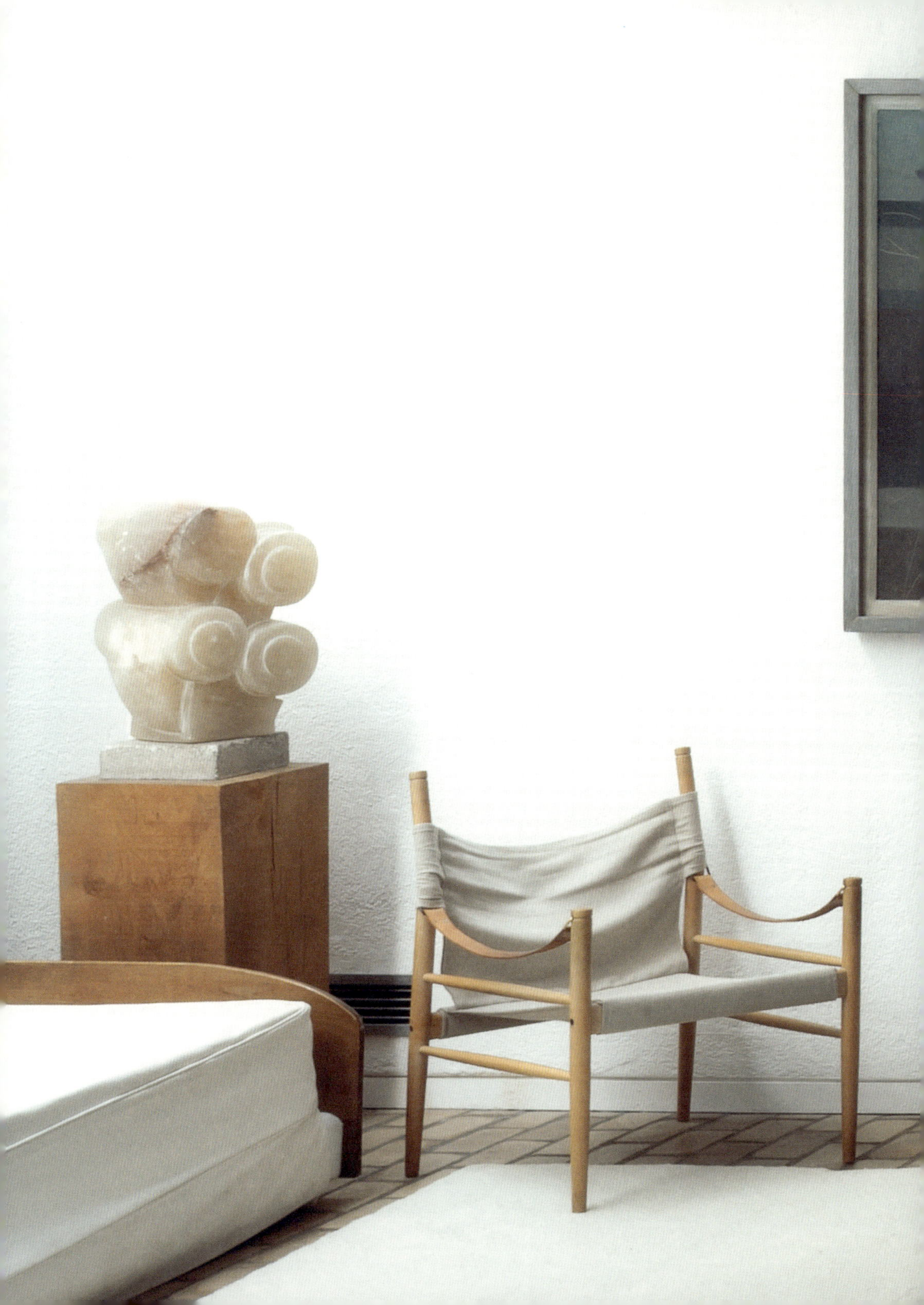

GEORGE KENNETHSON

(1910–1994)

George Kennethson was born Arthur Mackenzie in Richmond, Surrey and studied painting at the Royal Academy School in London 1929-32. He turned to sculpture around 1937, making work at a range of scales. His painstaking technique involved many weeks of work; for Kennethson, every chisel mark should be 'significant'. With his wife, the painter Eileen Guthrie, Kennethson lived and worked first in rural Berkshire. After the second world war, and with a growing family, they lived in Oundle, Northamptonshire, where Kennethson taught at Oundle School. There he continued to create a great many works in different types of stone, including alabaster and his favoured limestones. The Edes met Kennethson and Guthrie shortly after they moved to Cambridge, and acquired two of Kennethson's alabaster sculptures for display in the Kettle's Yard house. Many of the photographs used in *A way of life*, Jim Ede's large-format book about Kettle's Yard, were taken by George Kennethson and his son, the photographer Nicholas Mackenzie.

George Kennethson, letter to Jim Ede, 24 October 1982
Kettle's Yard Archive, Papers of Harold Stanley 'Jim' Ede. KY/EDE/1/1

> I keep reaching the absolute edge of despair at being quite unable to show my work anywhere, let alone sell it. In London everything I see seems either frivolous or sterile, or simply talentless, so that I am beginning to think mine must be the same [...] I am still obsessed by the problem of finding or developing a new language to deal with the life around one [...] Don't let me bother you with these reflections though. I hope particularly also that the Book [*A way of life*] is making progress, though I am occasionally anxious as to whether my photographs are good enough for it.

Forms, 1960s
Staffordshire alabaster,
48 × 29 × 31 cm
KY00942.EH

with (right)
Ben Nicholson
1933 (musical instruments), 1933
Oil paint on canvas,
103 × 90.5 cm
KY00644.EH

Jim Ede, *A way of life: Kettle's Yard*
(Cambridge University Press, 1984) p. 117

> The alabaster carving [*Construction (Birds)*] is a great asset to the house. It is a happy demonstration of form which does not spoil the material used, but brings out a beautiful and varied light as it passes through the stone. It makes of simple forms a block, containing and diffusing this light, the whole held together by the magic of sculpture.

George Kennethson, *Translations from Life and Nature: Stone Carvings 1950-1985* (Peterborough Museum and Art Gallery, 1986) p. 6

> In this particular medium with its methods, limitations and language, I search for a new approach to the balancing act between the claims of abstract values and natural perceptions - translations from life and nature is how I see them; as systems of rhythmic and expressive relationships in space, to me a kind of fusion of music and architecture, rather delicately drawn out of each individual, unique piece of material of a certain size, quality and nature.

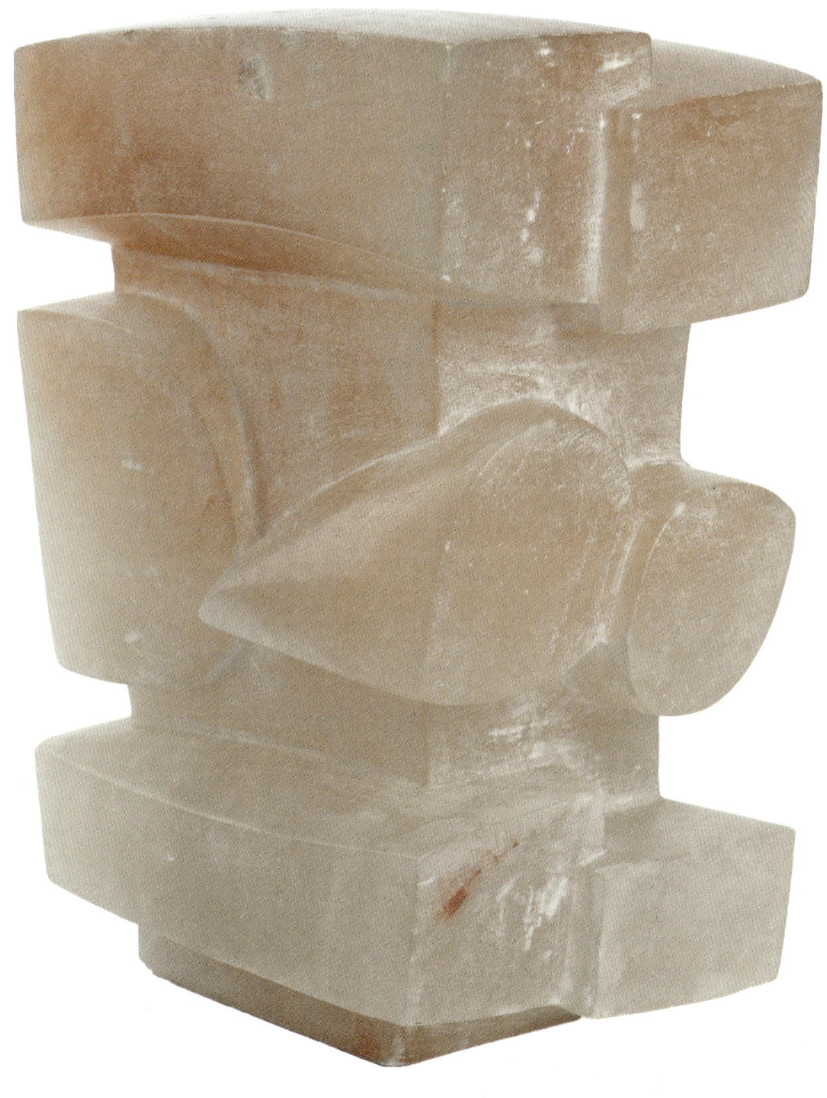

Construction (Birds), c.1966
Staffordshire alabaster, 29 × 20.2 × 15.3 cm
KY00917.EH

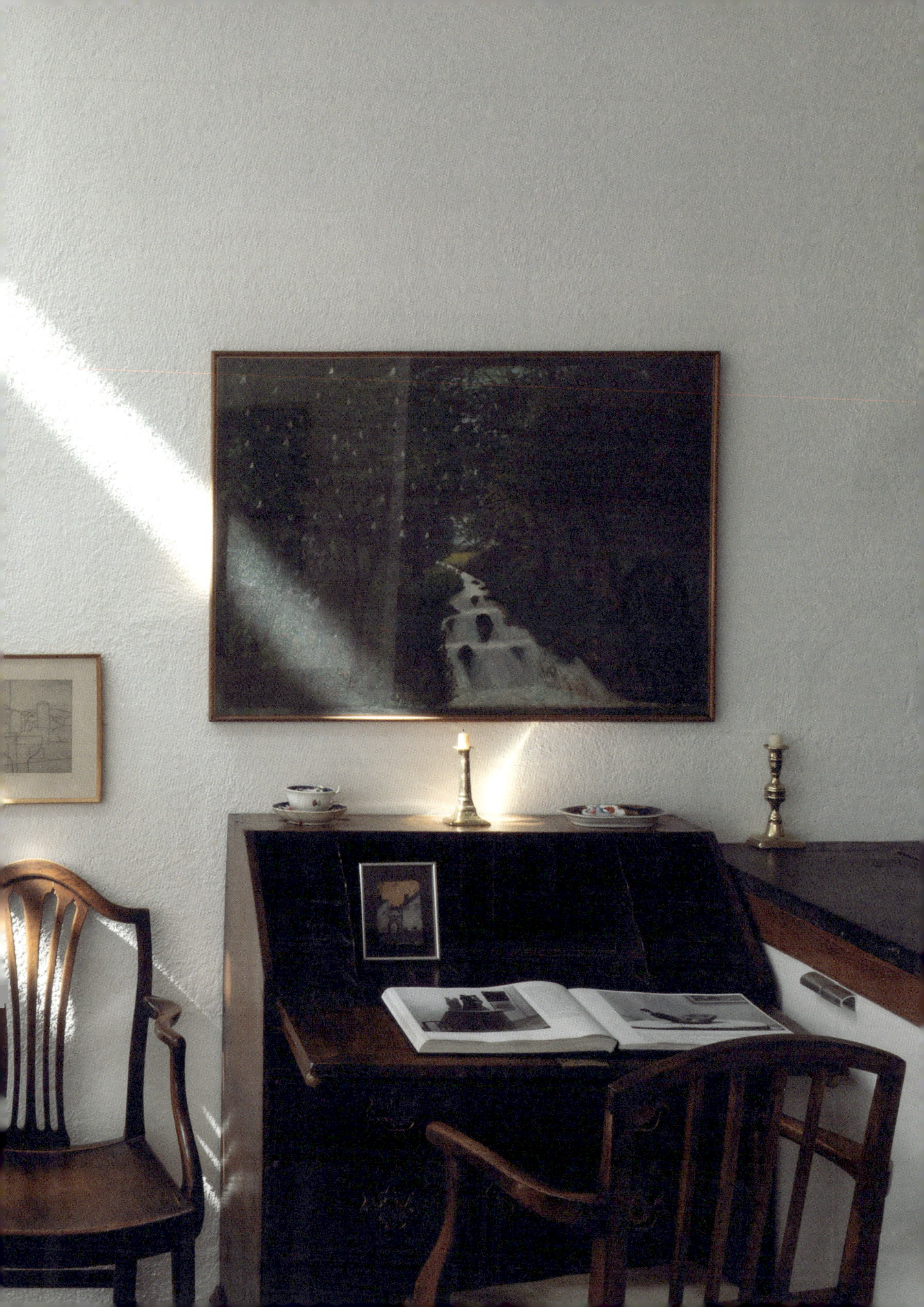

WINSTON McQUOID

(1909–1984)

Winston McQuoid was born in Glasgow and learned to paint in oils with Thomas Bond Walker in Belfast. McQuoid's first solo show was held in a space on Dublin Road, Belfast in 1924, when he was only fourteen years old. McQuoid then studied painting at the Verdin technical school in Northwich, Cheshire (1924-25) and at the Royal College of Art in London. While in London he lived on Sydney Street in Chelsea and came to love the paintings of John Constable and J.M.W. Turner on display at the Victoria and Albert Museum. McQuoid's landscapes and townscapes were exhibited in 1927 at London's Warren Gallery on Maddox Street and at the Redfern Gallery. McQuoid's collectors at this time included Lady Cunard, the writer Osbert Sitwell and civil servant Sir Edward Marsh. Between 1929 and 1949, McQuoid worked in the design studio at Odhams Press. He first met Jim Ede around 1930, and they continued their correspondence into the 1960s, while McQuoid was living in rented rooms in Upper Norwood, South London. In 1969, McQuoid moved to Ireland.

Waterfall in the Glen, 1927
Oil paint on plywood,
66 × 95 cm
KY00381.EH

with (left)
Ben Nicholson
Porta - San Gimignano,
1953
Etching on paper,
18 × 25 cm
KY00849.EH

and (below)
Alfred Wallis
Old Arch Digey (St Ives),
undated
Oil paint on card,
11 × 7.8 cm
KY00451.EH

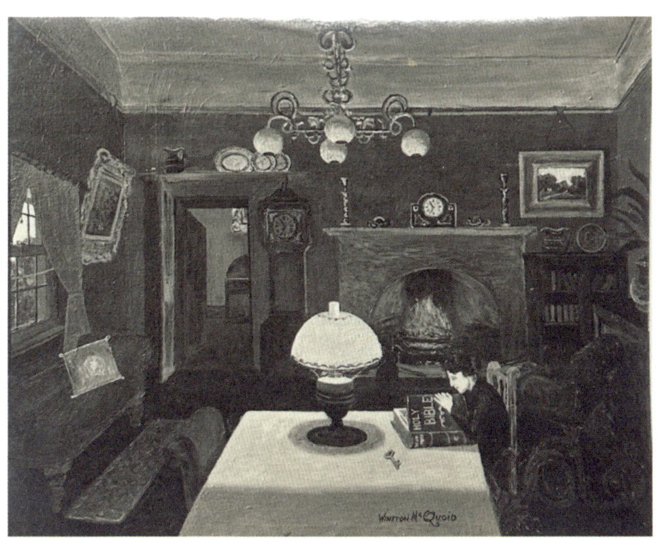

Photograph of a painting sent to Jim Ede, c. 1960s
Kettle's Yard Archive, Papers of Harold Stanley 'Jim' Ede. KY/EDE/1/1

Winston McQuoid, letter to Jim Ede, 17 June 1963

Kettle's Yard Archive, Papers of Harold Stanley 'Jim' Ede. KY/EDE/1/1

> [...] when I first came to London when I was fifteen, my first race was to the Victoria and Albert museum, and the first pictures I started to gaze at were Constables. Your view in liking my early work best when I was just about a schoolboy is in the way I am sure of the way I see John Constable's work. First, his sketches as he called them had fifty times the feeling of inspiration of his finished works. The *Sketch for the Leaping Horse* is to me worth fifty of the finished painting[s] of the *Leaping Horse*, and this is I feel sure the way you see my early work and what I do now.
>
> [...] I am pleased to see in your letter that you very much like the last picture I sent you, I painted it from a vague memory of Scotland, which I left when I was just six years old. My father took me on long journeys on some Sundays and this picture is a memory of where I do not know.

Jim Ede, *A way of life: Kettle's Yard*

(Cambridge University Press, 1984) pp. 188-189

> *The Glen* [...] was painted by a boy of twelve called Winston McQuoid. I met him when he was fifteen and he had just painted another remarkable work, *The Round Pond, Kensington* and *The Glen* hung in his home. He hadn't much idea of what he was doing, it was all just part of his life. [...] I thought he might be Great Britain's Douanier Rousseau. [...] I found in my London days that all artists who frequented One Elm Row had joy of this painting [...]
>
> He often came to see me at Kettle's Yard, always with umbrella, bowler hat and striped trousers, and a small Gladstone bag. I got his paints for him since he thought that artists' material could only be got at a particular shop in the West End, and though he lived in London he found it simpler to come to me in Cambridge.

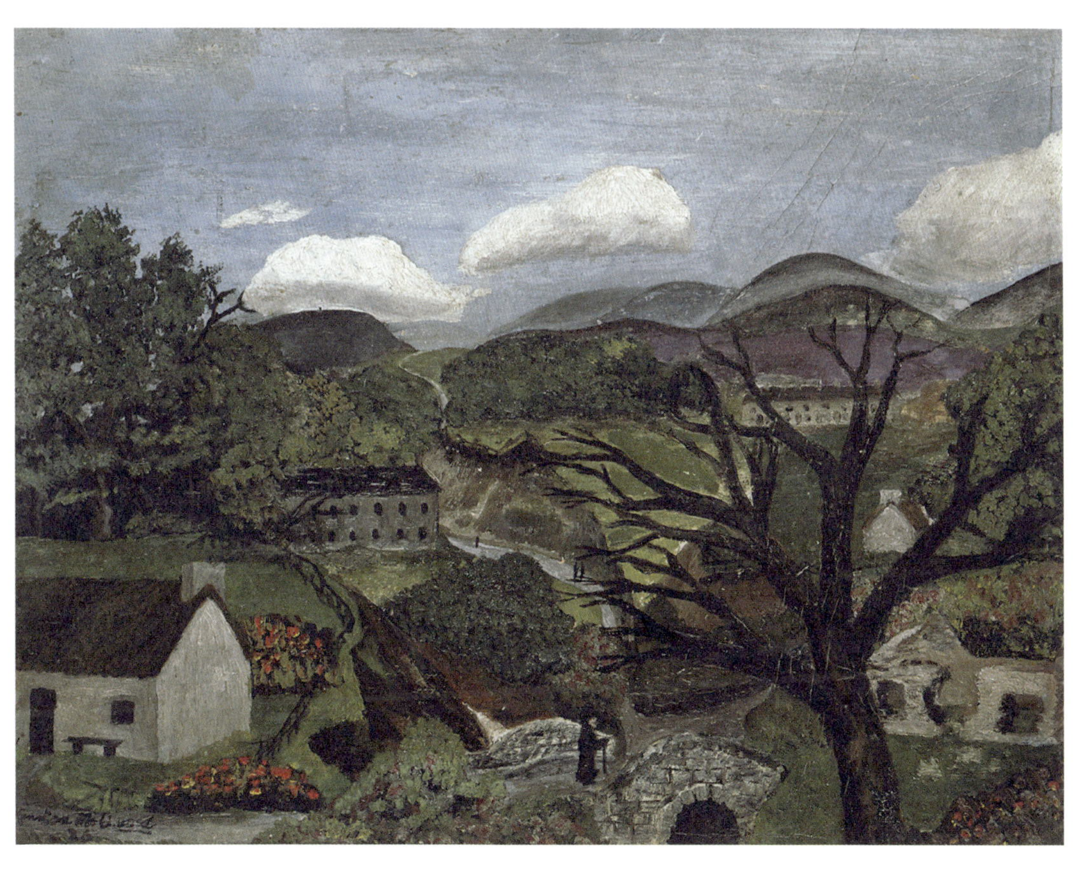

Cottages and Bridge, Ireland, 1926
Oil paint on card, 38.7 × 49.5 cm
KY00382.E

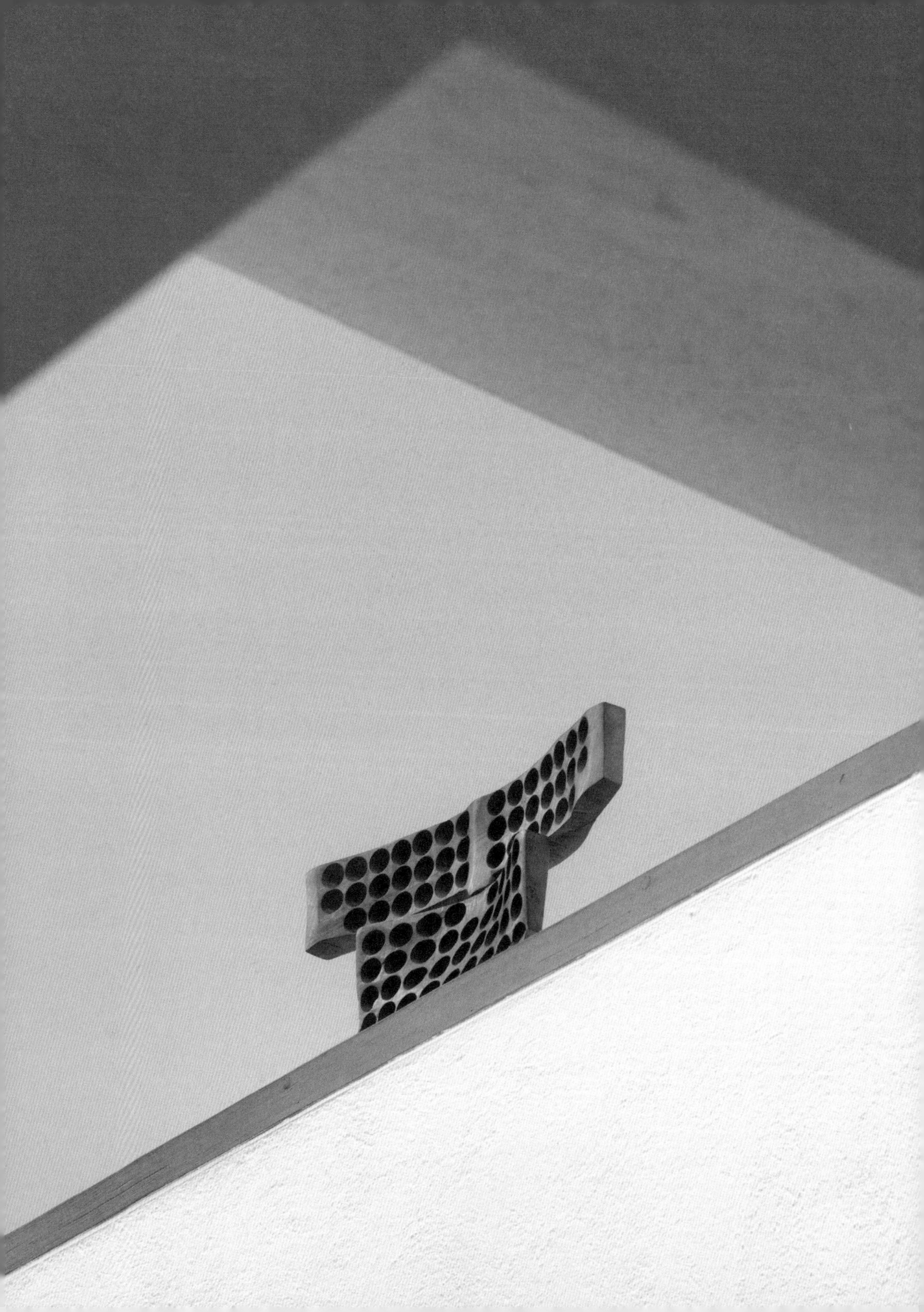

OVIDIU MAITEC

(1925–2007)

Ovidiu Maitec was born in Arad, Romania and studied at the Institutul de Arte Plastice (now the Universitatea Națională de Arte or UNArte) 1945–50, where he later worked as a teaching assistant 1950–56. He met his wife Sultana (born Sultana Tacu, 1928–2016), also an artist, at this time. Maitec received a number of commissions for public monuments in Romania under Soviet rule, but during the 1960s, his work became known in Western Europe, especially his smaller-scale intricately carved abstract works. Maitec was awarded the Romanian Academy prize in 1967, and Jim Ede first encountered the artist's work shortly afterwards. The Edes purchased two of Maitec's wooden sculptures in 1971, and an exhibition of his work was staged at Kettle's Yard in 1973. Maitec was elected a full member of the Academia Română (Romanian Academy) in 1991 and over the years received many awards for his artistic achievement, culminating in a knighthood (the Steaua României, National Order) in 2007.

Jim Ede, 'Ovidiu Maitec' in *Maitec: Sculpture*
(Kettle's Yard, Cambridge, 1973), unpaginated

> Ovidiu Maitec is a sculptor in the deepest tradition of Romanian art, sensitive, alert and purposeful. Like Brâncuși, he is immediately conscious of the needs of different materials; stone being stone and wood being wood. His work in whatever substance springs from a grand and living love, and although we are in the midst of a technological age he will, for instance, show the beauty of wood and the love of creating an object by hand. [...]

Barbu Brezianu, translated by Jim Ede in *Maitec: Sculpture*
(Kettle's Yard, Cambridge, 1973), unpaginated

Radar II, 1970
Walnut wood,
29.7 × 52.2 × 11.5 cm
KY01135.EH

> His works are like friends, whom one would like to caress. Sometimes they evoke the rustling of trees, the sough of

foliage, fluttering wings of unseen flocks of birds flowing over the crowns of the living forest. At other times, his sculptures hold symbolic meanings that awaken archaic moods and a feeling of perfect balance. Again, they suggest the loving calm and joining of two beings, or of the symmetric hinges which have been inspired by the frames of ancient town gates, those wooden gates, through which – when unfettered – one is likely to penetrate into the intimacy of another world, a harmoniously balanced universe. Ovidiu Maitec's metaphors are like the natural rhythm of long files of trees, sprung, as it were, from a miraculous seed and yet retaining old, indefinable and mysterious roots.

Ovidiu Maitec, letter to Jim Ede, 18 June 1974

Kettle's Yard Archive, Papers of Harold Stanley 'Jim' Ede. KY/EDE/1/1

I should like to tell you that I was exceedingly impressed by your letter and, though my work has come back to my studio, I am very happy to know that you believe my work to be of worth. Having been used – so far – to little success and recognition, and at the same time being neither morally nor materially spoilt, I go on toiling and learning to praise the genuine as well as a worthwhile word of praise. My having had the chance of showing my sculptures to you, my having had them exhibited at Kettle's Yard – due to your permanent appreciation and strenuous efforts make me happy and grateful to you.

Ovidiu Maitec, letter to Jim Ede, February 1979

Kettle's Yard Archive, Papers of Harold Stanley 'Jim' Ede. KY/EDE/1/1

You belong to the few and the first who singled out the significance of my work. You and your great achievement Kettle's Yard have always embodied – to my mind – the ideal meeting between two spirits in front of the mysterious altar of art, when hopes and the realisation of these hopes come true.

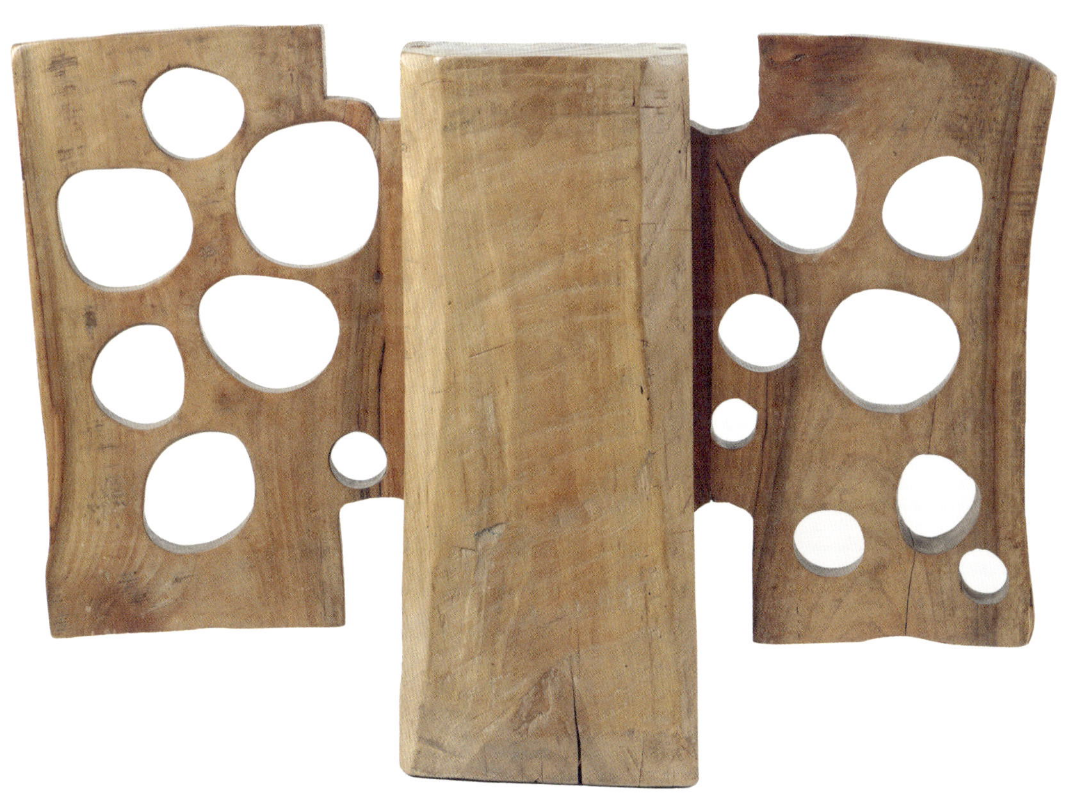

Bird, c. 1969
Walnut wood, 49 × 71 × 10 cm
KY01137.EH

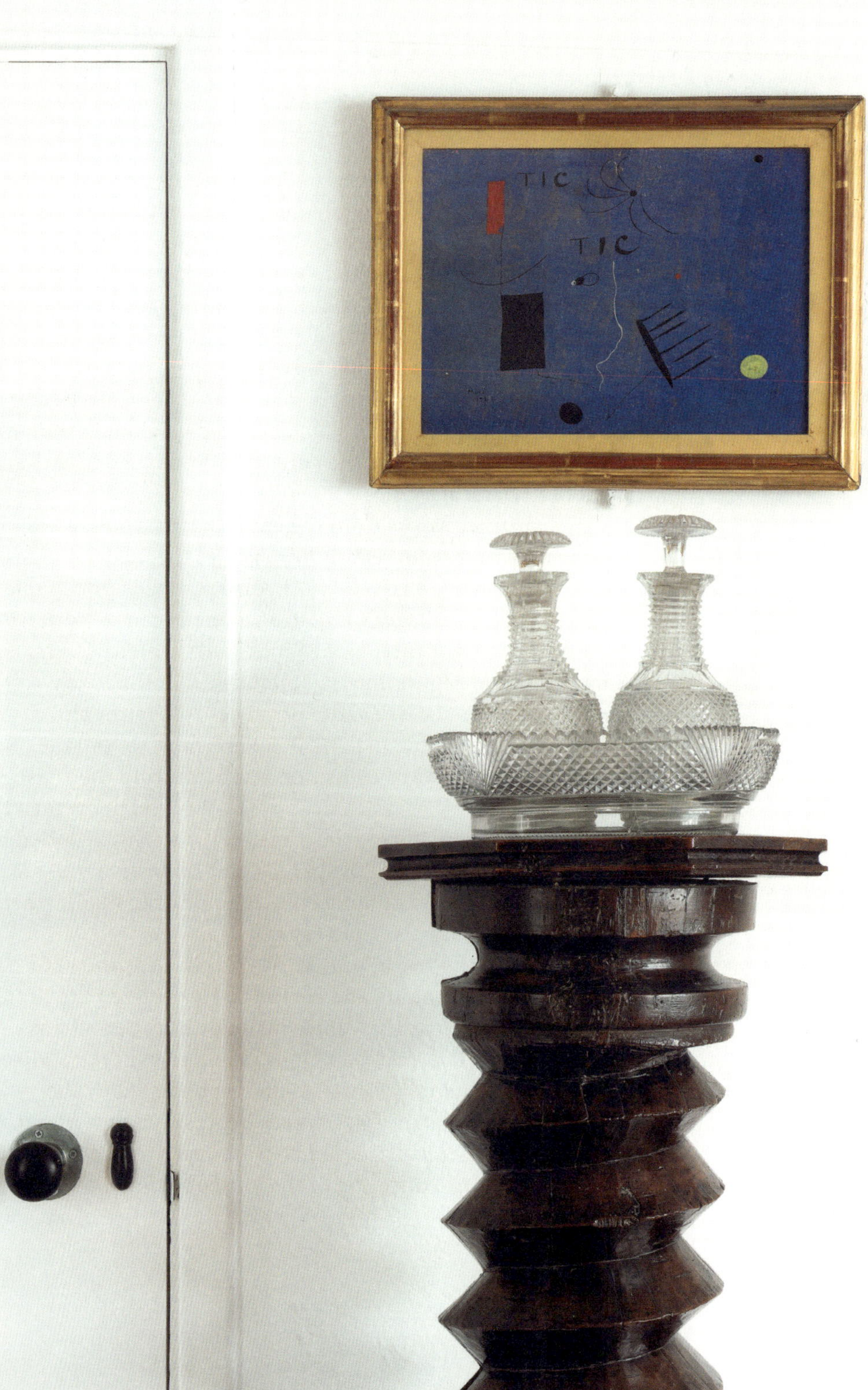
TIC
TIC

JOAN MIRÓ

(1893–1983)

Catalan artist Joan Miró was born in Barcelona. He trained at the Escuela de la Lonja in the city and later studied with Francesc Galí. In 1918, Miró was given a solo show at the Barcelona gallery of the dealer José Dalmau. In 1920, he made his first trip to Paris, where he met Pablo Picasso. From this period on, Miró divided his time between Paris and Montroig, Spain. In Paris, he came to know artists and poets, including Max Jacob and Tristan Tzara. Dalmau organised Miró's first Paris solo show at the Galerie la Licorne in 1921. Miró's work was included in the Salon d'Automne of 1923, and in 1924 he joined the surrealist group having earlier participated in Dada activities.

Miró's abstract works from the early twenties onwards incorporate text, and recurrent motifs such as the ladder, inspired by visits to the circus in Paris. In 1928, Miró made his first 'papiers collés' (pasted paper collages), and in 1929, he began to work with lithography and in sculpture, using found and painted objects. Miró's international reputation was established in the 1930s by the dealers Pierre Matisse and Pierre Loeb, the latter also a friend of Jim Ede's. Jim Ede met Miró in Paris in 1932, and the painting in the Kettle's Yard collection was a gift from the artist. Following the outbreak of civil war in 1936, Miró did not return to Spain for several years. During this time, his work was included in the exhibition *Cubism and Abstract Art* and *Fantastic Art, Dada, Surrealism* at the Museum of Modern Art, New York (1936), where a solo retrospective was also held (1941).

After the second world war, Miró's practice expanded to include work in printmaking and ceramics. He received the Grand Prize for Graphic Work at the Venice Biennale in 1954 and was included in the first *Documenta* exhibition in Kassel in 1955. Miró moved into a new studio in Palma, Mallorca, designed by the architect Josep Lluís Sert in 1956, where he was able to work on a larger scale, producing mural-sized canvases such as the *Triptych Bleu* (1961) now in the collection of the Musée National d'Art Moderne in Paris.

Tic Tic, 1927
Oil paint on canvas,
23.3 × 32.3 cm
KY00695.EH

Jim Ede, 'Introduction', *Kettle's Yard: An illustrated handlist of the paintings, sculptures and drawings*
(Cambridge: Kettle's Yard, 1970) p. 5

> Had it ever entered my head that I was collecting works of art I suppose this moment in Paris would have been my greatest opportunity; but all I thought of was trying to get my rich friends to buy the works of these new friends. But Miró gave me a small painting [*Tic Tic*] one sunny morning as we drank coffee in a Paris street. It was the day a President had been assassinated and as we drank our coffee there was a terrific explosion nearby and I quite thoughtlessly cried out 'Encore un Président' and everyone fell silent.

Jim Ede, *A way of life: Kettle's Yard*
(Cambridge University Press, 1984) p. 31

> The Miró was to me an opportunity to show undergraduates the importance of balance. If I put my finger over the spot at the top right all the rest of the picture slid into the left- hand bottom corner. If I covered the one at the bottom, horizontal lines appeared, and if somehow I could take out the tiny red spot in the middle everything flew to the edges. This gave me a much needed chance to mention God, and by saying that if I had another name for God, I think it would be balance, for with perfect balance all would be well.

Joan Miró, letter to Jim Ede, 24 September 1964
Kettle's Yard Archive, Papers of Harold Stanley 'Jim' Ede. KY/EDE/1/1

Translation: Dear friend, I was touched by your letter, and the pleasant memories it evoked. I only stayed for a short time in England, which didn't give me the chance to let you know. Please accept my warmest greetings, Miró.

M 44.170 reully 24.9.64

SON ABRINES - CALAMAYOR - PALMA DE MALLORCA

24/X/64

cher ami, j'ai été très touché par votre lettre et par les bons souvenirs qu'elle éveille en moi.

Je n'ai fait qu'un court séjour en Angleterre, ce qui ne m'a pas donné la possibilité de vous faire signe.

Recevez, je vous prie, mes plus cordiales salutations,

Miró

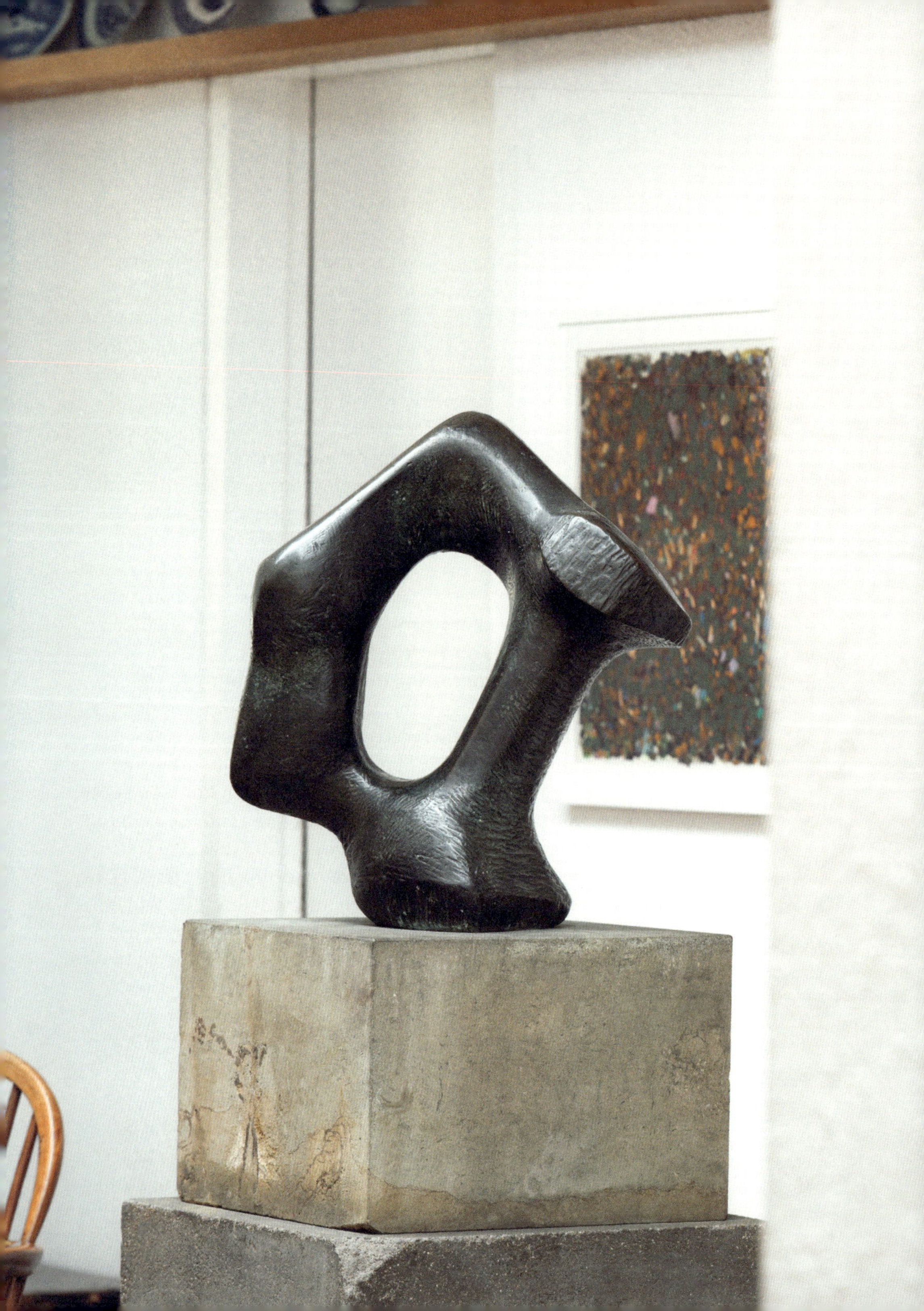

HENRY MOORE

(1898–1986)

Henry Moore was born in Castleford, Yorkshire and trained as a primary school teacher. During the first world war, Moore enlisted in the Civil Service Rifles and afterwards enrolled at the Leeds School of Art, funded by an ex-serviceman's grant. In 1921, he won a scholarship to train at the Royal College of Art, and in 1924 began working as a tutor there. During this time he made regular visits to the British Museum and the Victoria and Albert Museum, and came to know their collections of prehistoric, Cycladic, African and Mesoamerican sculpture, which proved influential for his work. During the following decade, Moore exhibited with London groups dedicated to modern forms of painting and sculpture, including the Seven and Five Society and Unit One, as well as the British surrealists. He also briefly taught at the academy of Amédée Ozenfant in London. During the second world war, Moore was employed as an official war artist, becoming widely known for his series of drawings of people sheltering in London Underground stations during the Blitz.

Moore had begun casting work in bronze in 1938, and continued this practice after the second world war, working on an increasingly large scale. He received many international public sculpture commissions, including for the UNESCO building in Paris and the University of Chicago. Moore first met Jim Ede when both were living in Hampstead, London in the 1920s, and the sculptor was a frequent visitor to the Edes' house on Elm Row. They renewed their acquaintance in the late 1950s upon the Edes' return to England from Morocco and France. In the 1960s, Ede sought Moore's advice on and assistance casting Henri Gaudier-Brzeska works at Kettle's Yard which he hoped to sell to museums in France.

Sculptural Object, 1960
Bronze on limestone base, 46.5 × 39 × 37 cm
KY00851.EH

with (right)
Gillian Ayres
Untitled, 1972
Gouache on paper, 45.5 × 58 cm
KY01387

Jim Ede, letter to Henry Moore, 3 August 1963
Kettle's Yard Archive, Papers of Harold Stanley 'Jim' Ede. KY/EDE/1/1

> I am ever so grateful to you for taking on what would be to me almost an impossible task & one which it has taken me so many years to get down to [...] I do so want to do all

in my power before I die to get Gaudier Brzeska into the public fame which I feel he should have. I doubt if France has potentially had a much greater sculptor […] With your agreement I think we should do 6 of each of the two things I brought […] I shall hope eventually to devote what profit I make to artists in need as Gaudier was […]

Henry Moore, letter to Jim Ede, 4 February 1964
Kettle's Yard Archive, Papers of Harold Stanley 'Jim' Ede. KY/EDE/1/1

At last I have found time to patinate one copy of the BIRD SWALLOWING FISH, and one copy of the GARDEN ORNAMENT, (I'll try to patinate the rest of them tomorrow, or the day after) […] I should like to keep here, if I may, one copy of the BIRD SWALLOWING FISH, because Irina [Moore] and I would like to have it for her collection […] I think the patina has made them much livelier and stronger than they were when they came from the foundry. I hope you'll be pleased with them.

Jim Ede, *A way of life: Kettle's Yard*
(Cambridge University Press, 1984) p. 50

I have always loved this Henry Moore [*Head*] which he gave to me so long ago. The stone is stone and the swift measure of its forms, or complex lines, enter into that still energy which was so characteristic of Mayan sculpture, and particularly so in our own day, of Gaudier-Brzeska. A stone, however carved, is first and foremost a stone; it belongs to things comparatively immobile, the rock from which it is separated, and must retain this parental force and immobility, yet it must also convey that strange admixture which is man; mutability of flesh and eternity of spirit. In this small head the equilibrium of sculpture is reached, its life contained within its own nature; it is hard to think of it being made - it just is.

Head, 1928
Stone on plaster base,
17.3 × 7.5 × 10.5 cm
KY00786.EH

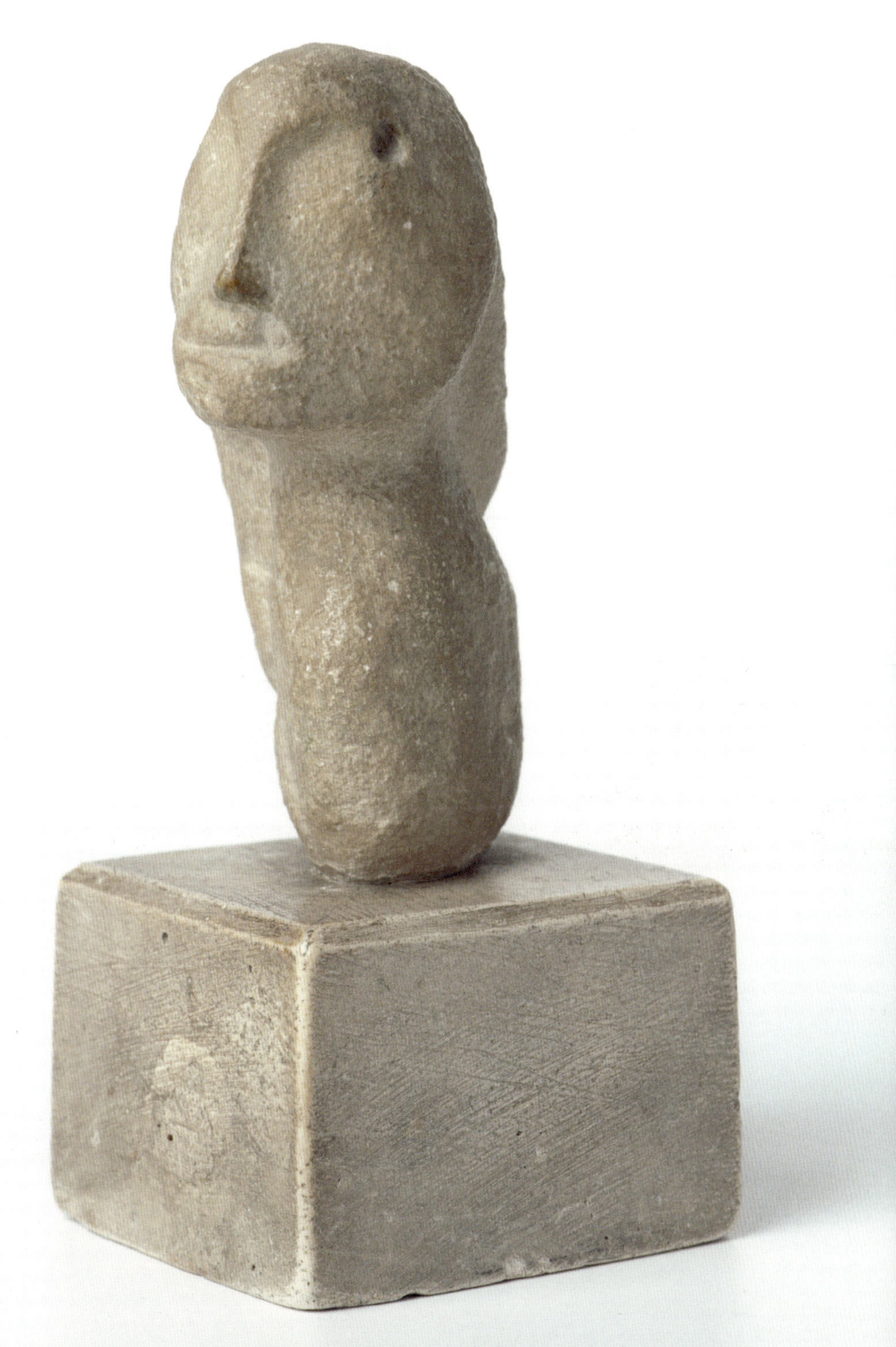

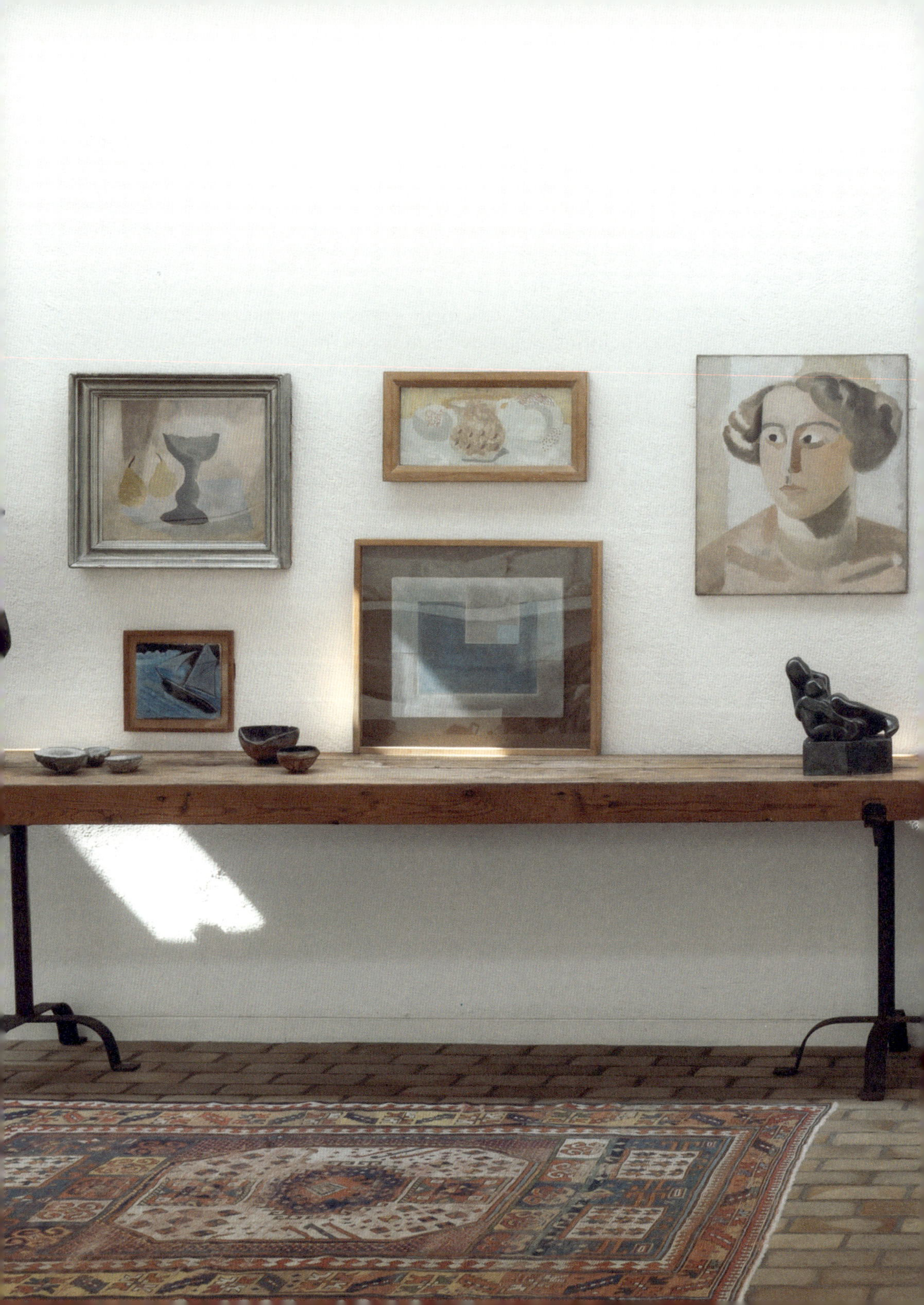

BEN NICHOLSON

(1894–1982)

Ben Nicholson was born in Denham, Buckinghamshire and studied at the Slade School of Art. During his formative years he travelled extensively in Europe and the United States. His early works were still lifes but in the 1920s, he began creating figurative and abstract works inspired by post-impressionism and cubism. In 1927, painting alongside his first wife Winifred (née Roberts) and Christopher Wood, he developed a consciously naïve landscape style, influenced by Alfred Wallis's example. By 1933, Nicholson was living in Hampstead, London with sculptor Barbara Hepworth (who he married in 1938) and producing his first geometric and abstract reliefs. Between 1939 and 1958, Nicholson lived in Cornwall, where other artists and critics had also relocated to during the second world war, including Naum Gabo and Adrian Stokes.

After the war, Nicholson's work became better known through British Council touring exhibitions. He won first prize at the Carnegie International in Pittsburgh in 1952, the Guggenheim International Award in 1956, the International Prize for Painting at the 1957 Bienal de São Paulo, and in 1964 exhibited a large relief wall at *Documenta* in Kassel, Germany. For Jim Ede, Ben Nicholson's friendship was formative, and for Nicholson, Ede's early support was vital. Nicholson did not withhold criticism of Ede and his activities over the years, but despite this, they corresponded throughout their lives.

Clockwise from left:
1924 (goblet and two pears), 1924
Oil paint and graphite on board, 35.5 × 43.3 cm
KY00337.EH

1924 (Bertha no.2), 1924
Oil paint and graphite on canvas, 61 × 56 cm
KY00330.EH

1930 (plate, cup and jug), 1930
Oil paint and graphite on board, 20 × 45 cm
KY00645.EH

1962 (argos), 1962
Oil paint and carved board on wood, 35 × 44.5 cm
KY00853.EH

with (left) Alfred Wallis
Small boat in a rough sea, c. 1936
Oil paint on card, 19.5 × 23 cm
KY00692.EH

with (right) Henri Gaudier-Brzeska
Maternity (Mother and Child), 1913 (cast 1960s)
Bronze, 28 × 27 × 18 cm
KY00809.EH

Jim Ede, 'Ben', not dated [unpublished note]

Kettle's Yard Archive, Papers of Harold Stanley 'Jim' Ede. KY/EDE/4/2/4/12

> Art for him has been a continuous process of exploration and discovery, and each conquest of a new territory has served as the base for a new expedition. Certain symbols remain constant, jug, colour – with these constant symbols the artist creates infinite variations, & it is in the exploitation of these variations that he arrives at the extremes of realism & abstraction. Beauty is a product of self-imposed difficulties, takes very few symbols but with these few it creates a multiplicity of variations – note Mondrian – still less symbols. Achievement is clearly considerable & the consistency of that achievement, its unfailing revelation of a faultless sensibility and its fountain-like projection of varied forms from a seemingly inexhaustible source, require us to recognise in BN one of the major artists of our time.

Ben Nicholson, letter to Jim Ede, 1926

Kettle's Yard Archive, Papers of Harold Stanley 'Jim' Ede. KY/EDE/1/11

> As for finding some 'form of expression' why I should have thought you were obviously expressing something – only you're going through a sort of transition stage & you're now rather uncomfy, suspended somewhere about midway between being a guardian of the Past & becoming a guardian of the Future [...] It is precisely people like you, who can like an old house so much & chuck everything for it, who can like a new house so much & chuck everything for it [...] I expect you get an awful lot of fun out of living too carefully for your house. We had a wonderful time in Switzerland living too carefully for our villa – we invented a game of squash as a substitute for fires – you played it before work, in rests & after work – such a good game.

Letter from Ben Nicholson to Jim Ede, 1932

Kettle's Yard Archive, Papers of Harold Stanley 'Jim' Ede. KY/EDE/1/11

> We felt the £2 very generous of you, & really about the £22 I don't quite know what to say – it is such a very big sum.
> As for helping me you have done that ever since you first liked the idea in those 2 small goblets – but really this £22 is most charming of you – & thank you ever so much.
> It is especially welcome at the moment, as we had nothing left at all & had been breaking open a small money box to get our bus fares – & the food bills had reached a point where there was no more credit left!
> So your 22 seems more like 222 & gives us liberty to work.
> We have divided it in half & been paying some urgent bills (even before writing to you!)
> (I know too what a v. big chunk £22 is out of your savings, earned in that Tate)
> You must have a ptg [painting]. Love from Ben
> I was so pleased you liked the new developments in our work.

Ben Nicholson, letter to Jim Ede, 29 March 1937

Kettle's Yard Archive, Papers of Harold Stanley 'Jim' Ede. KY/EDE/1/11

> [...] to be English as the peculiarly English expression of an international, universal movement (life) is completely vital. Kit [Wood] had a link with Rousseau & had sensed but not yet realised in his work the link with his contemporary Picasso – David [Jones] & Winifred [Nicholson] had their link with – Cézanne? something with Matisse – ? but these are not their contemporaries? & Ben – ??? – ! – ??
> Anyhow the charming & delightful personal artistry of one or two human creatures – that is something – because something can grow from that – but personal artistry is only a very small peg in an immense & marvellous universal construction.
> Not only that – the Cubist & the present non-figurative Constructive movements are two of the most important in the whole short history of painting & in the structure of the world.

Ben Nicholson, letter to Jim Ede, 3 February 1968

Kettle's Yard Archive, Papers of Harold Stanley 'Jim' Ede. KY/EDE/1/11

> I'm sure your K.Y. cat. [1968 catalogue of the Kettle's Yard collection] will help the collection and a good idea all the little reproductions. You should surely be careful not to claim this good collection as 'contemporary', it is contemporary with Jim Ede - & what more can one expect? Well I suppose contemporary indicates 'today'? [...]
> Your Wallis collection must be superb, and the only one I expect where you had a relatively free hand with cash [...]
> You know Jim you can't call this collection 'contemporary' - you do it harm to do so - it simply is not that as things are today - you could, just, say 'sprinkled with contemp. work'.

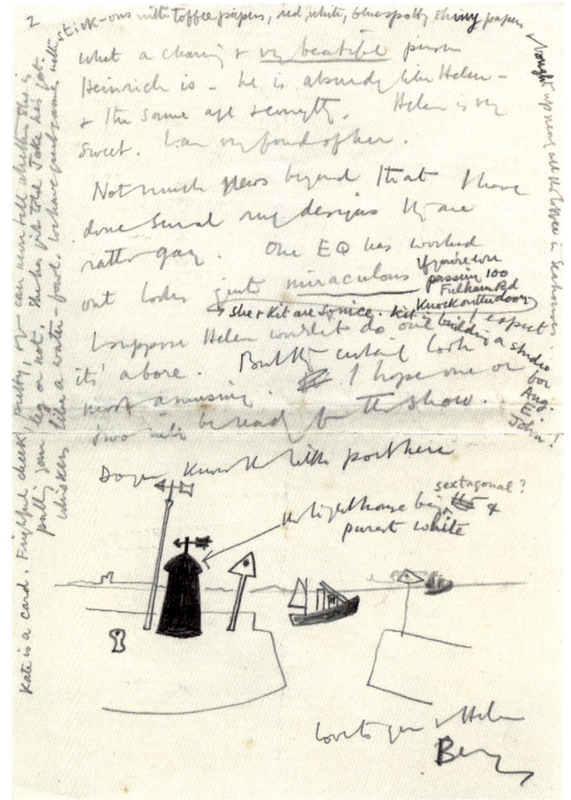
2

stick-ons with toffee papers, red, white, blue spotty shiny paper

what a charming & very beautiful person Heinrich is – he is absurdly like Helen – & the same age seemingly. Helen is very sweet. I am very fond of her.

Not much news beyond that I have done several rug designs they are rather gay. One EQ has worked out looks quite miraculous

If you're ever passing 100 Fulham Rd knock on the door

She & Kit are so nice. Kit is building a studio I expect

I suppose Helen wouldn't do one it's above. But they certainly look most amusing. I hope one or two will be ready for the show.

Do you know the little port here

sextagonal?

the lighthouse bright & purest white

love to you & Helen

Ben

Ben Nicholson, letter to Jim Ede, 1933

Kettle's Yard Archive, Papers of Harold Stanley 'Jim' Ede. KY/EDE/1/11

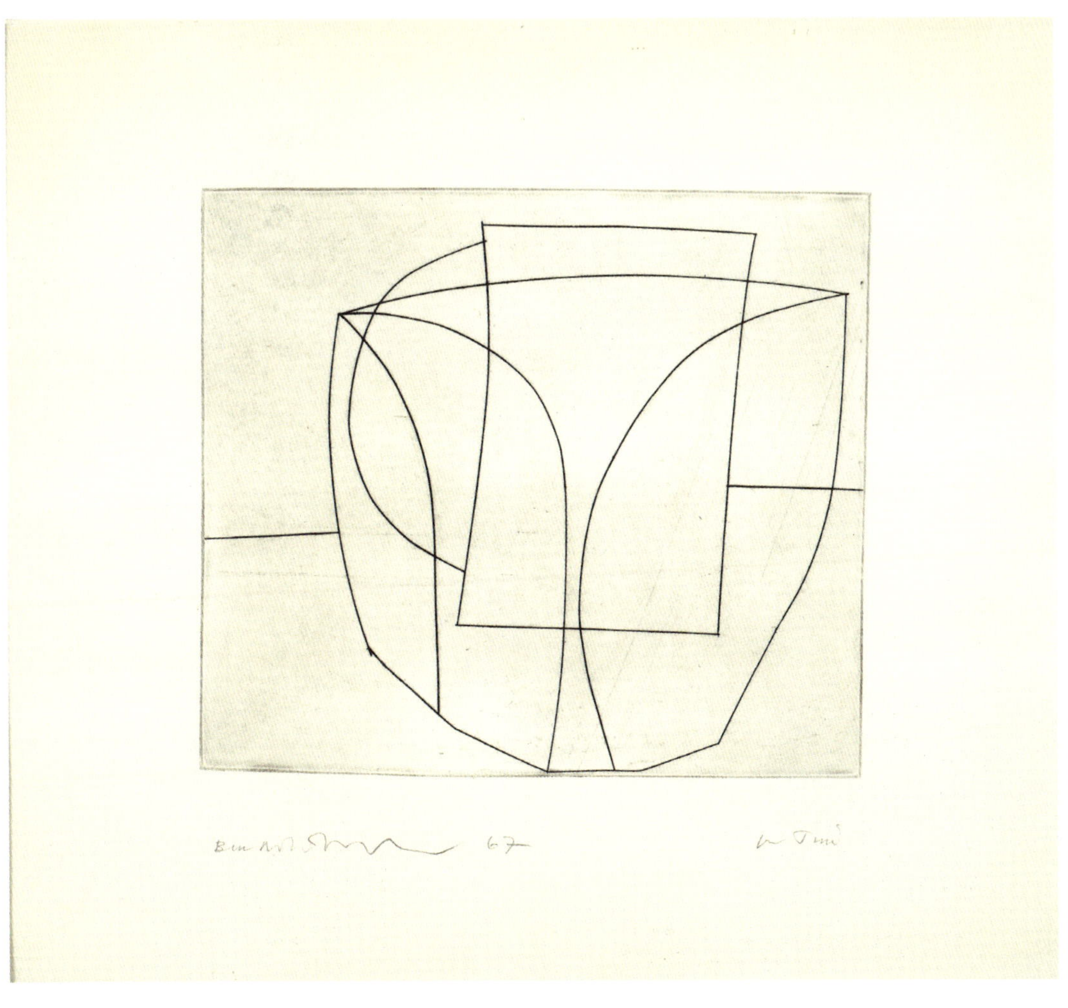

sexagonal, 1967
Engraving on paper, 19 × 22 cm
KY00926.EH

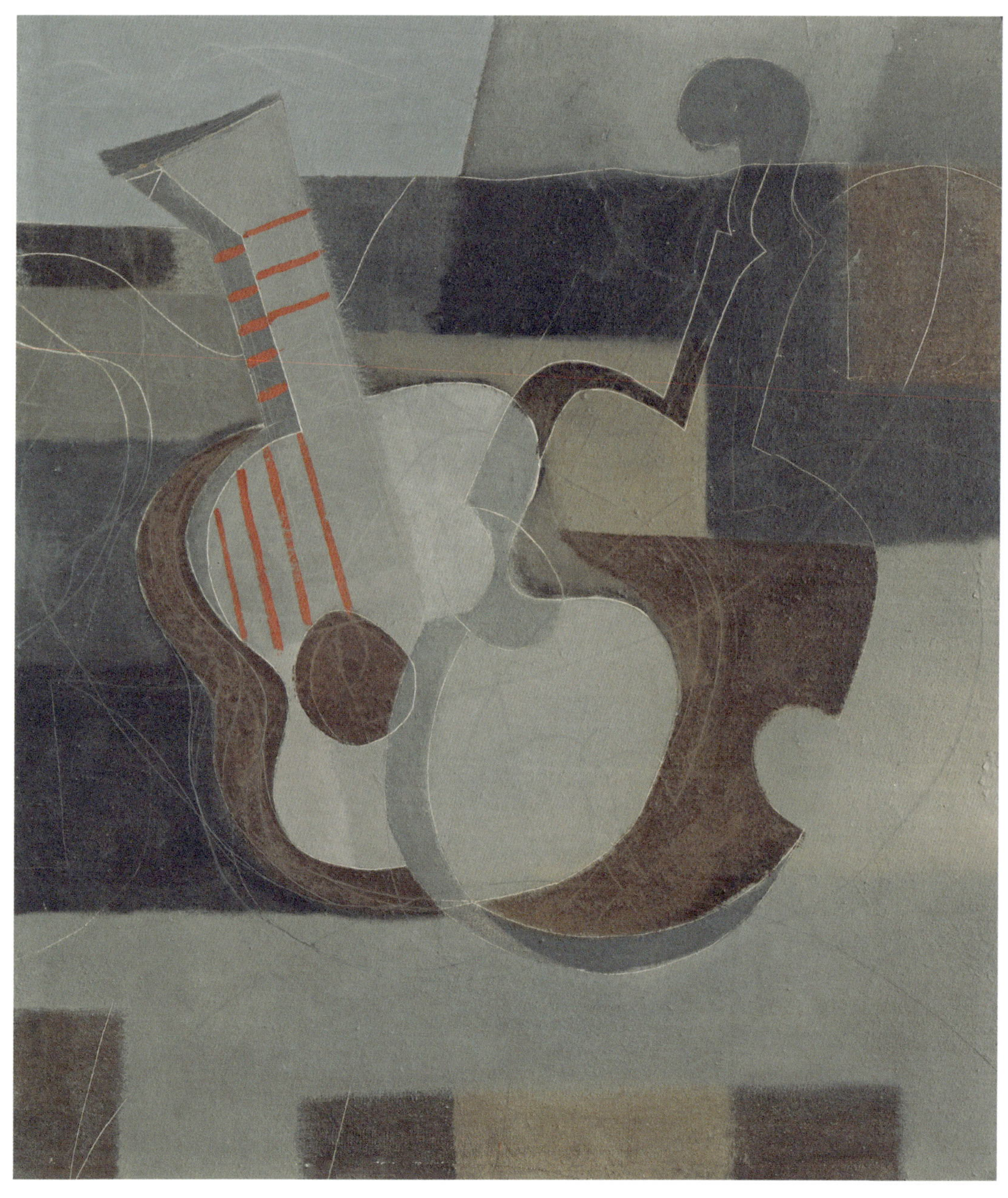

1933 (musical instruments)
Oil paint on canvas, 103 × 90.5 cm
KY00644.EH

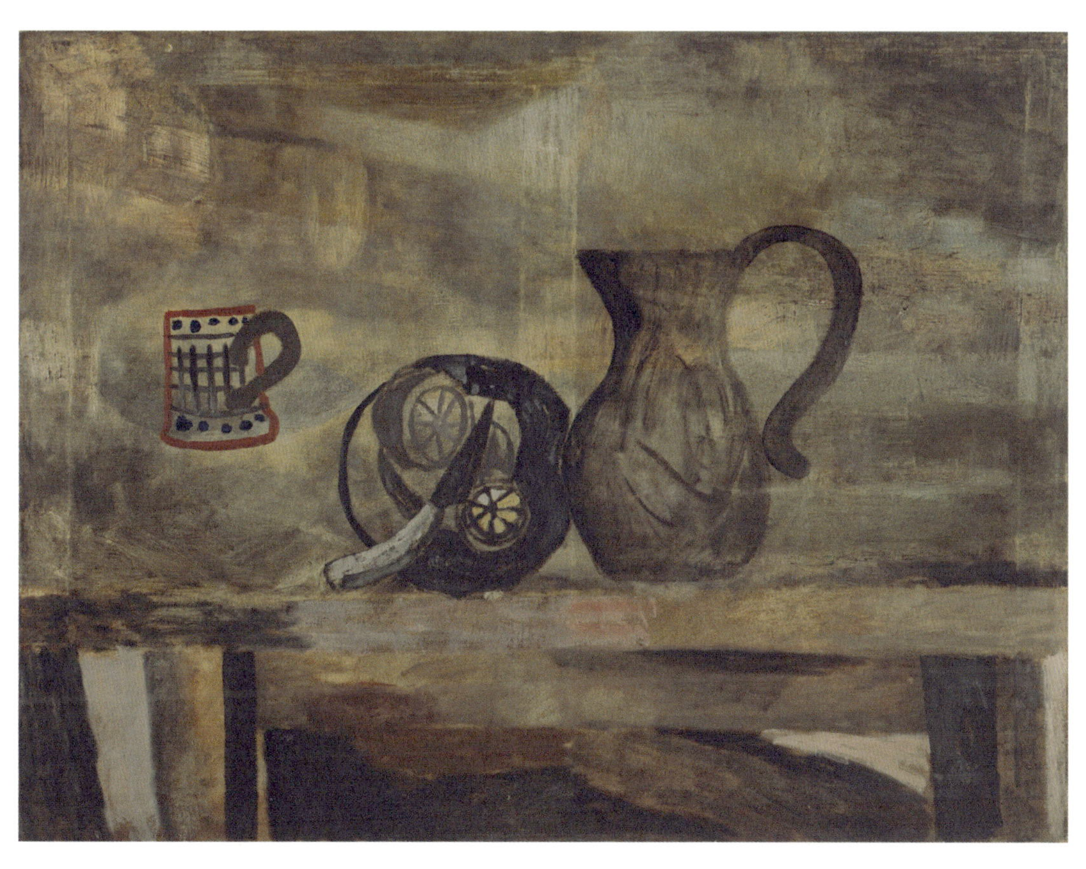

May 1927 (still life with knife and lemon)
Oil paint on canvas, 91.5 × 122 cm
KY00333.EH

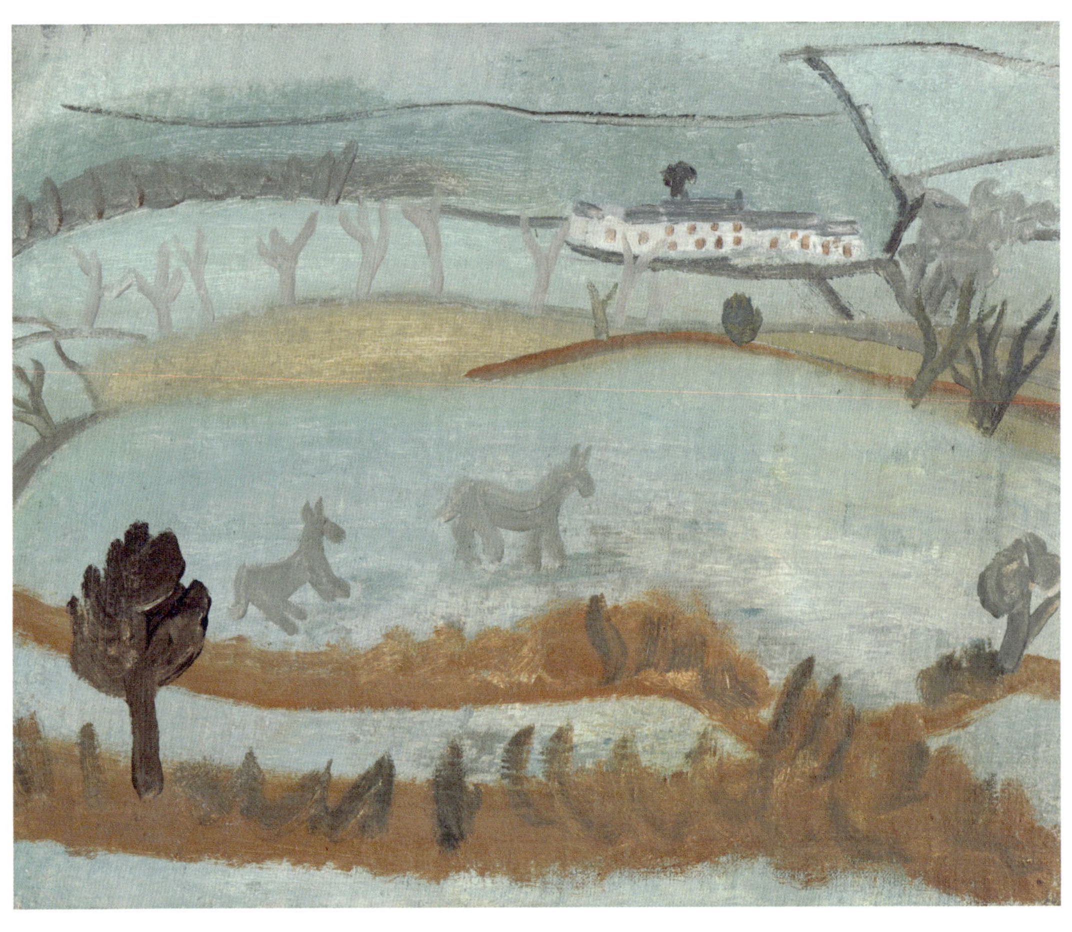

1928 (Banks Head - Cumbrian Landscape)
Oil paint on canvas, 45.3 × 55.6 cm
KY00628.EH

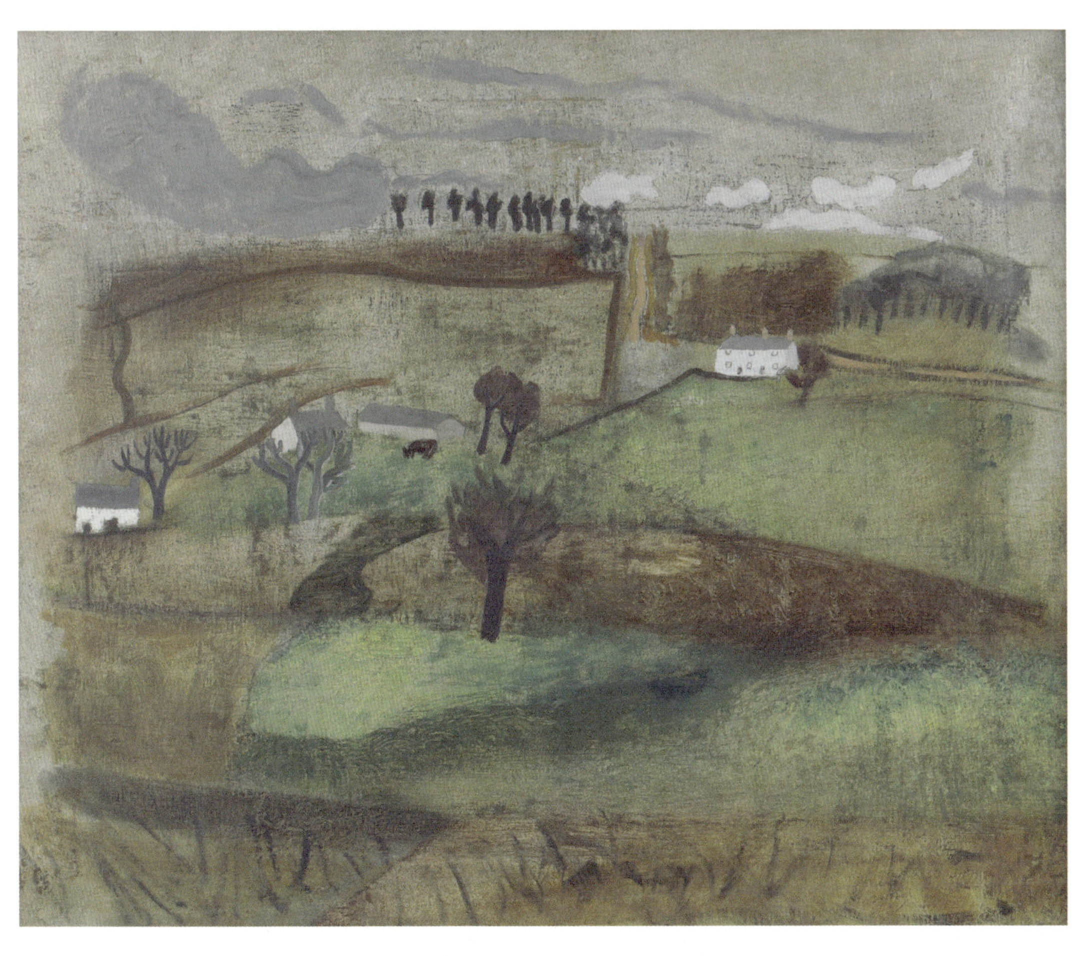

1929 (Kingwater Valley, Cumberland), 1929
Pencil and oil paint on canvas, 56.5 × 68.5 cm
KY01426

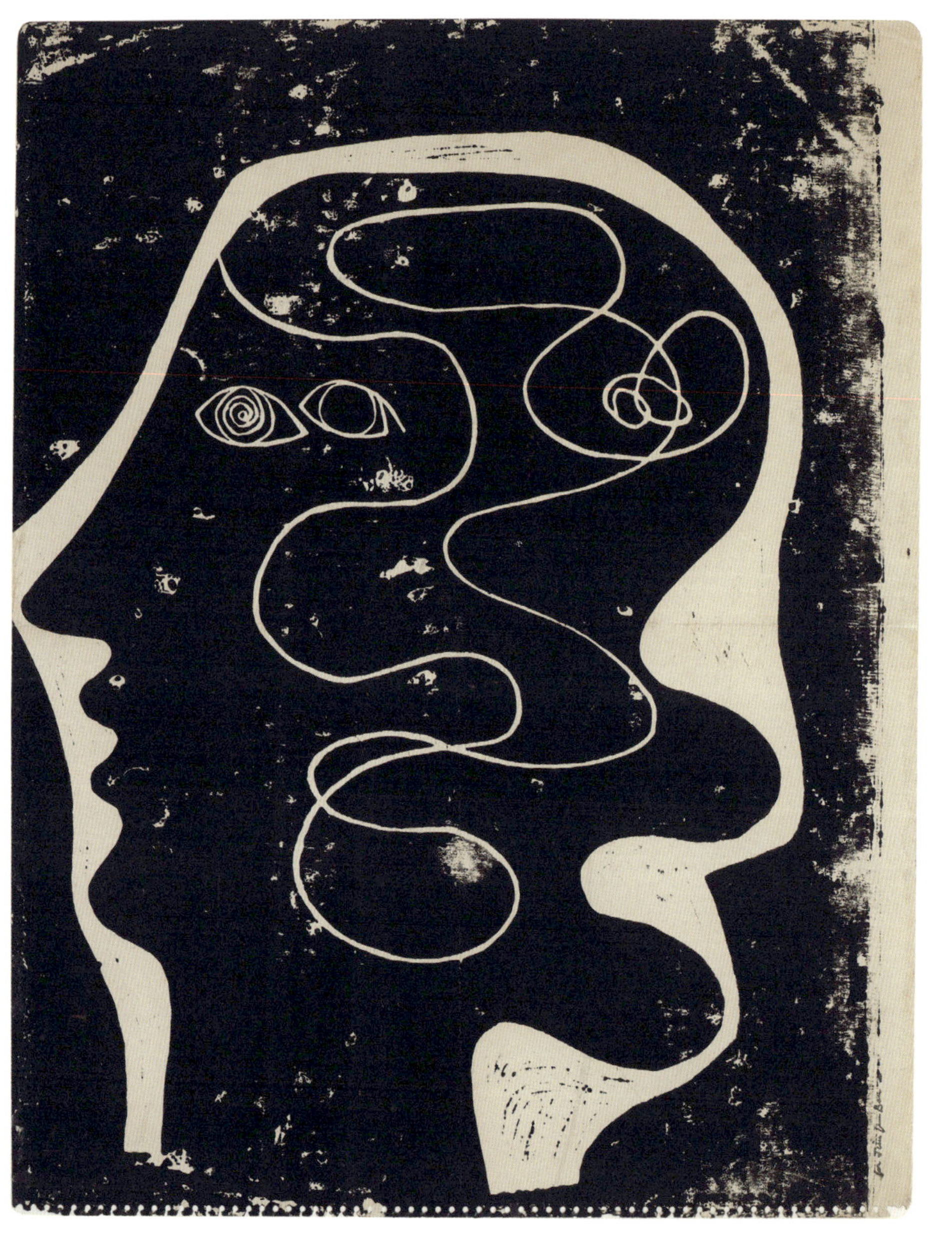

head, c. 1933
Linocut print on card, 42 × 33 cm
KY00647.EH

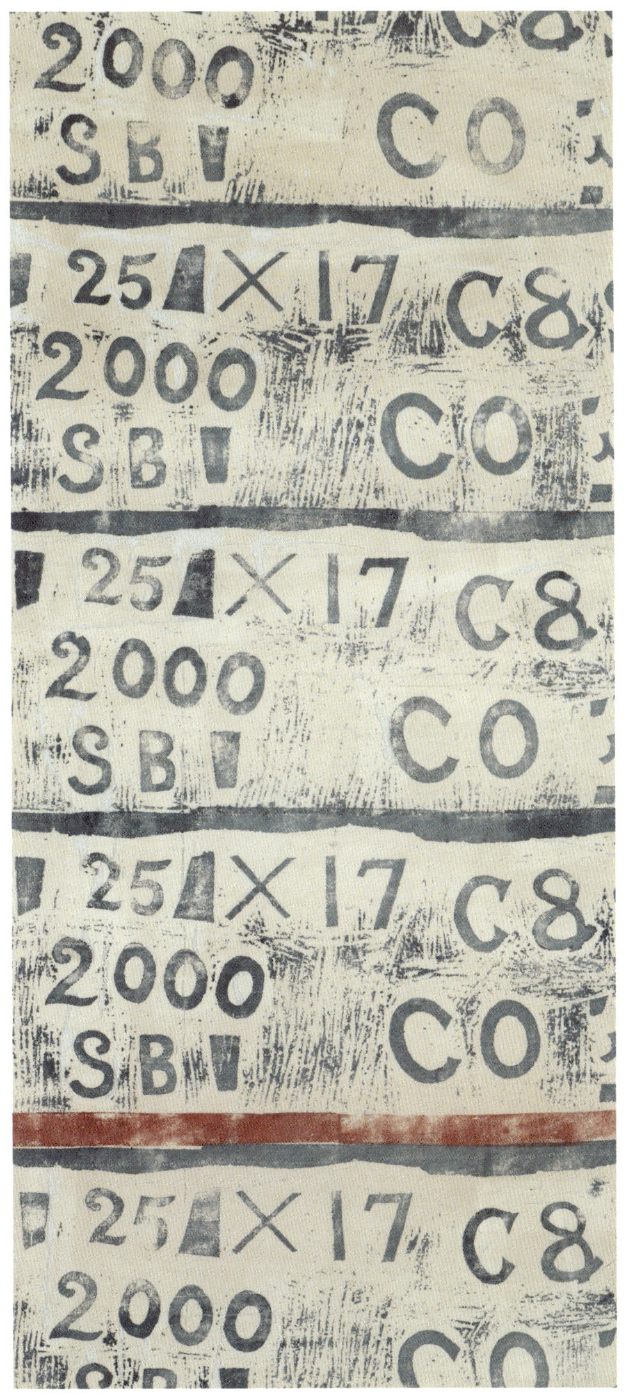

letters and numbers, c. 1933
Linoblock print on cotton, 72 × 32 cm
KY00705.EH

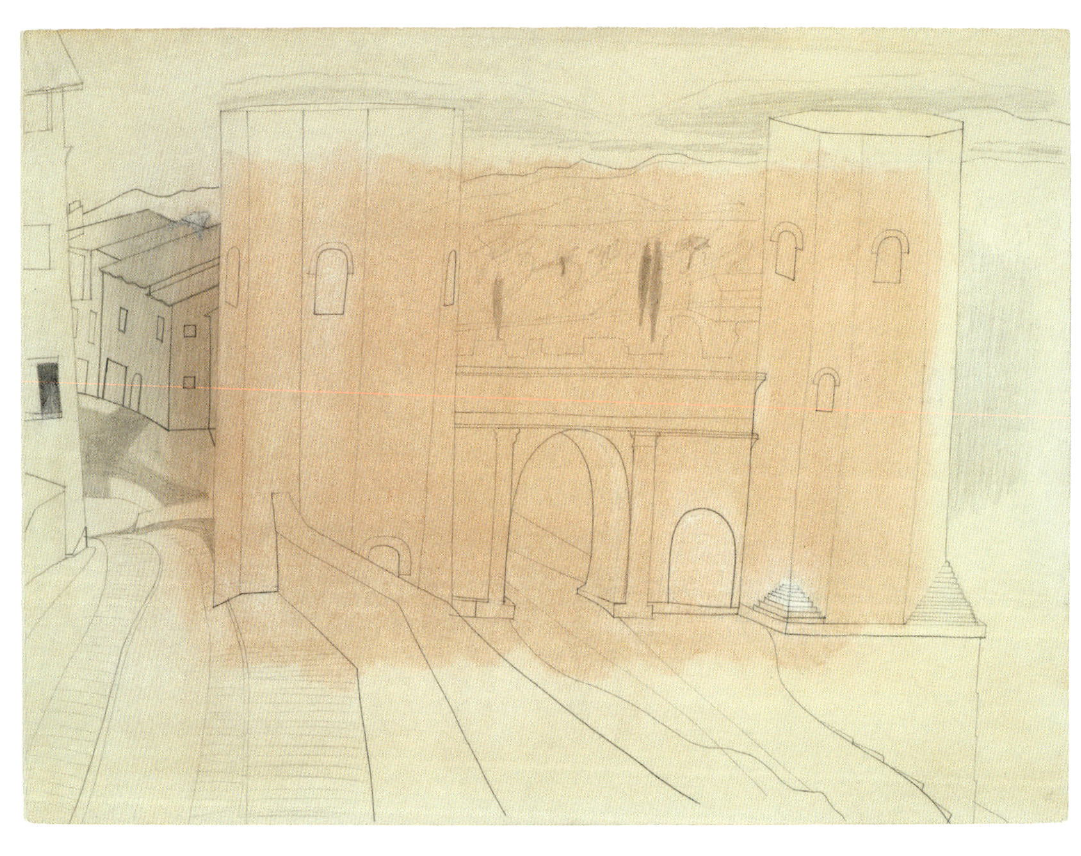

1955 (spello), 1955
Graphite and watercolour on card, 38 × 52 cm
KY00763.EH

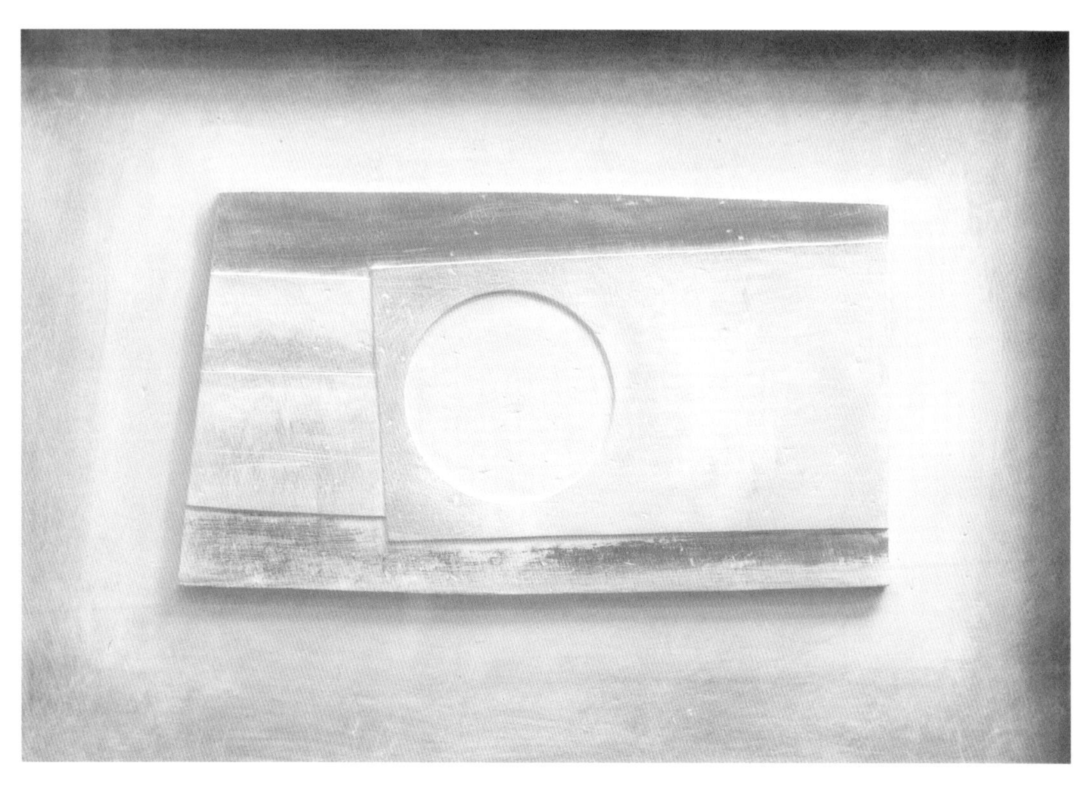

1965 (Kos - project for freestanding relief wall), 1965
Oil paint on carved board, 32 × 47 cm
KY01428

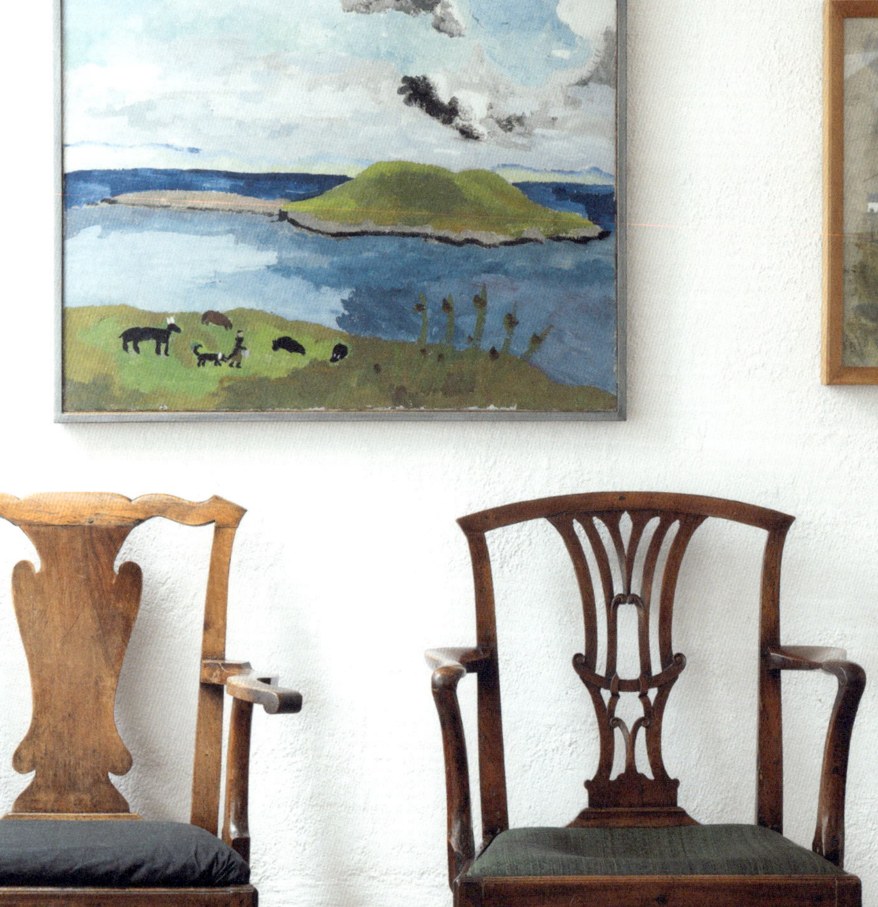

KATE NICHOLSON

(1929–2019)

Kate Nicholson was born in Brampton, Cumberland (now Cumbria). She studied at Carlisle College of Art and Camberwell School of Arts and Crafts before enrolling at the Bath Academy of Art 1949-53, where she was taught by William Scott and Peter Lanyon. In addition to this formal education, Nicholson learnt much from her parents, the artists Ben and Winifred Nicholson. After leaving Bath, she taught at Totnes High School in Devon, before moving to St Ives in 1955, where she lived and worked alongside her father. In Cornwall, Nicholson became an active member of the Penwith Society, and her first solo exhibition was with the Waddington Galleries in 1959. Later exhibitions were staged at the Marjorie Parr Gallery in London. Kate Nicholson accompanied her mother, Winifred, on painting trips to Scotland and Greece, and in 1962, they also stayed with Jim and Helen Ede at Kettle's Yard. Earlier that year, Jim showed his support for Kate by swapping a work of hers he had previously acquired for two new ones.

Isle of Skye, 1948
Oil on canvas, 68.5 × 89 cm
KY00758.EH

with (right) Ben Nicholson
1929 (Kingwater Valley, Cumberland), 1929
Pencil and oil paint on canvas, 56.5 × 68.5 cm
KY01426

Kate Nicholson, letter to Jim Ede, not dated

Kettle's Yard Archive. KY/EDE/1/1

> What a beautiful photo of a poised shell you sent me for Xmas. I wonder if you took the photo yourself? It is very good of you to take the trouble to interest colleges to buy paintings of living artists. [...] Have you got any students who are especially keen on painting? It must be a good way to show them pictures in the natural setting of a living house with stones and raw wood. [...] I have just been working on a painting of that fragile Japanese pink, a strident green and a small bit of glowing red. Also I find that the winter skeleton plants are marvellous to draw, all the essence of the plant is retained in the dried up plant. Dried bamboos are good to work from.

Jim Ede, *A way of life: Kettle's Yard*

(Cambridge University Press, 1984) p. 195

> Kate Nicholson's land- and seascape [*Isle of Skye*, 1948], so vibrant in its sweeping width of outlook, even at the age of seventeen, was totally disregarded as children's nonsense - the animals are a little queer and she burst into laughter when she saw them some twenty years later - but they are individuals, and all so open and full of air.

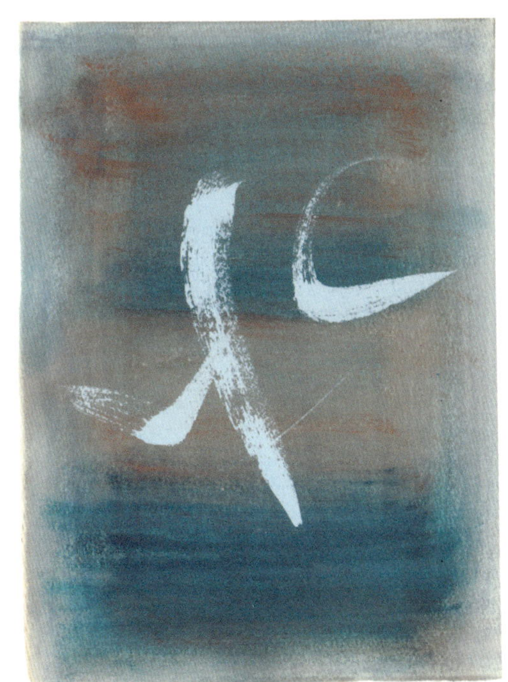

Alcestes, 1963
Gouache on paper, 38 × 28.5 cm
KY00823

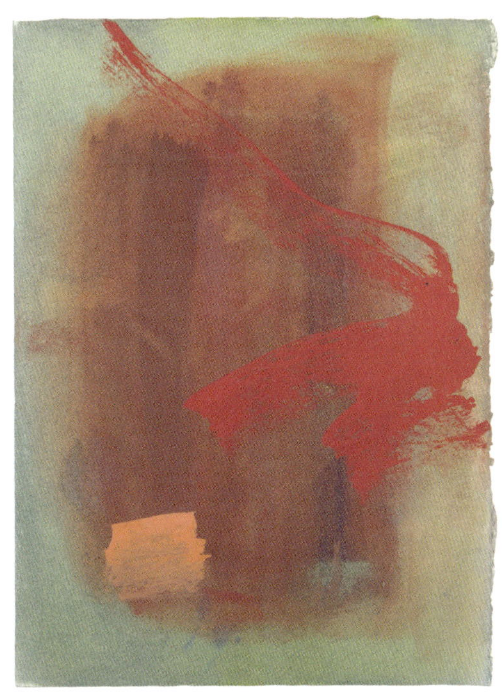

Thola's Tomb, 1962
Gouache on paper, 38 × 28 cm
KY00821

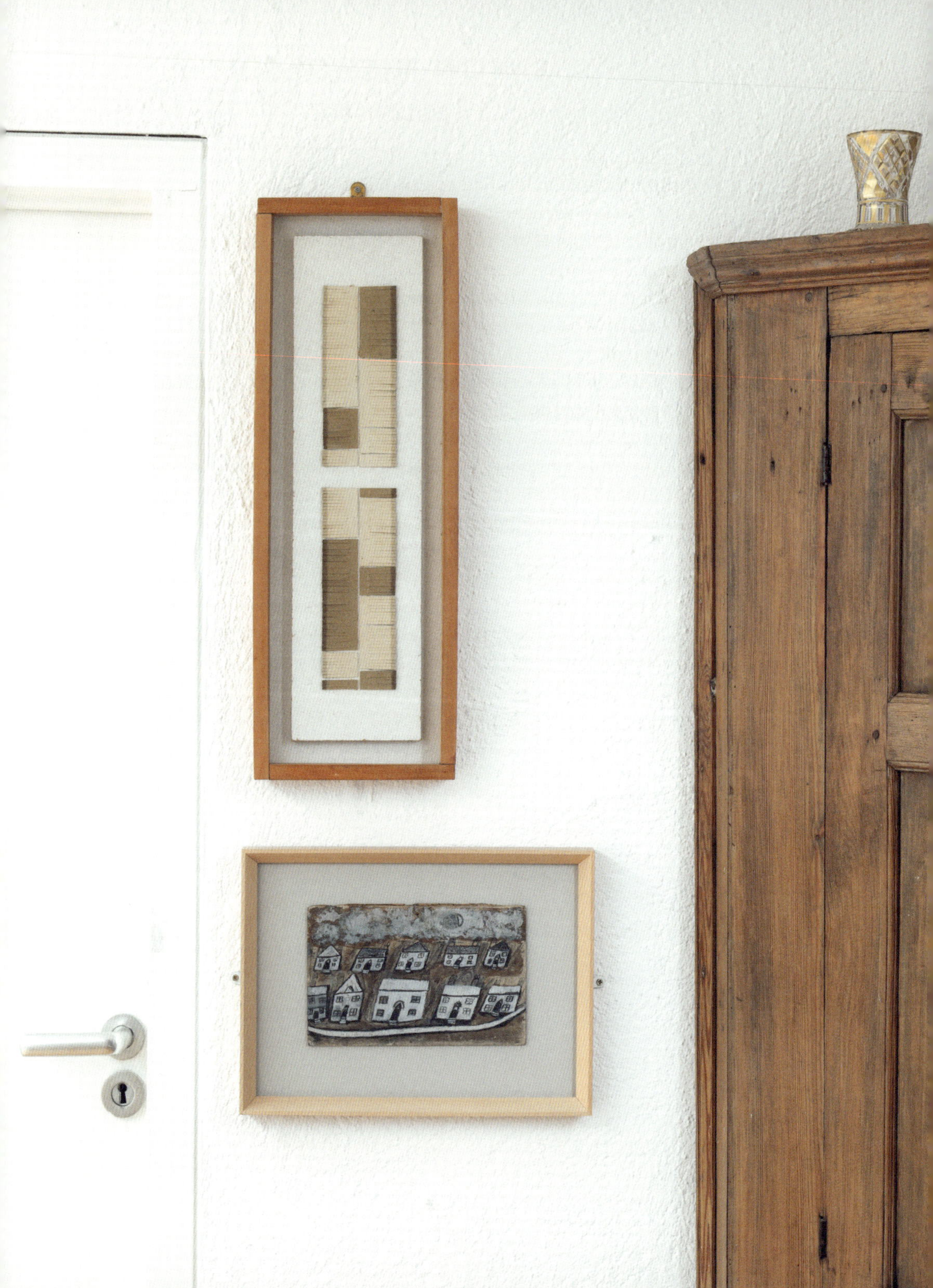

SIMON NICHOLSON

(1934–1990)

Simon Nicholson studied sculpture at the Royal College of Art 1953-54 and archaeology and anthropology at Trinity College, Cambridge 1954-57. Afterwards, he moved to St Ives, Cornwall where his artist parents, Ben Nicholson and Barbara Hepworth also lived. Simon Nicholson moved to the United States in 1964 to take up a post as Visiting Professor of Sculpture at the Moore College of Art and Design in Philadelphia. From 1965, he taught at the University of California, Berkeley, where he promoted play as a principal method of design and invited children to participate in the assessment of students' projects in local schools, parks, playgrounds and hospitals. Solo exhibitions of his work were held at Galeria Carl van der Voort in San Francisco (1968) and the Gallery for Contemporary Art in Pittsburgh (1969).

In 1971, Nicholson returned to England to teach at the Open University, where he wrote a syllabus titled 'Art and Environment'. In 1972, he published an influential article titled 'The Theory of Loose Parts' in which he argued that children's engagement with art is predicated on the presence of open-ended materials that could be transformed. Nicholson's work was exhibited in group shows at the ICA (*Play Orbit*, 1970) and in video exhibitions at the Musée d'Art Moderne in Paris and the Palais des Beaux-Arts in Brussels (1974).

St. Ives 12, 1962
Matches on strawboard, 56.5 × 18.5 cm
KY00940.EH

with (below)
Alfred Wallis, *White houses - Hales Down, near St Ives*, 1930-32
Oil paint and graphite on card, 14.9 × 23.2 cm
KY00784.EH

Simon Nicholson, letter to Jim and Helen Ede, 5 September 1962
Kettle's Yard Archive, Papers of Harold Stanley 'Jim' Ede. KY/EDE/1/1

It is very kind of you to mention all these most splendiferous objects re: wedding. You really ought not bother at all about such a thing. The shell sounds like a very well designed object and exactly our tea of cup. We like Wallis paintings extraspecially and please do not think that such an object would not be appreciated. In fact I think Wallis is one of the very very few people who painted who we do like and possibly would always be more interested in his work more than Brzeska [...] But on the other hand we also like any thing in the sort of goblets and [...] spoons very much. I think the only possible qualification here is that we prefer simple things to decorated things but then we are sure you do also.

Simon Nicholson, letter to Jim Ede, 9 August 1961
Kettle's Yard Archive, Papers of Harold Stanley 'Jim' Ede. KY/EDE/1/1

NICHOLSON
WINDEMERE
SAINT IVES
CORNWALL

9 8 61

Dear Jim

Many thanks for your card.

The bookseller/printseller in question has left and the shop is in diff hands : we will see Barbara should she know anything about the print sometime : meanwhile we wondered could it be Still Life Spotted Curtain in the Aberdeen Art Gallery ?,,, ? ? ? ? ? ? ? ? ? ? ?? ? ? ? ? ????? ?? ?????? ????? ? ? ? ? ? ? ?? ?? ? ? ?? ?

which is the only repro of Bens work anywhere N E A R 18" X 18" if what you have in mind looks like this

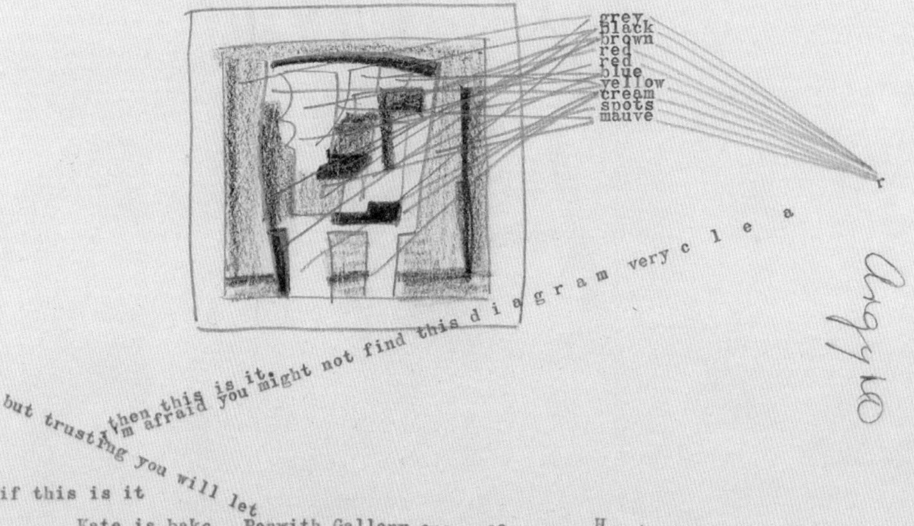

then this is it. I'm afraid you might not find this d i a g r a m very c l e a r but trusting you will let us know if this is it

Kate is bakc . Penwith Gallery opens 23rd Sept. Hop to hear from you. Love

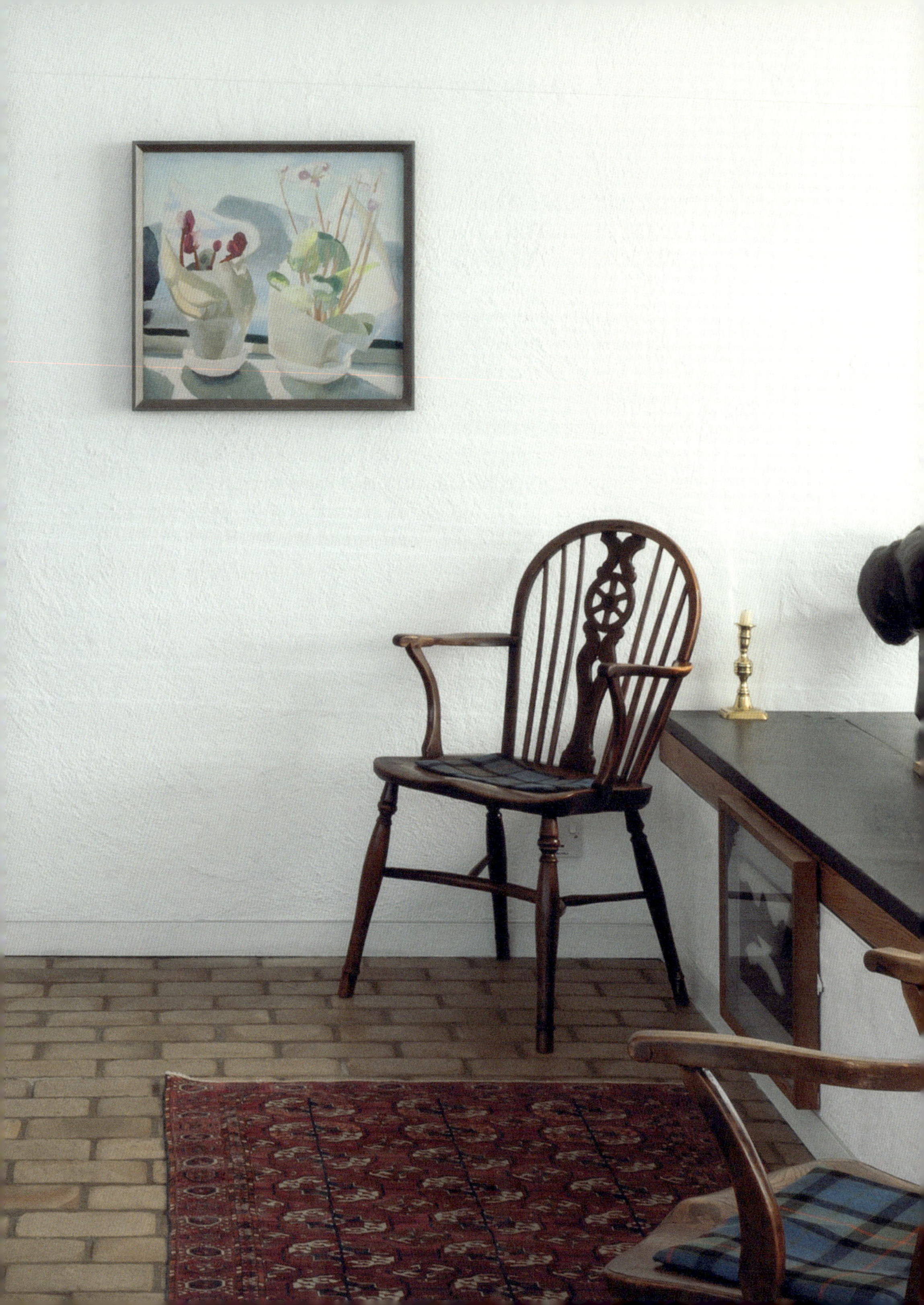

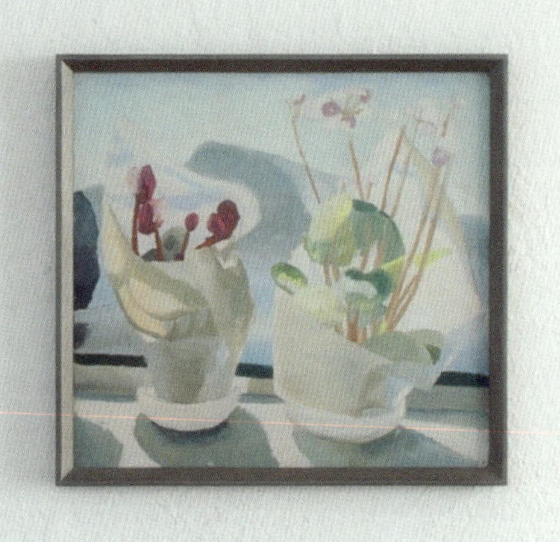

WINIFRED NICHOLSON

(1893–1981)

Winifred Nicholson (née Rosa Winifred Roberts) was born in Oxford and studied painting with her grandfather, George Howard, 9th Earl of Carlisle, before enrolling at the Byam Shaw School of Art in London. Her early works comprised still lifes, landscapes and carefully observed portraits in domestic settings. In 1920, she married fellow artist Ben Nicholson. They moved to a villa near the village of Castagnola, north of Lake Lugano in Switzerland. Winifred Nicholson's *Cyclamen and Primula*, now in the Kettle's Yard collection, was painted during this period. Nicholson began to follow the Christian Science movement and her and Ben's three children were born in 1927, 1929 and 1931. In 1924, she purchased a stone farmhouse on Hadrian's Wall in Cumberland (now Cumbria), where she would spend much of her later life in the company of friends and fellow artists, including Li Yuan-Chia (1929–1994) who lived nearby from 1968.

Nicholson exhibited with the Seven and Five Society in London from 1926 and had several solo exhibitions during the interwar years and subsequently. In 1937, under the name Winifred Dacre, she wrote a text on colour for the 1937 publication *Circle: International Survey of Constructive Art*, alongside contributions from artists and architects including Lázsló Moholy Nagy, Piet Mondrian and Walter Gropius. In the 1930s, having separated from Ben Nicholson, Winifred Nicholson lived in Paris, and during the 1950s, she often visited the Hebrides and Western Scotland, making several paintings there. Many of her works most admired by the Edes were bought by their mutual friend, the collector Helen Sutherland and subsequently donated to Kettle's Yard by Nicolete Gray.

Cyclamen and Primula, c. 1923
Oil paint on board,
50 × 55 cm
KY00767.EH

with (below, right) L.S. Lowry, *Mountain Lake*, 1943
Oil paint on board
KY00986.EH

and (shelf) Henri Gaudier-Brzeska, *Head of Mlle Borne*, 1914 (posthumous cast)
Bronze,
40 × 29.8 × 34.2 cm
KY01276.EH

Winifred Nicholson, letter to Jim Ede, c .1929

Kettle's Yard Archive, Papers of Harold Stanley 'Jim' Ede. KY/EDE/1/12

Masculine is one half. Feminine the other - each equally potent, living beautiful, purposeful. Each totally distinct. Each only reaching its full flowering point in fusion with the other, by marriage, by friendship, by some momentary sparky contact of love, or by being united in one body as they were in Shakespeare or in my grandmother [...]

There has always been some element of fusion, however slight to bring life. The more fusion the more life.

Now we are off. We start from the masculine pivot and look out from his point of consciousness, as the world up till now has done. He is elemental masculine - in a lazy primitive forest. He is conscious of the warmth of the sun and then of an urge to be up and active. He does not query where this urge comes from, he starts chasing in the forest. He runs through the trees and exults in running, through the green leaves he sees glimpses of fleeting loveliness. It is mysterious beyond his understanding, it has not entered into his world. He runs the faster to discover what it is, all his prowess are employed and his invention, he makes nets and arrows, and then telescopes and microscopes and aeroplanes and wirelesses to discover the unknown - and what he has discovered he expresses in all the art he knows. He is Botticelli, Jane Austen, Modigliani, Marie Laurencin, Goya, El Greco, Giorgione etc, etc, etc. And the thing he discovers is Beatrice, Clara, Heloise, Platonic ideas, America, the North Pole, Uranus, the Banking System, the Law of Relativity, etc, etc, etc. And when he has discovered it, according to the fairy tale he lives happily ever afterwards, and says so as Raphael said so.

That is Chapter 1 and the fairy tale thought that was the end. But they discovered dimly that it was not - and that put out all their calculations - Woman not a lovely ethereal Doe, with panting flanks and soft scared eyes, and trails of pale convolvulus torn off in her mad flight through the wet undergrowth? The search not sufficient for itself? Art clamouring for some reason, some basis for itself, why then the world's a snare, and a delusion, and they invented cynicism, and Voltaire, and Descartes and Debussy and Dostoyevsky and Freud and the Word Sex. And all the time that doe in the bushes was having the laugh of her life [...] She could not trust the raw masculine principle with her secret [...] the secret was terrible as well as beautiful and true, and needed as high courage to bring to maturity, as all his fighting and speculation after Abstract truth. And she knew that she must play her part in silence and alone, for any word spoken would mean that he would use his pride of masculine force and spoil the secret - not understanding it [...]

But the moment has nearly come for change [...] Masculine speculation has explained nothing, chiefly because it did not start at the beginning [...]

The change is just coming and the other pivot is going to open its mouth to speak [...] It will not look upon things and events as things to chase and explore and possess, i.e. understand. It will not search for Truth [...]

There is no such thing as action, and strenuous endeavour and capturing things through prowess - things just come and also go - the right things come, many different ones, from many different places and nestle beneath her smile - and stay - and in stillness and quiet, she places them so near one another that they cease to exist and pass through death to become something one [...]

Winifred Nicholson, letter to Jim Ede, not dated

Kettle's Yard Archive, Papers of Harold Stanley 'Jim' Ede. KY/EDE/1/12

> There seems too little time to write anything worthwhile. All my spare time off housekeeping and mothering I spend trying to delve further, to find more. When one is young one is satisfied with a flower petal or a sparkle. Now I want more [I] want the rainbow scale of the flower and the reason and the travel of the sparkle - and most of all a long quiet time of intense peace and uninterrupted thought - none of which one can get. Nobody can ever get. They have to put all the interruptions in to the cauldron and boil them along with the rainbows - that one can never catch or hold.

Winifred Nicholson, letter to Jim Ede, late 1940s

Kettle's Yard Archive, Papers of Harold Stanley 'Jim' Ede. KY/EDE/1/12

> I paint a lot and am improving I think and I hope. Country and earth and being under the sky are good for my kind of painting and working hard at other things and not being able to paint when one wants too, that's a great help too. Kate teaches me a lot. It's all so easy to her, all inside her head like Ben's vision. Please give my love to Helen and to yourself, and forgive haste. I must go out and milk in the frosty moonlight all hay, mist and animal smells.

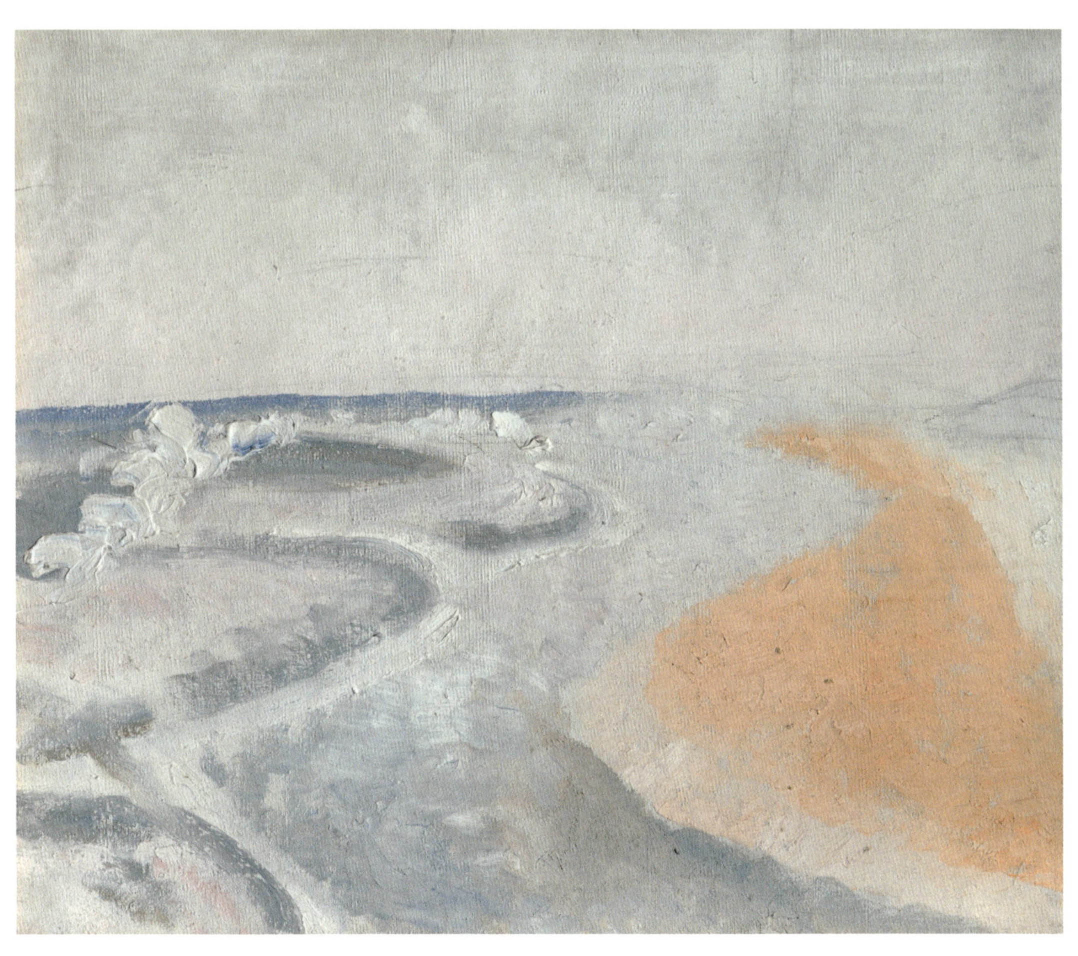

Seascape (Sea and Sand), 1926
Oil paint on canvas, 49 × 59 cm
KY00387.EH

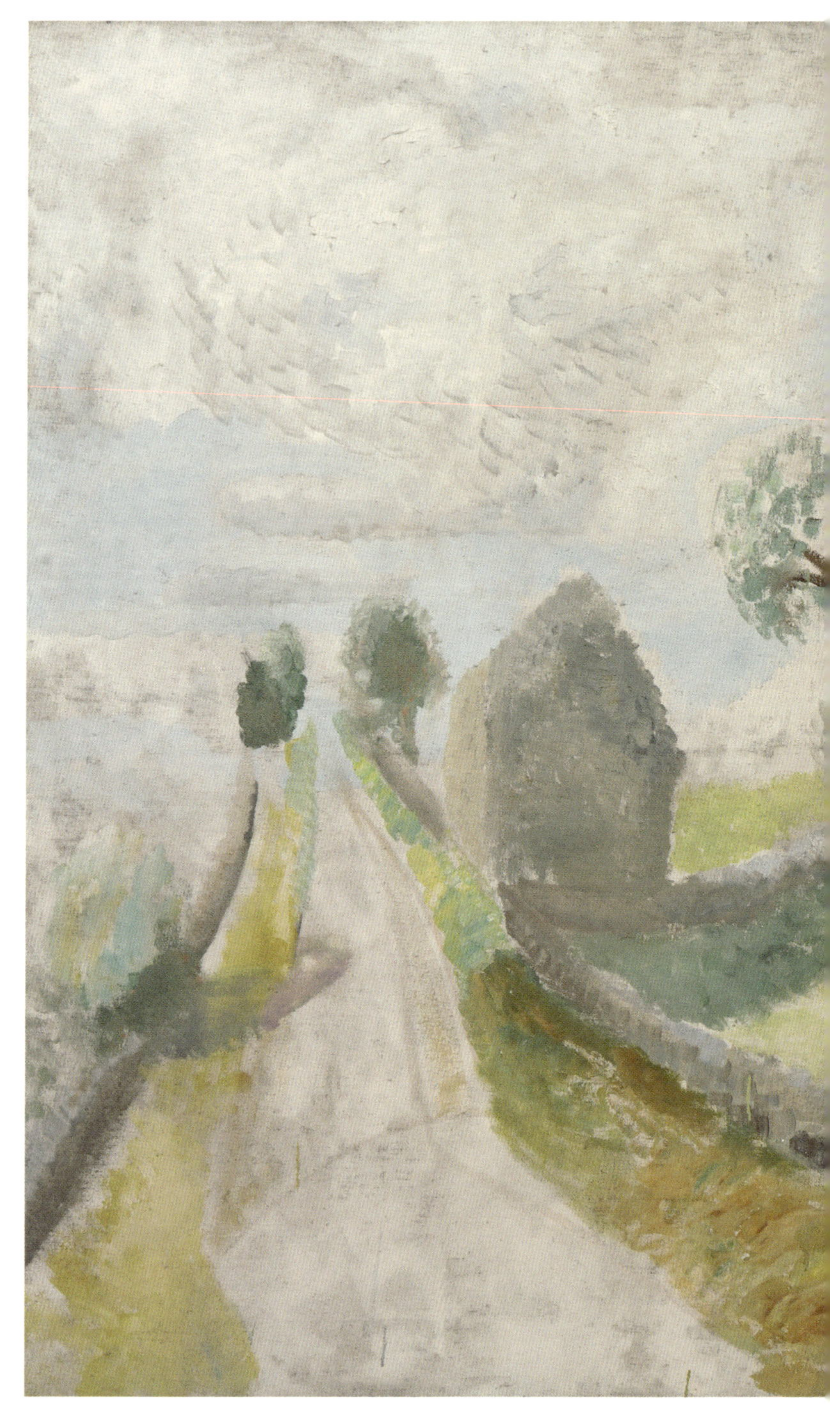

Roman Road (Landscape with House and Barn), 1926
Oil paint on canvas, 126.5 × 189.5 cm
KY01260.EH

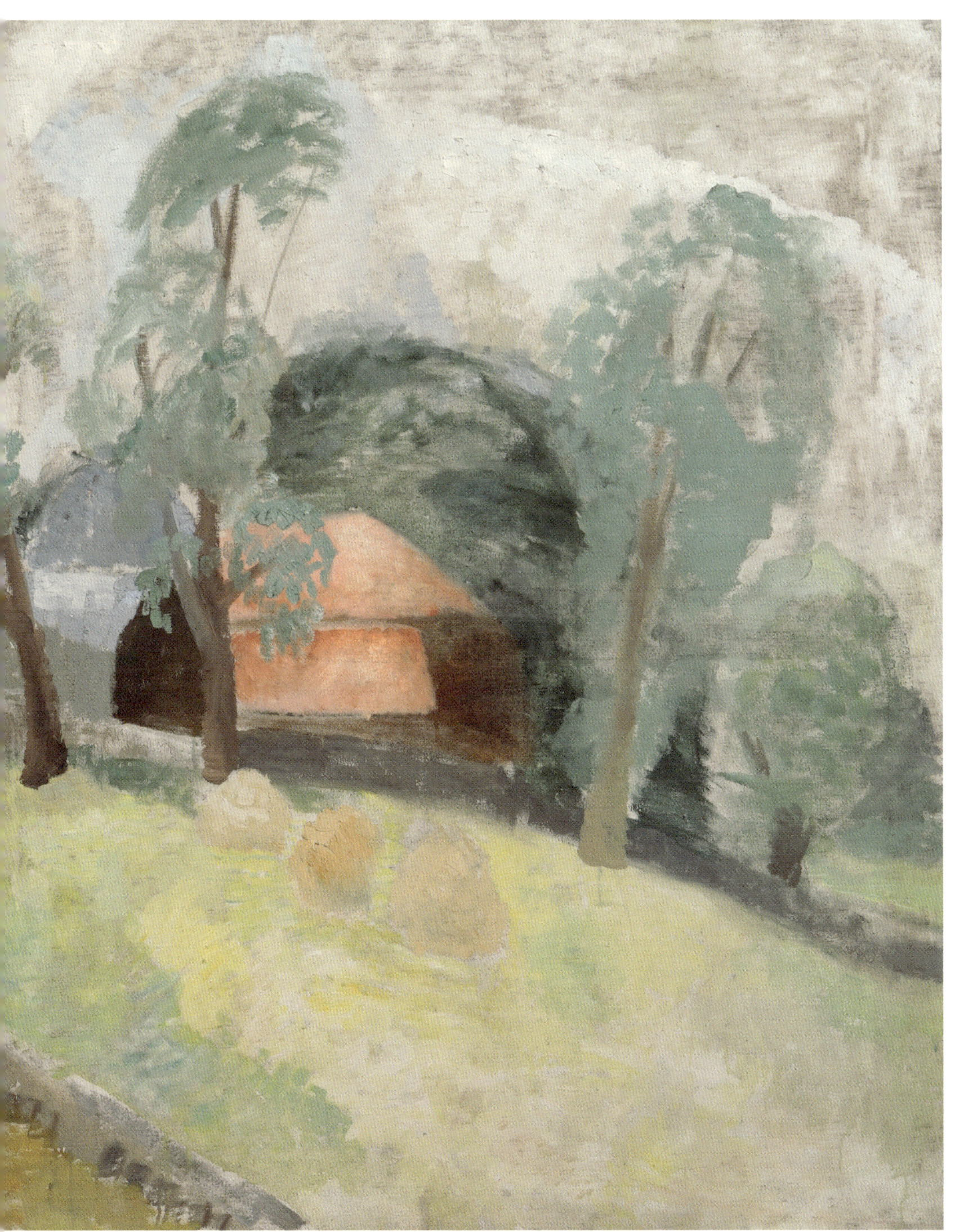

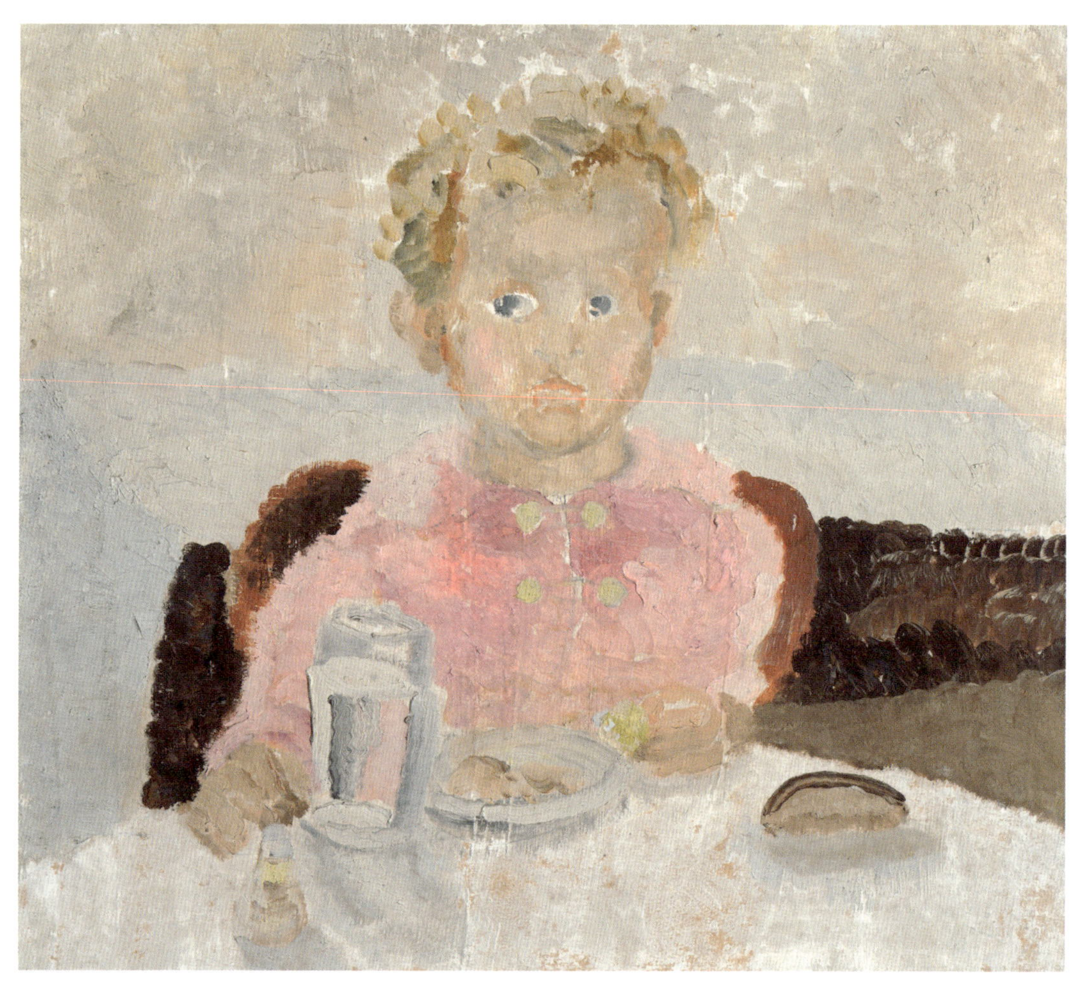

Sam Graves, c. 1930
Oil paint on board, 53 × 61 cm
KY00674.EH

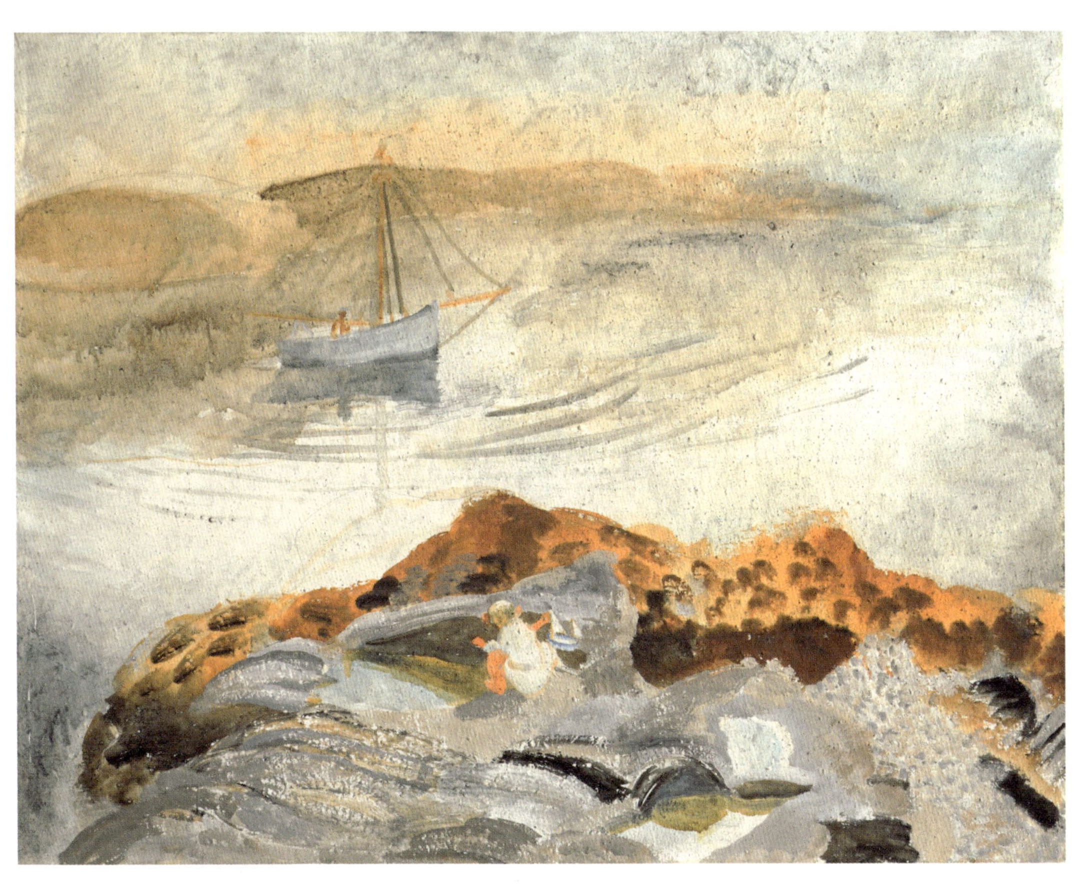

Seascape with Dinghy (or Seascape with Two Boats), 1932
Oil paint on canvas, 68 × 87 cm
KY01261.EH

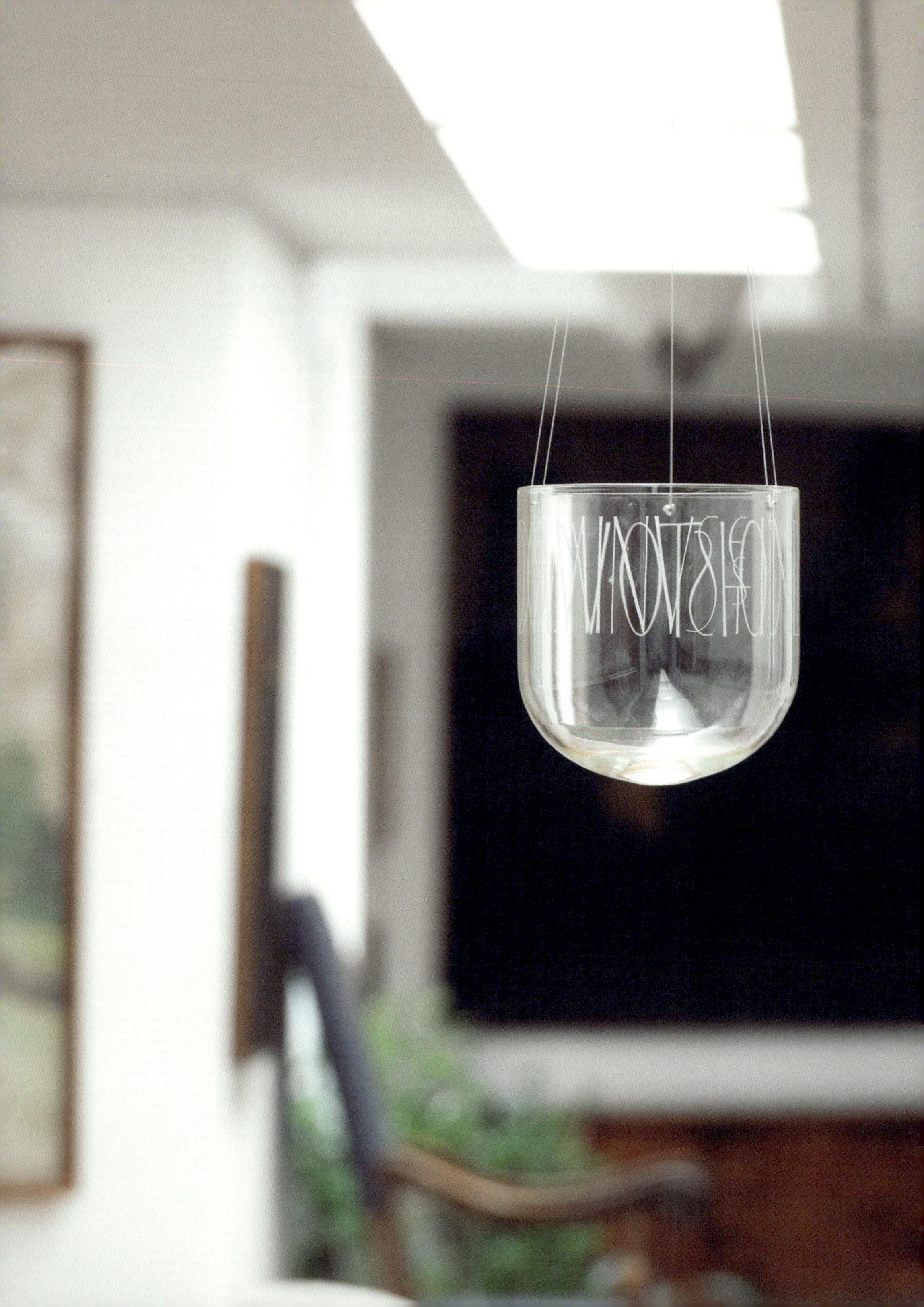

DAVID PEACE

(1915–2003)

David Peace was born in Sheffield. He became fascinated by lettering during childhood and worked as a glass engraver from 1935, making presentation glass and designing church and college windows from 1956. As well as being a master engraver of glass, Peace was a well-regarded town planner, working in Staffordshire throughout the 1950s. He moved to Cambridge in 1961, where he served as the County Council's Head of Environmental Planning 1975-80, receiving an MBE for his services in 1977. Soon after arriving in Cambridge, Peace met the Edes, who acquired five of his pieces for Kettle's Yard between 1969 and 1977. David Peace was Master of the Artworkers' Guild, 1973 and the first Chairman of the Guild of Glass Engravers 1975-86.

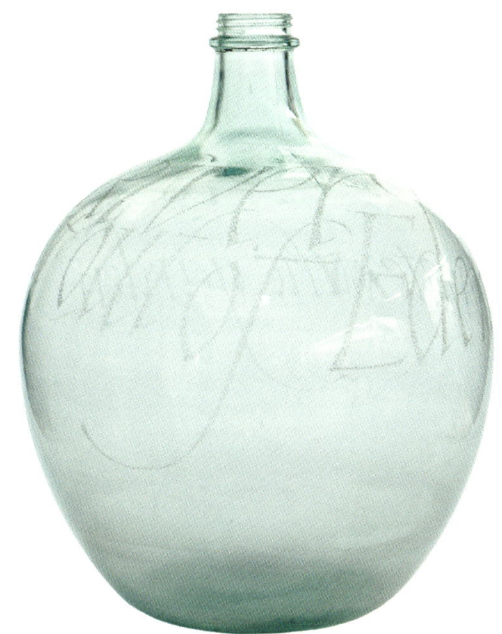

Left:
Sanctuary lamp, 1955 (remade 1994)
Engraved glass, 23 × 23 cm
KY01000B.EH

Right:
And a River went out..., 1970
Engraved glass carboy
KY01001B.EH

H.S. Ede, 'Introduction' in David Peace, *Engraved Glass*
(Abbots End, Hemingford Abbots, Huntingdon, 1980) p. ii

It seems to me that art is a great miracle - it is the showing forth of the Holy Spirit, a transubstantiation. It is to find and proclaim the poetry of life, without which there *is* no life. [...]

A translation from French into English must become English, both in words and thought; so an engraved glass must become, all the more, glass; lines and shapes, proportion and spaces pressing towards this end.

David Peace is a master of all this. Glass is sharp, his line cuts; glass is brittle, his design fragments it; glass is hard, the clearness of his incision reveals it; glass is transparent, his engraving fills it with transparent light. We learn that to cut glass is quite other than to cut stone - that an engraving on glass is in no way an engraving on paper. David Peace is also a great respecter of the shape or a goblet, a bowl or whatever form he uses, and the marks he makes upon its surface reveal that shape, giving a new dignity and a new life to the material object. The beauty of the glass itself is seldom obstructed by his markings, but instead vibrates and glitters; [...] the never ending changes of light, its warmth, its coldness, its mysterious pervasion and enfoldment [...] it becomes indeed miraculous.

Canst thou bind the cluster of the Pleiades or loose the bands of orion, 1961
Engraved glass, 95 × 46.5 cm
KY01138.EH

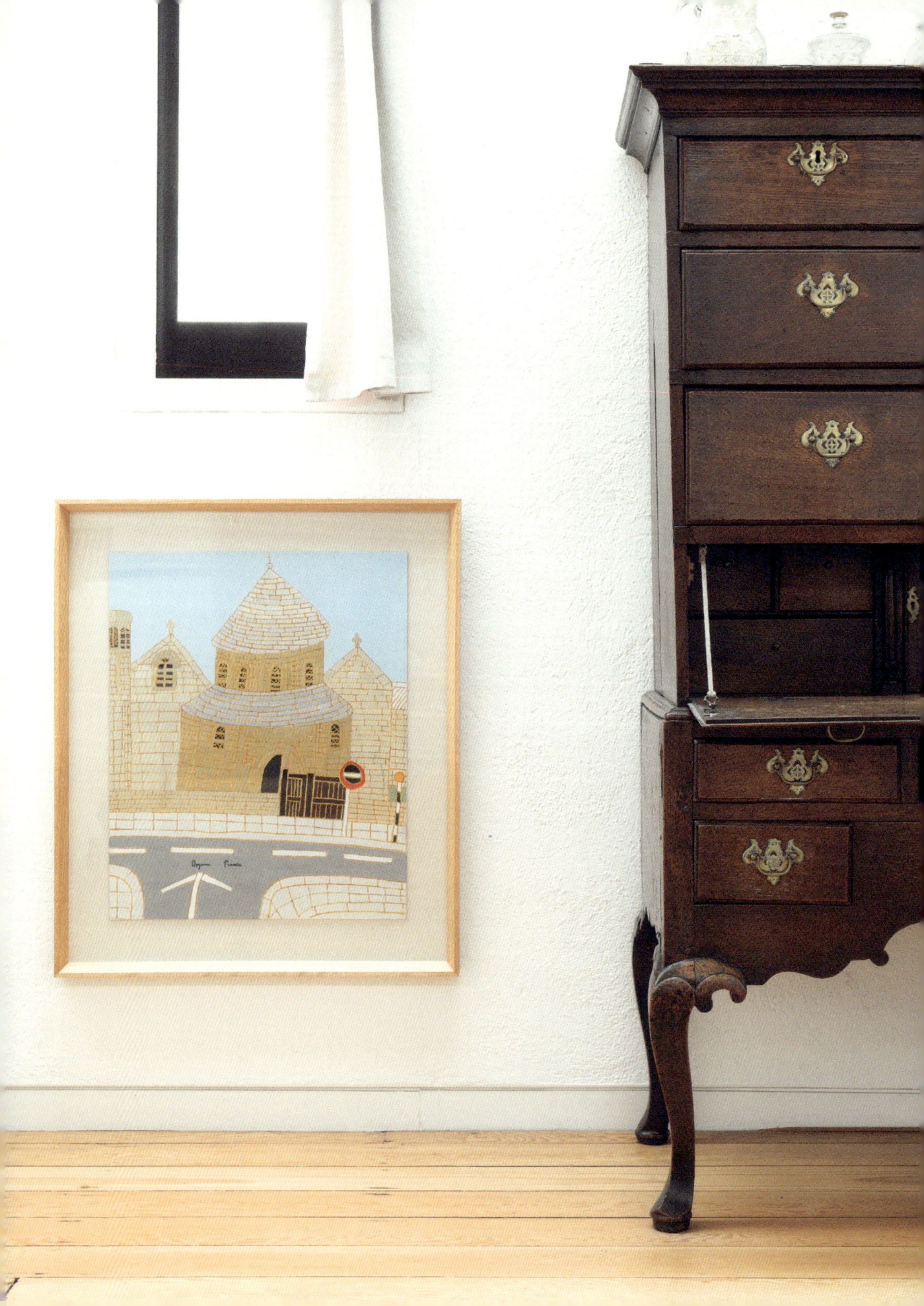

BRYAN PEARCE

(1929–2007)

Bryan Pearce was born in St Ives, Cornwall and studied at the St Ives School of Painting under Leonard Fuller between 1953 and 1957. He joined the Penwith Society in 1957 and the Newlyn Society in 1959. A solo exhibition of his work was staged at the Newlyn Gallery in 1959, and the Penwith Society held a retrospective in 1966. Pearce was born with the rare genetic condition, phenylketonuria (PKU) which, if untreated, can lead to brain damage. He was originally encouraged to draw and paint by his mother Mary Pearce (née Warmington) for its therapeutic effect. Pearce developed a characteristic style comprising a steep perspective, bold outlining, and flat, bright colours. His subjects were always closely observed, most often the buildings and boats of St Ives and the surrounding countryside.

Jim Ede met Bryan Pearce in the early 1960s, having been introduced through Barbara Hepworth. Ede became an advocate of Pearce's art, helping to arrange exhibitions of his work. He also invited Pearce and his mother to Cambridge, where they stayed for two weeks at Kettle's Yard. Pearce exhibited with the St. Martin's Gallery and the New Art Centre in London in the 1960s and 1970s. Solo exhibitions were staged at Modern Art Oxford (1975), the Plymouth Art Centre (1984) and the Royal West of England Academy (1995).

The Round Church, c. 1966
Oil paint on hardboard, 61 × 50.8 cm
KY00913.EH

Jim Ede, 'Foreword', *Bryan Pearce: Early Paintings*
(Falmouth: Falmouth Art Gallery, 1982) p. 1

> If anyone is in need of peace, trust and joy, they will find it in the work of Bryan Pearce. [...] I know of no artist with whom I can compare him in this direct simplicity and devotion save Fra Angelico who would place one colour against another with assurance and tenderness [...]

Mary Pearce, letter to Jim Ede, 11 February, c.1970
Kettle's Yard Archive, Papers of Harold Stanley 'Jim' Ede. KY/EDE/1/1

> Many thanks for your letter & the very nice catalogue [...] It was so interesting to read your introduction for I knew so little of where you had lived etc. etc. [...] It is so nice when people have lived with Bryan's paintings for a while & then buy another, it is so encouraging & it was wonderful to open your catalogue and see so many listed - thank you [...] Recently we have seen a lot of porpoises crossing over from the Island to Clodgy [Point] & masses of gannets diving for fish. There were so many diving at the same time that it looked like a heavy snowstorm as they fell into the sea [...] Kate [Nicholson] was here yesterday to answer some questions to an American poet who wants to do an article [...] He was thrilled to know that Kate would talk to him about Bryan's work - so much has been written about his handicap & less about his work, which Kate has always said is wrong.

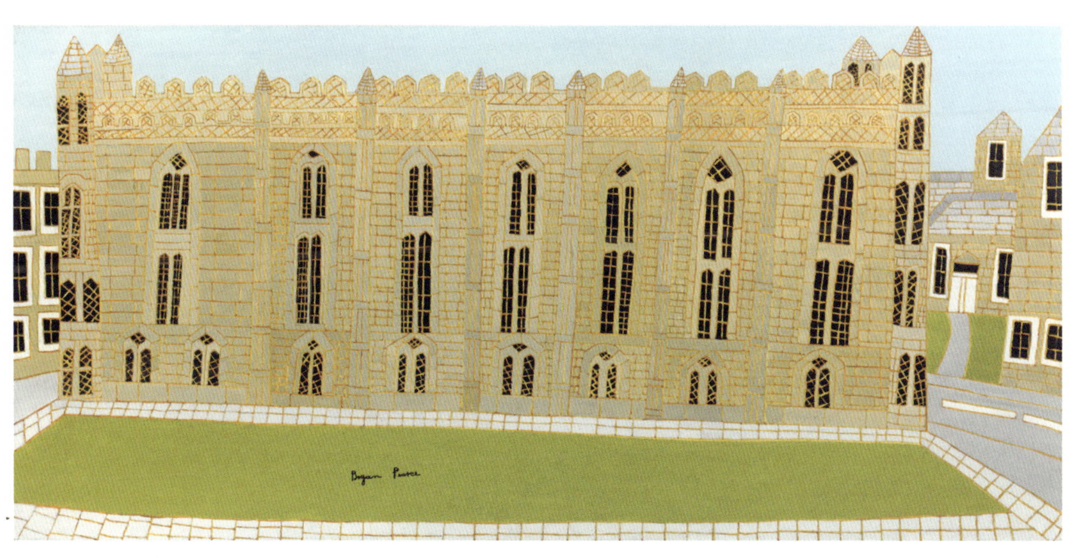

King's College Chapel, 1966
Oil paint on hardboard, 55.7 × 117 cm
KY00914.EH

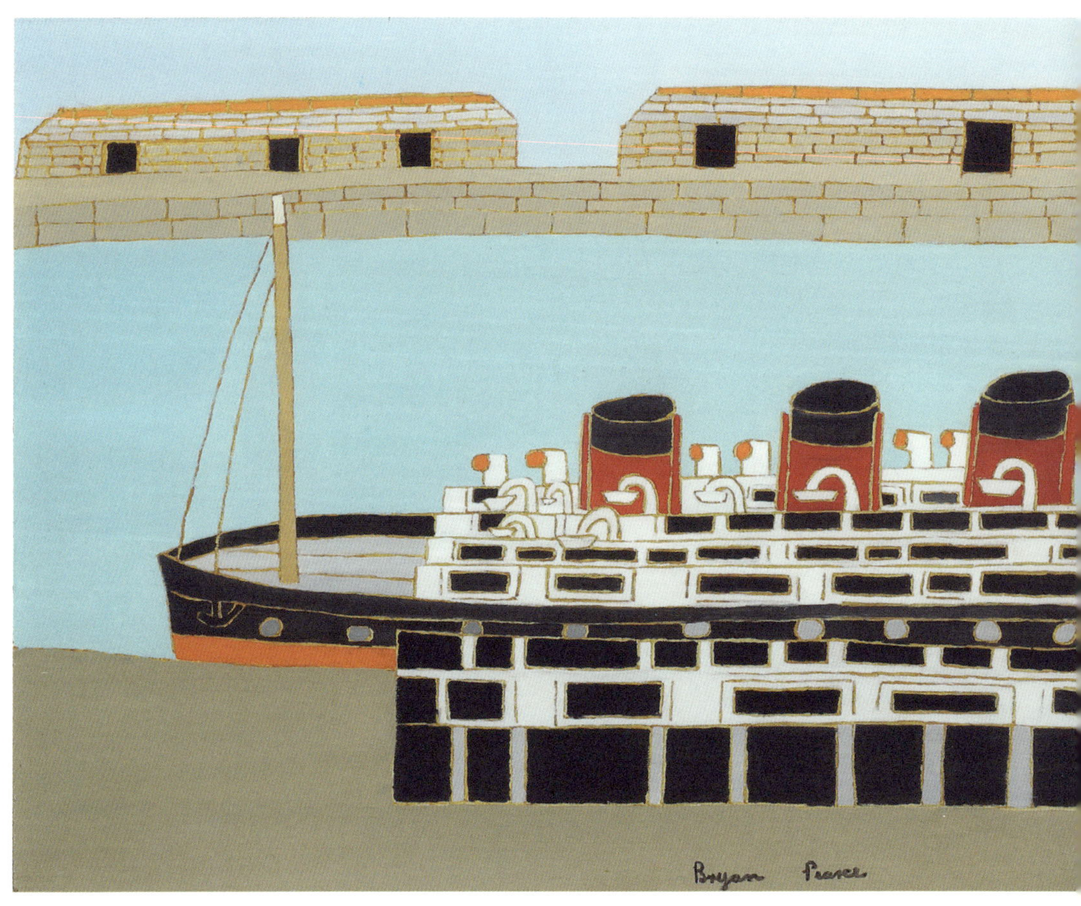

The Queen Mary, undated
Oil paint on hardboard, 40.6 × 109.7 cm
KY00796.EH

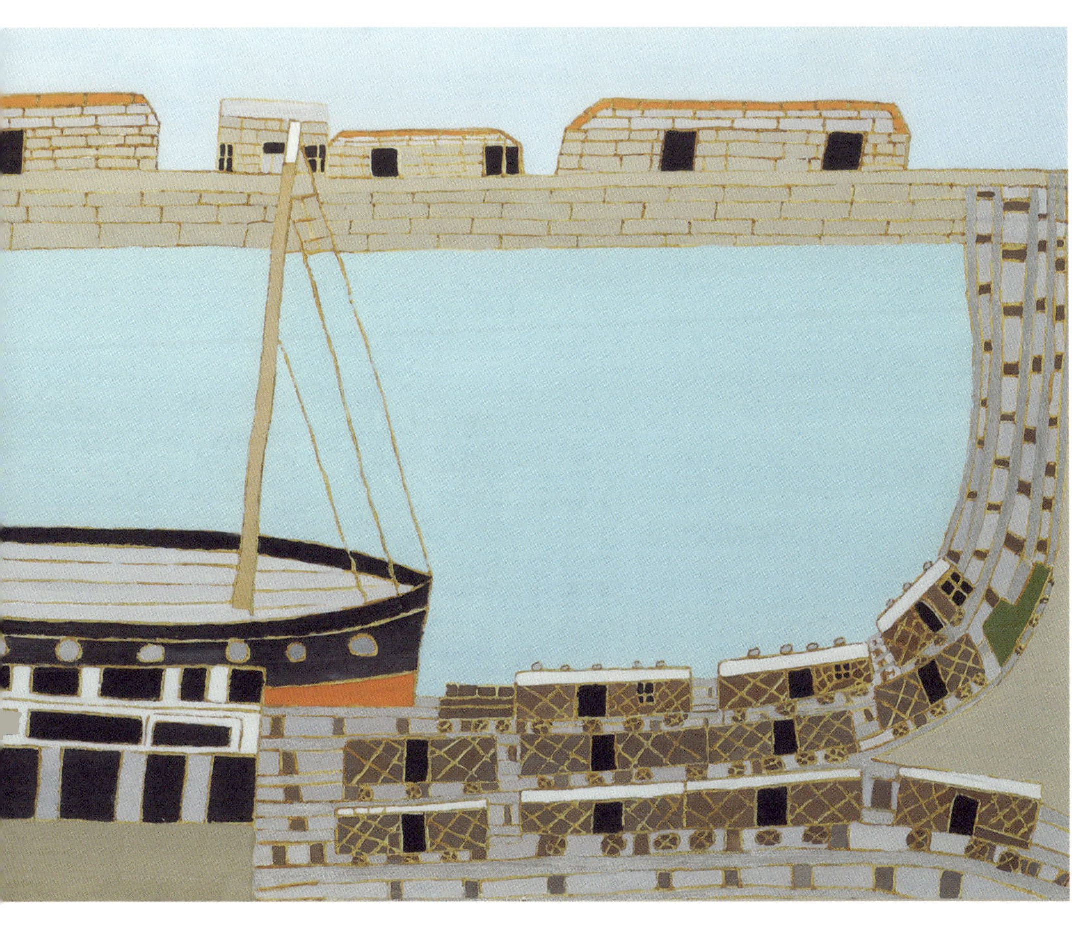

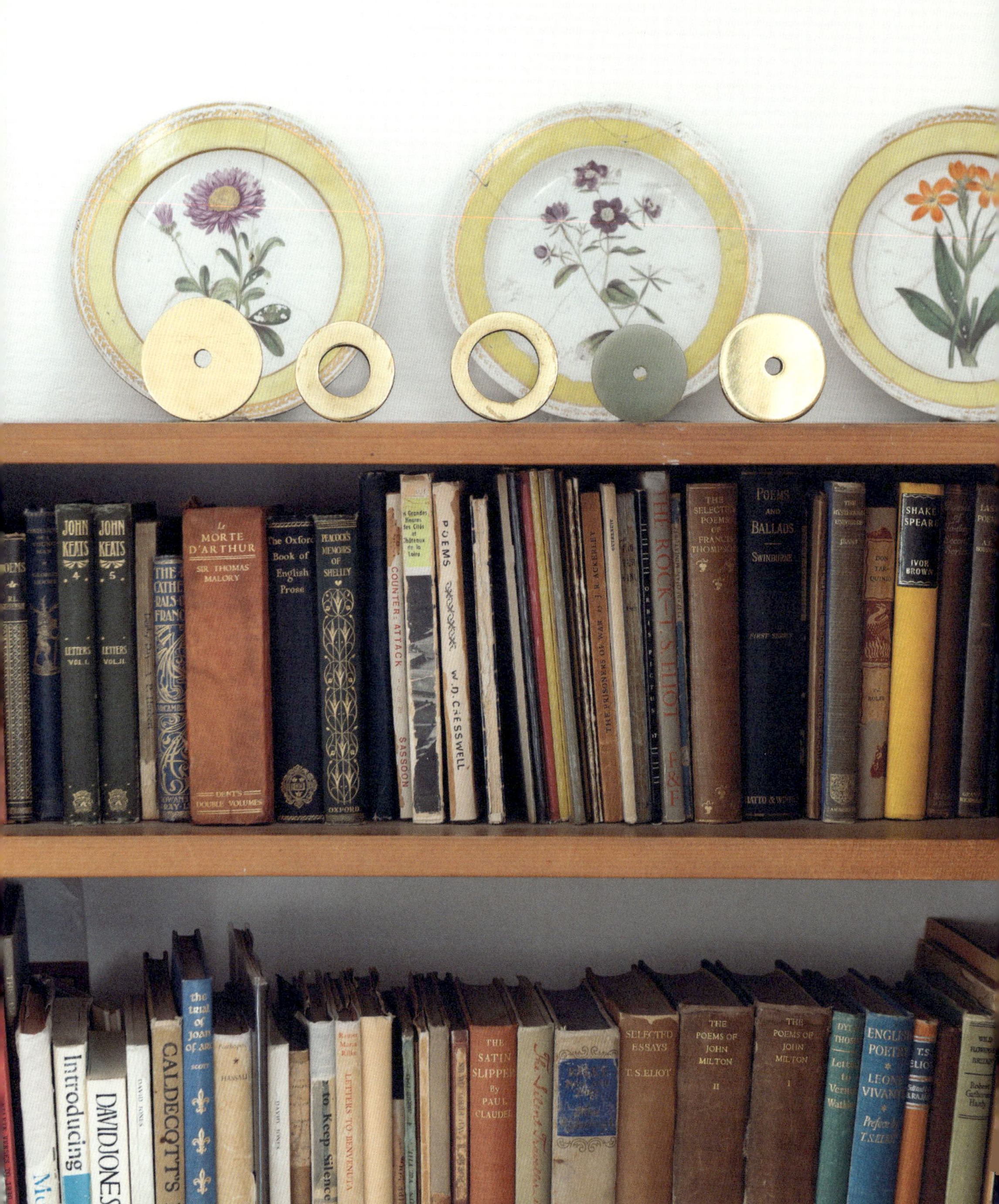
JOHN KEATS 4 LETTERS VOL. I.
JOHN KEATS 5 LETTERS VOL. II.
Le MORTE D'ARTHUR SIR THOMAS MALORY
DENT'S DOUBLE VOLUMES
The Oxford Book of English Prose
PEACOCK'S MEMOIRS OF SHELLEY
OXFORD
COUNTER-ATTACK SASSOON
POEMS W. D. CRESSWELL
THE PRISONERS OF WAR J. R. ACKERLEY
THE ROCK — T. S. ELIOT
THE SELECTED POEMS OF FRANCIS THOMPSON
POEMS AND BALLADS SWINBURNE FIRST SERIES
SHAKESPEARE IVOR BROWN
the trial of Joan of Arc
Introducing
DAVID JONES
to Keep Silence
LETTERS TO BENVENUTA
THE SATIN SLIPPER By PAUL CLAUDEL
SELECTED ESSAYS T.S. ELIOT
THE POEMS OF JOHN MILTON II
THE POEMS OF JOHN MILTON I

RICHARD POUSETTE-DART

(1916–1992)

Richard Pousette-Dart was born in Minnesota in the USA. He attended Bard College, New York State for one semester in 1936, before leaving to move to New York City, where he worked as an assistant to the sculptor Paul Manship and in the photographic studio of Lynn T. Morgan. In 1941, the Artists' Gallery, New York, hosted Pousette-Dart's first solo exhibition, and subsequent group and solo exhibitions included those at 67 Gallery, Betty Parsons Gallery, and Peggy Guggenheim's Art of This Century. He was initially associated with abstract expressionist painters including Barnett Newman, Jackson Pollock and Clyfford Still, but preferred to work independently, living outside the city in New York State.

Pousette-Dart was influenced by European modern artists, especially the work of Henri Gaudier-Brzeska, as well as transcendentalism and his lifelong commitment to pacifism. He taught at the New School between 1950 and 1961, and a retrospective of his work was held at the Whitney Museum of American Art in 1963. Pousette-Dart later taught at other institutions, including Columbia University, Sarah Lawrence College and Bard College. He and Jim Ede first met in 1940 and continued a wide-ranging and intimate correspondence. Pousette-Dart gave the Edes several works, including the brass and jade rings that are on permanent display in the house.

Group of Rings, c. 1940–50
Brass and jade
KY00739a.EH
KY00739b.EH
KY00739c.EH
KY00739d.EH
KY00739e.EH

Richard Pousette-Dart, letter to Jim Ede, 17 November 1940
Kettle's Yard Archive, Papers of Harold Stanley 'Jim' Ede. KY/EDE/1/13

> Before me, lying on the table, are the two lovely little shells which you so kindly brought to me. I like best the smaller of the two - it is exquisite. How the Universe, how God, is revealed in this little bit of asymmetry. How this little shell is a window upon God, upon all Creative Principle, to any seeing eyes [...]
> I did not mean to give you the impression that I do not like Brancusi, for I like the sort of thing he has done tremendously, except that he does not feel forms but rather surfaces, nor does he feel space as he should but again falls back upon a superficial value. Craftsmanship is important but never dominant in a living work. Gaudier is far far more the true artist and achieved far more with his small allotment of time in which to work. Both of these artists perceive the spirit variously - Brancusi almost all intellect - result coldly contemplative. Gaudier - a fine balance of feeling - intellect - which tends to move the observer's whole being. Gaudier's work is more primal - direct and in harmony with the workings of nature itself. My opinion of Brancusi is relative. I do not dislike him. Brancusi takes art away from the moving energy which life is [...] Life is not among the stars but upon the earth. His work may appear awesome to the ignorant, but to the artist's eye it must appear as bright and as ineffectual as an automobile radiator ornament. Brancusi in his art has no soul! I speak too much of him.

Richard Pousette-Dart, letter to Jim Ede, November 1940
Kettle's Yard Archive, Papers of Harold Stanley 'Jim' Ede. KY/EDE/1/13

> We have known each other quite a while now - have we not? and I believe - achieved quite some creative awareness of one another - at least - it feels good - Happy from my part of the fence [...] I have a new circle for you which I will send in the mail as soon as I find it convenient - it is large & open & with a certain more gracefulness - great is a circle! all is in a circle! a circle is an eye to God! a circle is God! all life is uniquely

> a circle! all persons are qualities of becoming circularity or realizing God! All is nature & symbol in God [...] I am happy you like & keep & consider with love the circles - they are each attitudes of the one same - & each the entire realization from its own cosmic self - I should like for you to have about 12 - so to make a lovely circle of circles for my friend.

Richard Pousette-Dart, letter to Helen Ede, 21 February 1941
Kettle's Yard Archive, Papers of Harold Stanley 'Jim' Ede. KY/EDE/1/13

> Art is the matter of a joint of one finger only: life is the count, art is part of life: it should be a richness growing out of a full & normal relationship of family [...] But now I come to wonder if we all, not with pen but with all our actions & total self do not rather write some sort of mystic book of life - records of trace within the closing waters of stillness [...] poetic prose & poem.

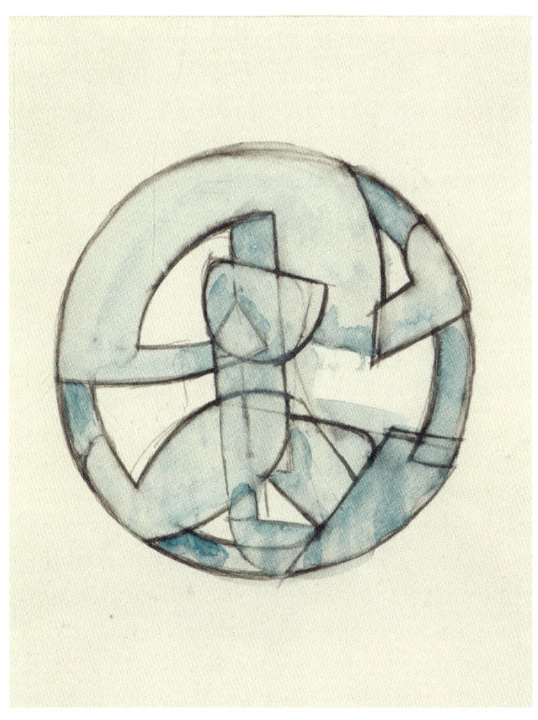

Roundel, c. 1940s
Ink and watercolour on paper, 28 × 22 cm
KY00747.E

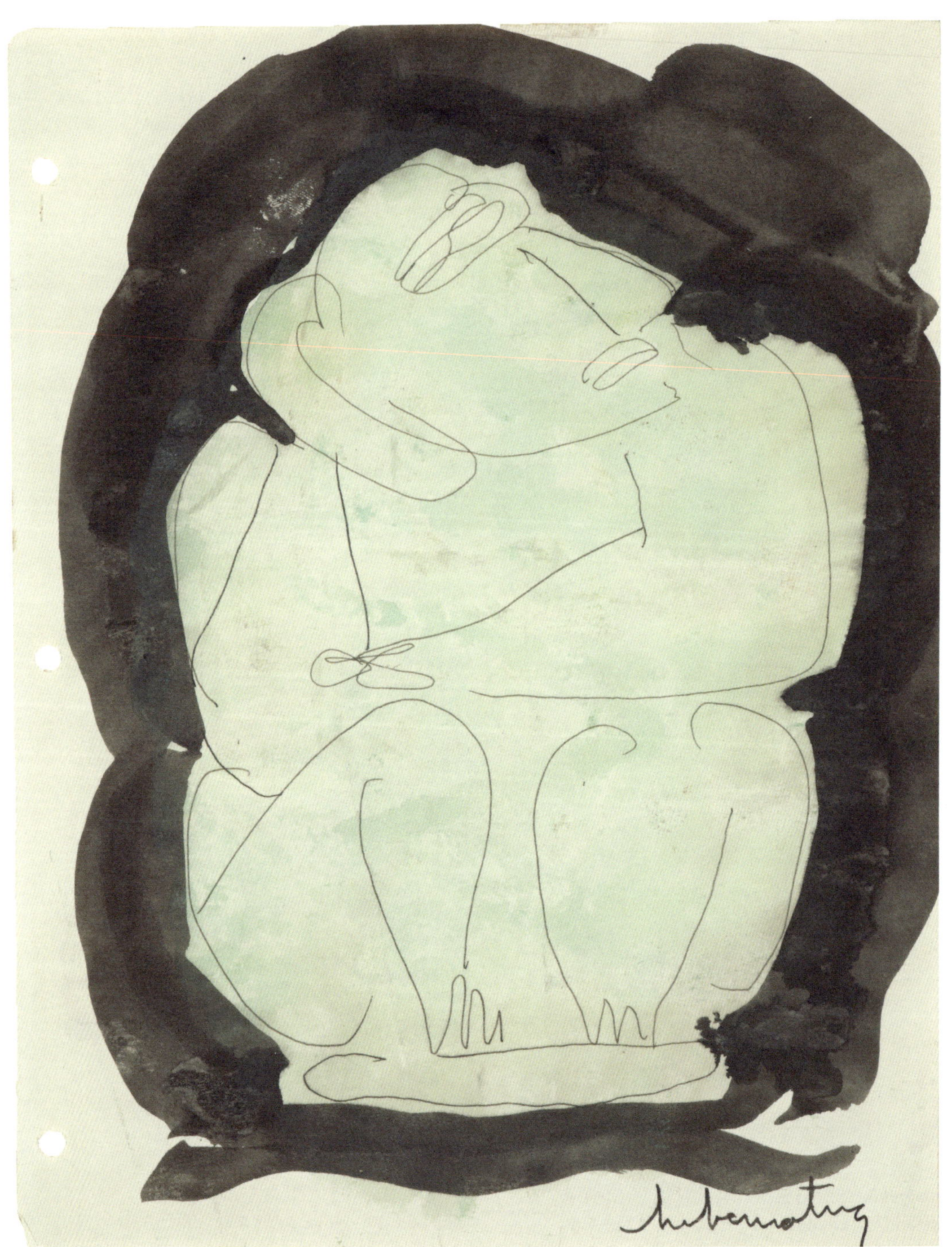

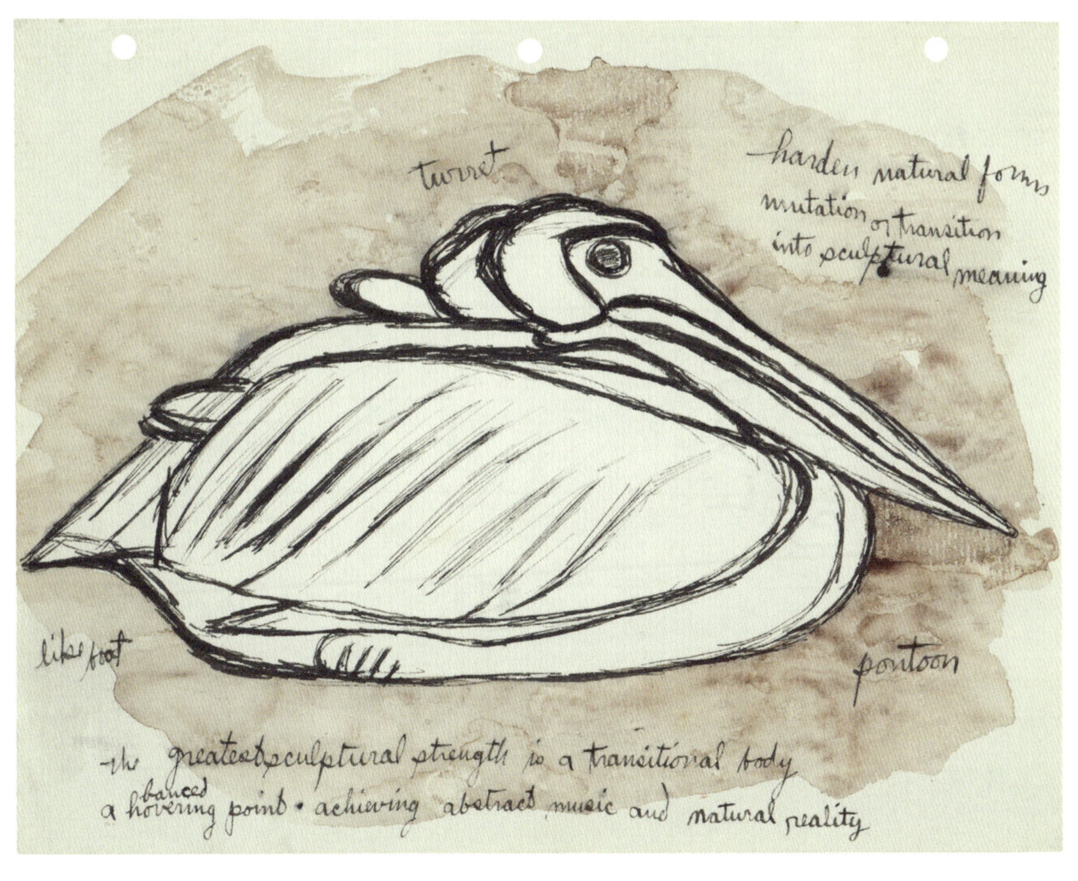

Hibernating, c. 1940s
Ink and watercolour on paper, 27.3 × 22.2 cm
KY00748.E

Bird, 1930s
Ink and watercolour on paper, 22 × 28 cm
KY00745.E

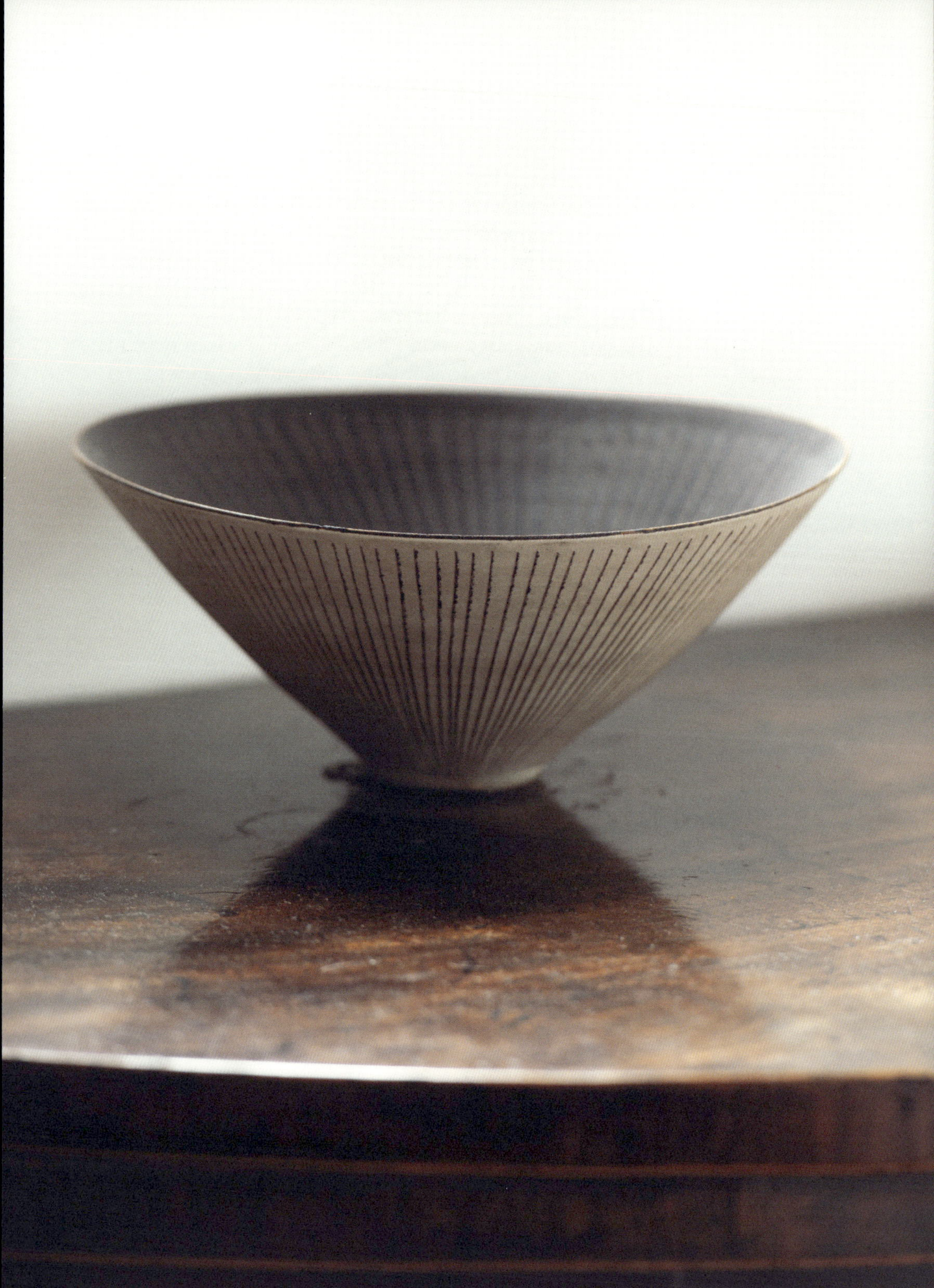

LUCIE RIE

(1902–1995)

Lucie Rie (née Gomperz) was born in Vienna, Austria and trained at the Kunstgewerbe Schule in the city, where Michael Powolny and Josef Hoffmann were her tutors. Rie established her own ceramics studio in Vienna, where her reputation grew, culminating in the award of a silver medal at the Exposition Internationale des Arts et Techniques dans la Vie Moderne in Paris in 1937. In 1938, Rie was forced to flee her home following the annexation of Austria by Nazi Germany. As a Jewish refugee in London, Rie found work producing ceramic buttons for the fashion industry, and slowly re-established herself as a potter. She became known for her distinctive tableware and one-off pieces, all created from her modest studio at Albion Mews in London. While retaining conventional vase and bowl shapes, Rie's highly expressive formal language was influenced by a variety of traditions, from Islamic fritware to the sgraffito technique of Bronze Age vessels. Her work was technically innovative, combining earthenware with stoneware glazes and, later taking increasingly complex forms. Jim Ede was introduced to Rie's works through exhibitions organised by Henry Rothschild at Kettle's Yard in the 1970s, acquiring five for his collection.

Bowl, c. 1960
Glazed porcelain, 8 × 20 cm
KY01104.EH

Lucie Rie, letter to Jim Ede, 5 October 1976
Kettle's Yard Archive, Papers of Harold Stanley 'Jim' Ede. KY/EDE/1/1

> I enjoyed your card so much - and all the nice things which you say - thank you. And thanks for sending me your lovely pot-pourri - even though it has not arrived - your idea to send it was very kind and sweet and gives me a lot of pleasure. I do hope that you will come to London one day - I am so hoping to meet you again - I shall never forget my visit with Barbara [Hepworth] at Kettle's Yard. It was a unique experience. My best wishes for you and your wife and much love.

Betty Thompson, Kettle's Yard Supervisor, Interview with Sebastiano Barassi, 1999
Kettle's Yard Archive, House & Gallery Records

> Jim particularly prized 'The Wave' [*Conical Bowl*], which was in the 1971 exhibition and was given to him as a gift by a friend. Every evening during the show, he would remove the pot from the temporary exhibition space and place it where it now sits in the house extension, spending many hours enjoying its flared shape, pitted glaze and the gleam of the bowl under the skylight.

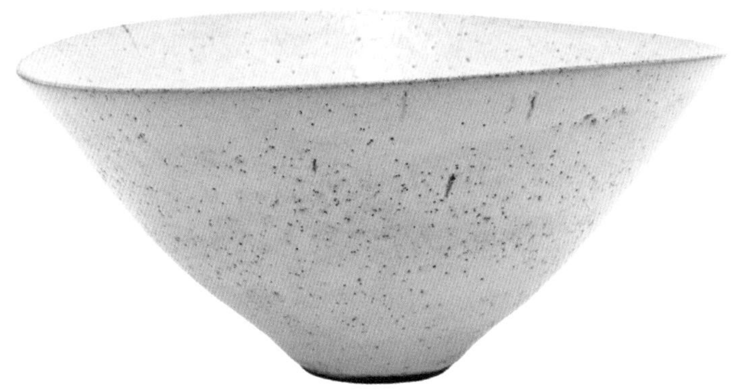

Conical Bowl, 1971
Stoneware with shiny white pitted glaze, 16.8 × 36.7 × 34.5 cm
KY01130.EH

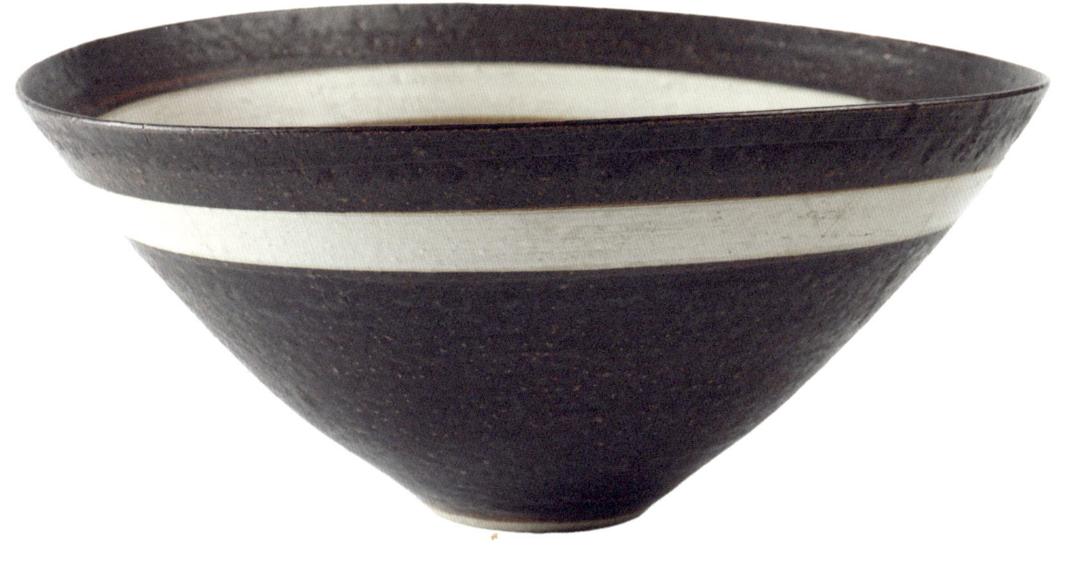

Bowl, 1971–74
Porcelain, 13 × 29 cm
KY01140.EH

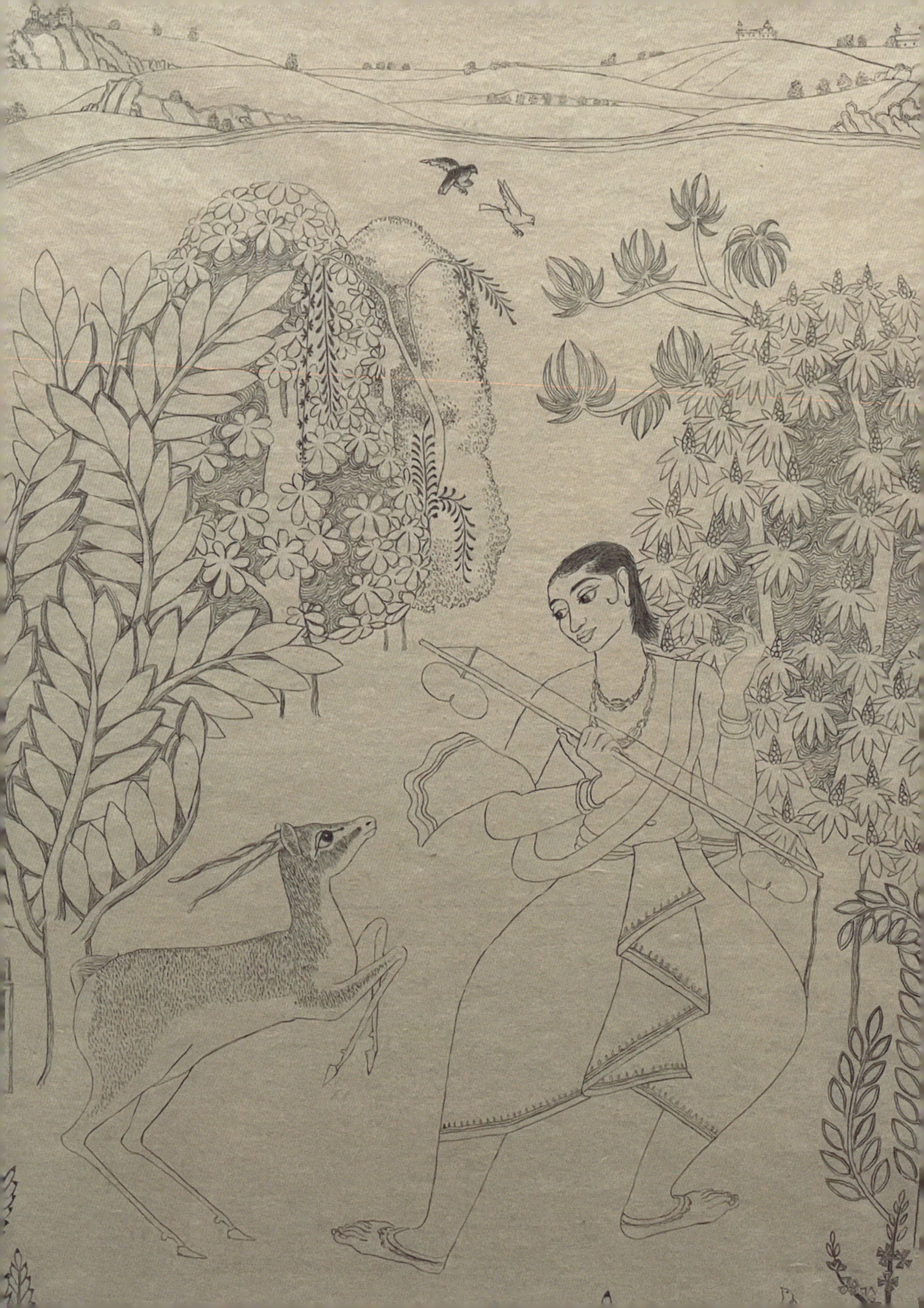

ABANI ROY

(1904–1975)

Abani Roy was born in 1904 in Bengal, India, and trained as an artist in Kolkata. He came to know the Edes while they were living at 1 Elm Row in London in the 1920s, and the couple supported Roy while he found it difficult to earn an income from his art. In 1931, Roy was commissioned by Sir Akbar Hydari to create a picture of the historic Round Table Conference on India which took place at St. James's Palace in London and was attended by Mahatma Gandhi. The primary work that resulted was a large copperplate engraving, exhibited at the India Office in 1938. Related prints are now in the collection of the National Galleries of Scotland, having been presented to the museum by Jim Ede in 1977. Ede sought to champion Roy in society and find buyers for his work. He introduced T.E. Lawrence to Roy's work, who in turn wrote to Philip Kerr, Lord Lothian - in attendance at the 1931 conferences - to recommend the artist. Roy's work was included at the Royal Academy Summer Exhibitions of 1931-33 and 1936, where his talent was noted by critics.

Jim Ede, *A way of life: Kettle's Yard*
(Cambridge University Press, 1984) pp. 57-58

> At One Elm Row all these artists were familiars, constantly coming in and out, and what is more bringing their work, hot from its making, to show or give. [...] It was a rambling old house [...] It had lovely windows and shapely rooms, and an abiding sense of quiet [...] [Abani Roy] who arrived unexpectedly into all this bareness said that he hoped Mrs Ede would not mind his having seen it, he thought we had just moved in and the furniture had not come.

Indian Scene, undated
Pen and ink on paper, 29.5 × 19 cm
KY00386.E

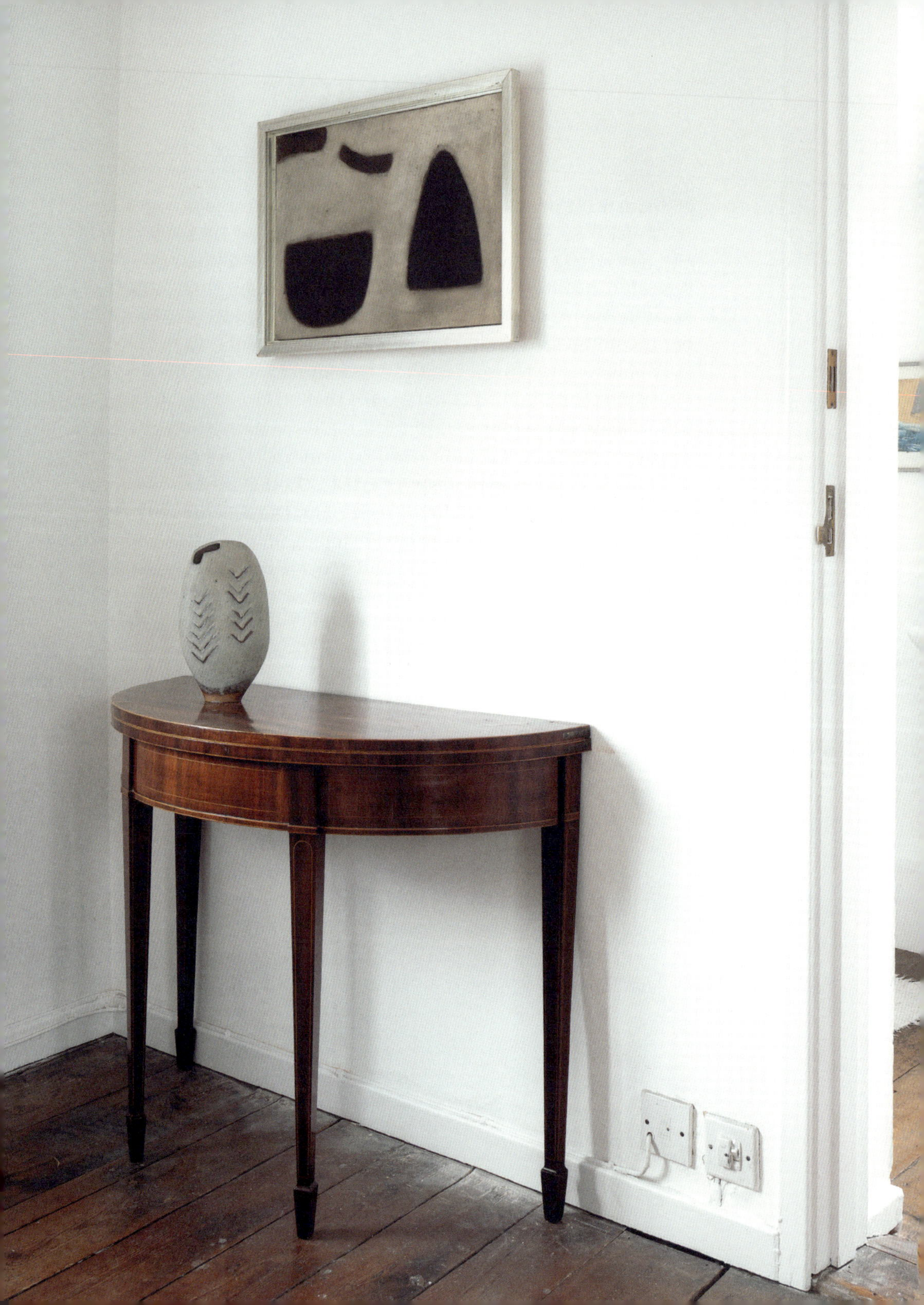

WILLIAM SCOTT

(1913–1989)

William Scott was born in Greenock, Strathclyde and brought up in Enniskillen. He trained at the Belfast School of Art 1928–31 and moved to London in 1932 to study at the Royal Academy Schools until 1935, initially based in the sculpture department. Scott lived and worked in France in the late 1930s, where he became interested in still-life painting, but returned to Britain in September 1939. He served in the British army during the second world war, from July 1941 to January 1946.

Scott was Senior Painting Master at the Bath Academy of Art 1946–56 and made frequent trips to Cornwall, where he associated with the St Ives group of abstract artists. Scott exhibited as part of the Festival of Britain celebrations in 1951. During a trip to North America in 1953 Scott met artists including Mark Rothko and Willem de Kooning. In 1964, he undertook a one-year residency in Berlin, funded by the Ford Foundation. The Tate Gallery staged a retrospective exhibition of Scott's work in 1972. Jim Ede acquired three paintings by Scott for Kettle's Yard in the 1960s.

Message Obscure I, 1965
Oil paint on canvas, 37 × 53 cm
KY00928.EH

with Zoë Ellison
Grey flattened vase, c. 1959
Stoneware (glazed), 28 × 16 × 7 cm
KY01206

William Scott, letter to Jim Ede, 1 March 1962

Kettle's Yard Archive, Papers of Harold Stanley 'Jim' Ede. KY/EDE/1/1

> It was very nice hearing from you and nice to know that you would like to have another of my paintings in your collection, especially a new one. I have been working on very large canvasses for the last three years and I have nothing that has yet spilled over into any dimension less than 4' × 5'. I have hopes that my scale might contract a bit shortly and I will certainly let you know.

William Scott, letter to Jim Ede, c. 1962

Kettle's Yard Archive, Papers of Harold Stanley 'Jim' Ede. KY/EDE/1/1

> I am wondering whether you would care to exchange a painting rather than buy one.
> I have one or two small pictures [...] I have no idea how valuable Wallis is or how we compare in the commercial market. If you are interested in a swap I should like to hear from you.

William Scott, letter to Jim Ede, 5 December 1962

Kettle's Yard Archive, Papers of Harold Stanley 'Jim' Ede. KY/EDE/1/1

> I collected the Wallis paintings and I have selected one. Miss Briggs will return the others to you with two small paintings of mine. I would have been happier if you had been able to select one yourself from my studio. I have several rather bigger than these but you ask me to use my own choice and I prefer myself these small ones to the larger size. I am sending you two to choose one. The painting I prefer is the one like this [drawing of *Bowl (White on Grey)*] but it would not obviously be everybody's taste.

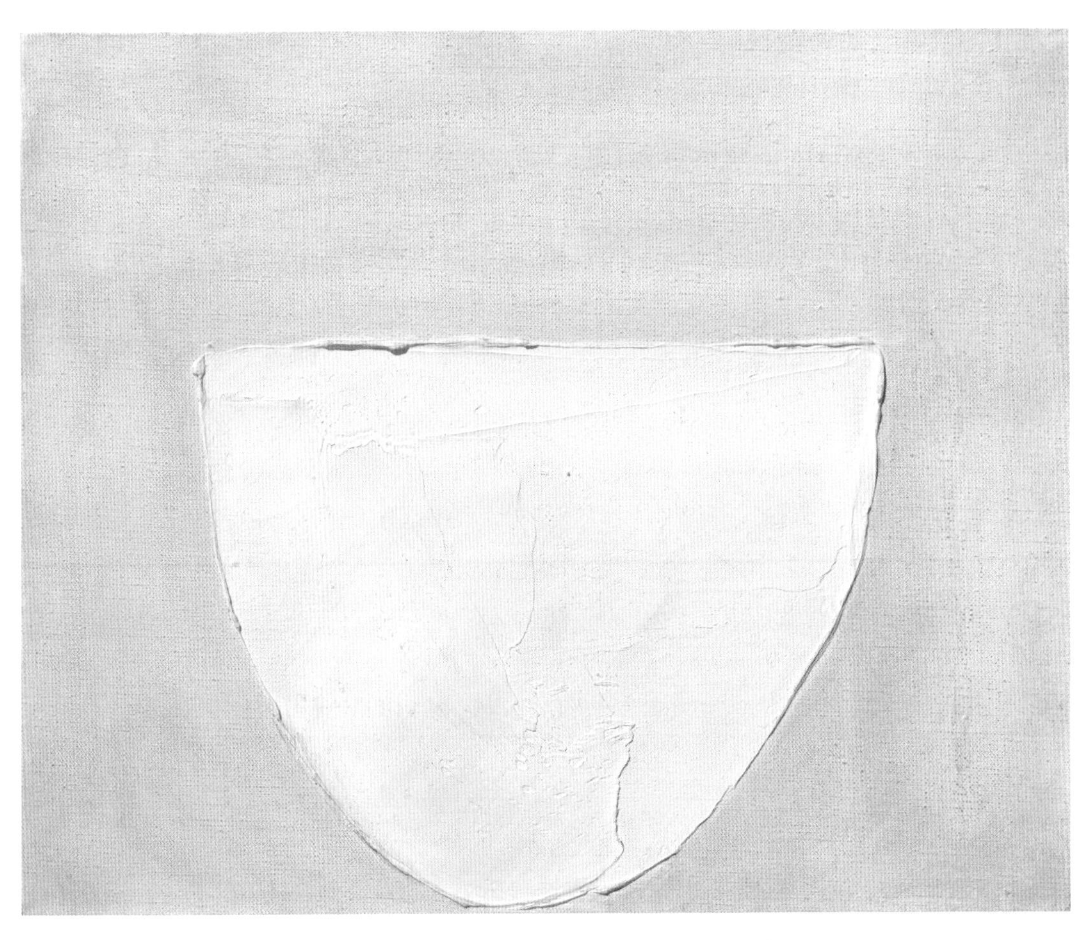

Bowl (White on Grey), 1962
Oil paint on canvas, 22 × 27 cm
KY00921.EH

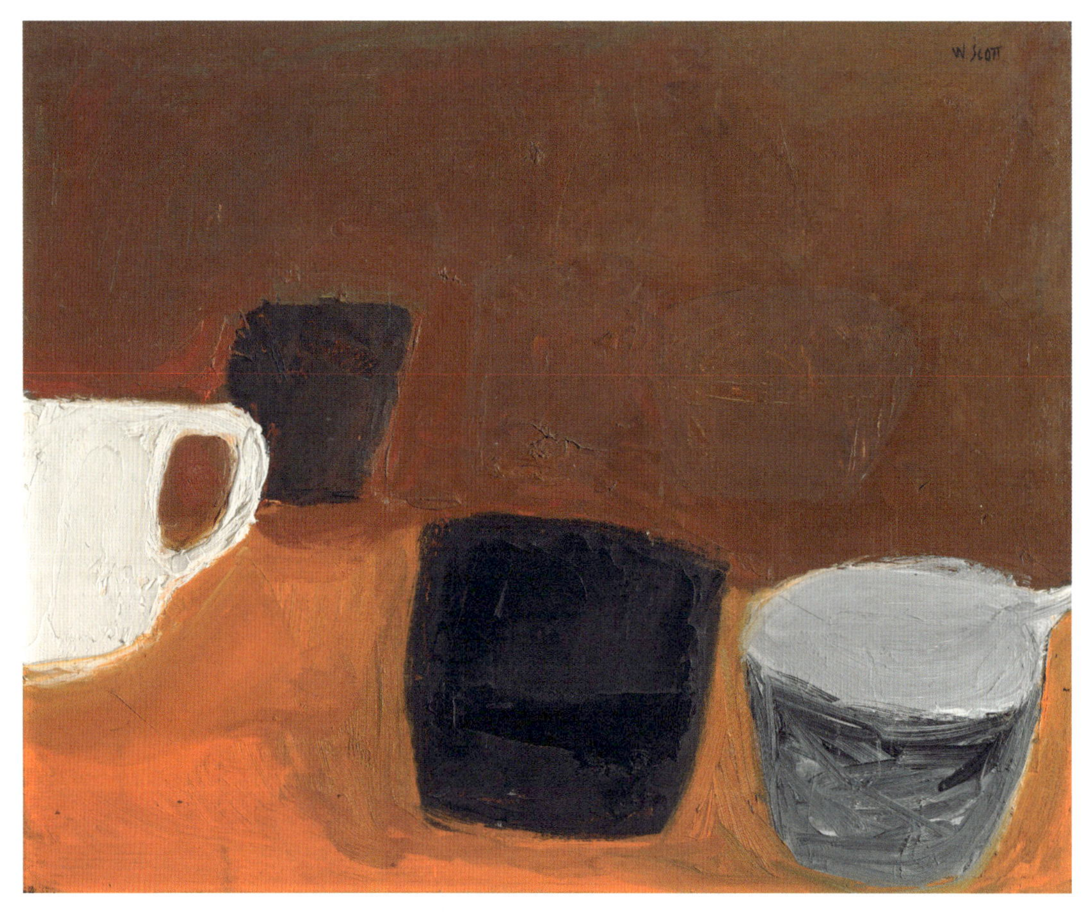

Still Life with White Mug, 1957
Oil paint on canvas, 40 × 49.7 cm
KY00852.E

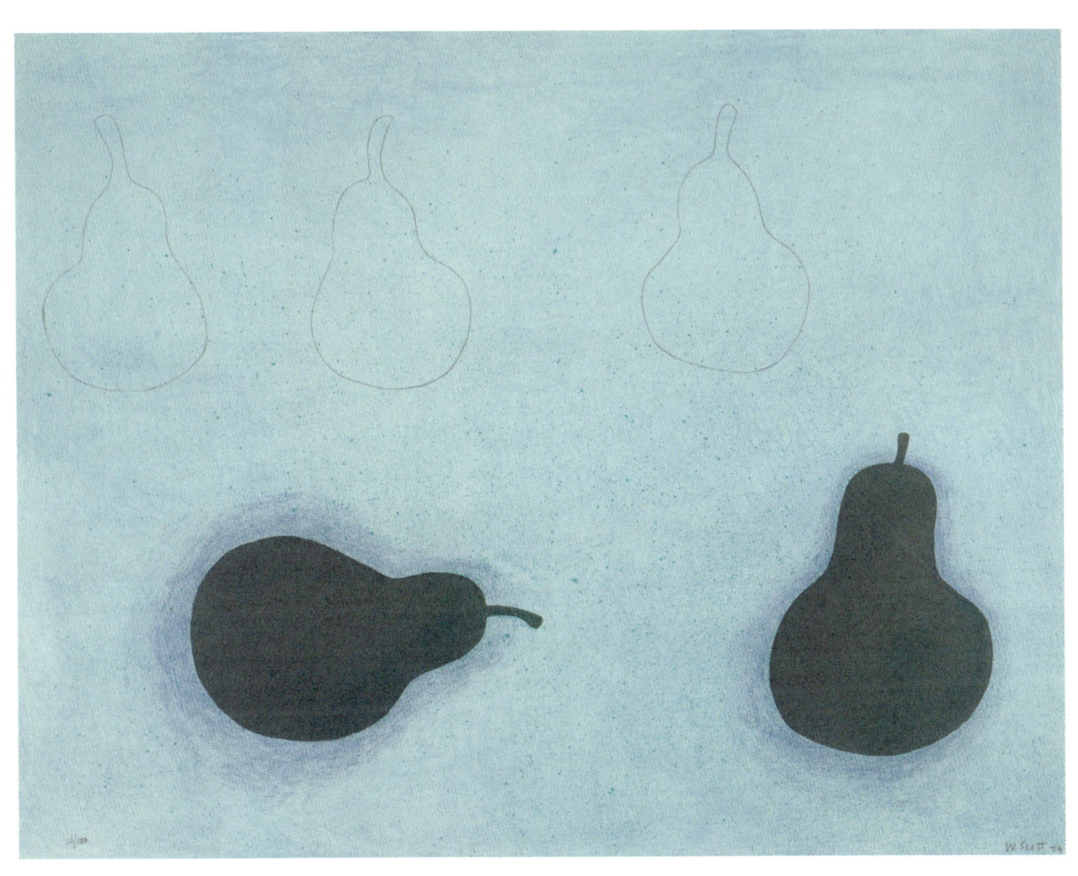

Pears, 1979
Lithograph on paper, 49.5 × 65 cm
KY01213

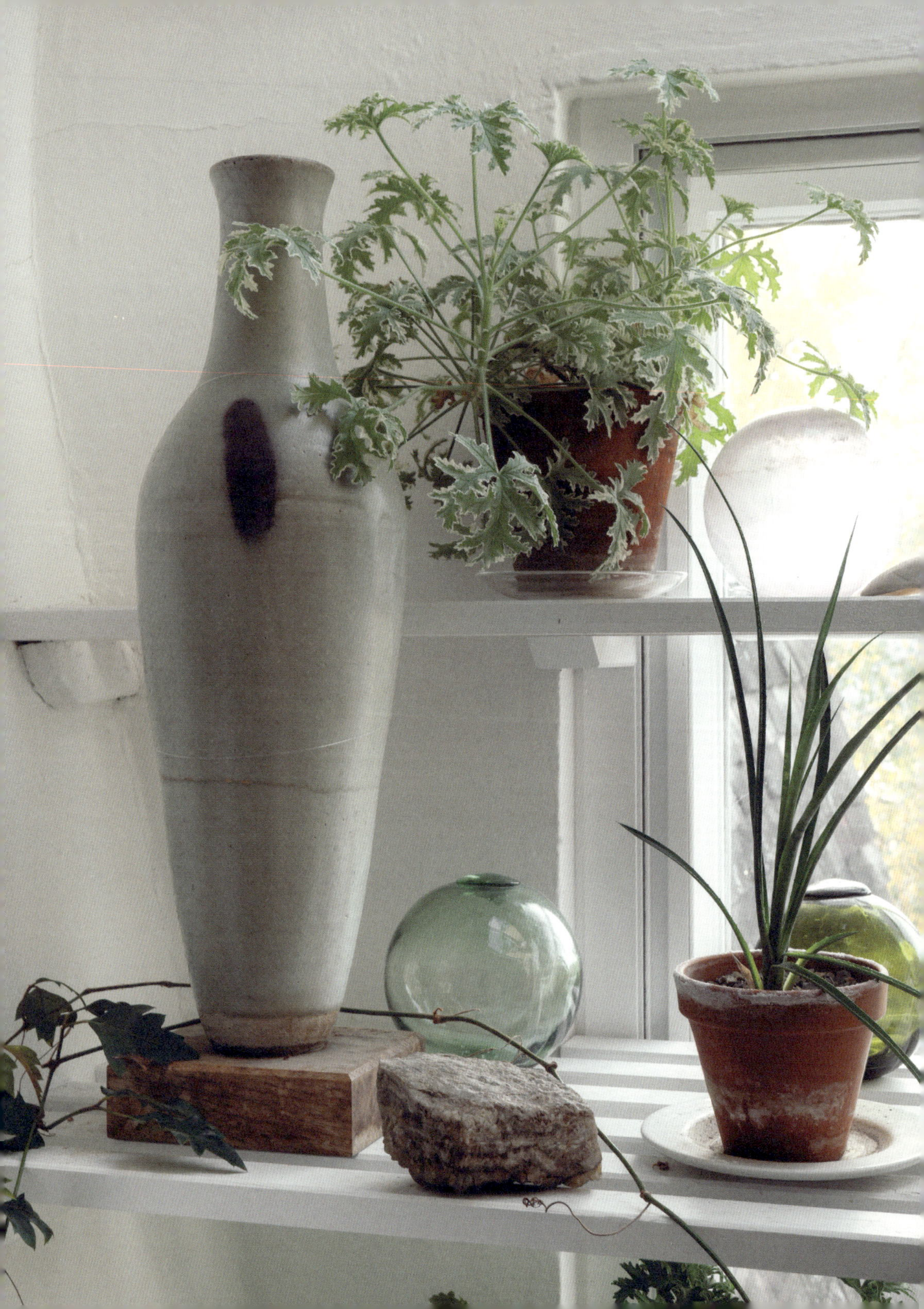

WILLIAM STAITE MURRAY

(1881–1962)

William Staite Murray was born in Deptford, south London and studied painting before enrolling in pottery classes at Camberwell School of Arts and Crafts in London. In 1919, he set up his own pottery and in 1926, Staite Murray was appointed Head of Ceramics at the Royal College of Art in London, where he taught until 1940. In 1927, he was introduced to the Seven and Five Society by Ben Nicholson, exhibiting with them in 1928, when he showed twenty-two pieces of stoneware. In the same year, Staite Murray exhibited alongside Ben and Winifred Nicholson at the Lefevre Galleries, and Jim Ede contributed a short text to the catalogue. In 1939, Staite Murray travelled to Zimbabwe (then a British colony known as Southern Rhodesia). Unable to return to the UK after the outbreak of the second world war, he and his wife settled in the country long-term, where he served as a Trustee of the National Arts Council.

Jim Ede, *A way of life: Kettle's Yard*
(Cambridge University Press, 1984) p. 93

> *The Heron* had just been given to me by its maker William Staite Murray when David Jones came to stay and knocked it off the window-sill of his bedroom. It was in several pieces. With much anxiety I told W.S.M., but he was delighted since it gave him the opportunity to mend it in the traditional way with gold. He had never liked to break one of his pots just in order to mend it.

Jar (The Heron), c. 1928
Glazed stoneware, 52 × 17 cm
KY00635.EH

Jim Ede, [typescript] 'Ben Nicholson, Winifred Nicholson and William Staite Murray', 1928

Kettle's Yard Archive, Papers of Harold Stanley 'Jim' Ede. KY/EDE/4/2/4/13

William Staite Murray would like to make pots which couldn't be seen, pots so inevitably lovely in shape and colour that they become one with the beauty of created life. It is the wish of all and Murray reaches very near to his ideal. Pottery is midway between sculpture and painting - the alternating point of abstract and concrete plastic formal expression. It is the art of suggestion with the utmost economy, for its immediateness of expression in abstract form approaches more nearly to a songlike quality than any other medium. It has been neglected by artists and exploited by commercialism to such an extent that it has fallen from the high position it held in the art of the great peoples of the past. Staite Murray's work is doing much to restore to pottery its ancient dignity; its execution is perfect and controlled and takes no mean position amongst other branches of plastic art. In his hands the melody of concrete idea emerges from the expressive urge of its architectural harmony and pottery becomes again a thing vigorous and intimate in which art and craft are deliciously balanced.

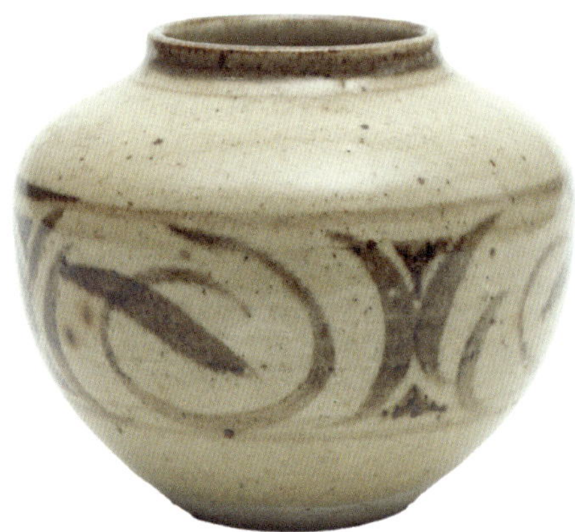

Vase, 1922
Glazed earthenware, 11.5 × 14 cm
KY01363

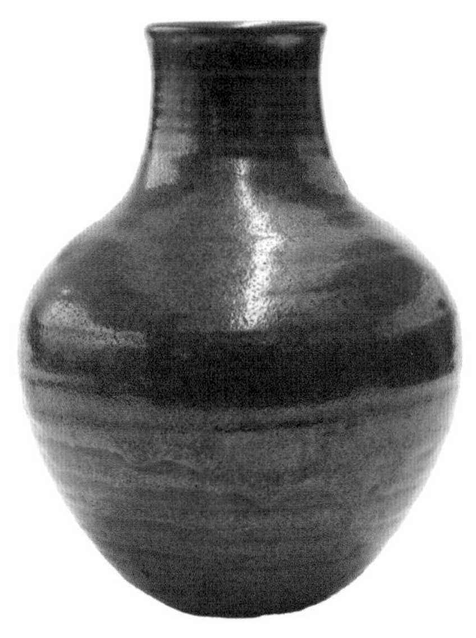

Vase, 1930s
Glazed terracotta, 23 × 17 cm
KY01116.EH

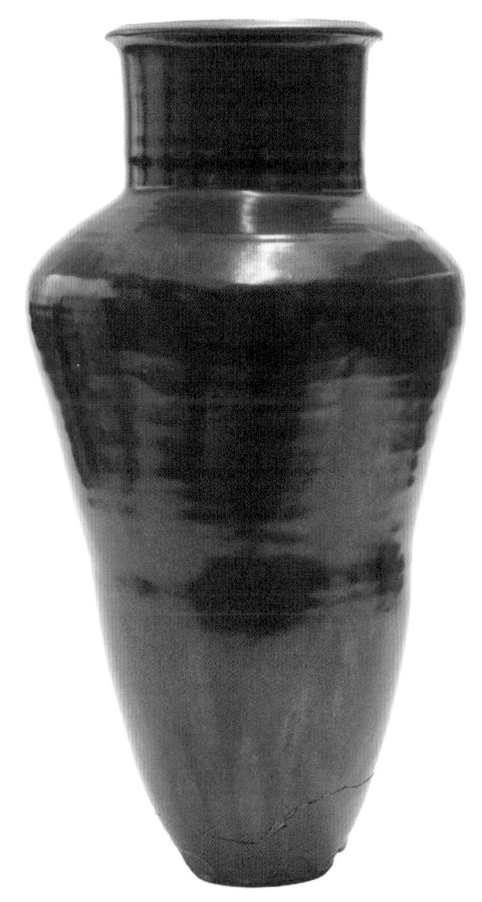

Vase, 1930s
Glazed terracotta, 43 × 21 cm
KY00640.EH

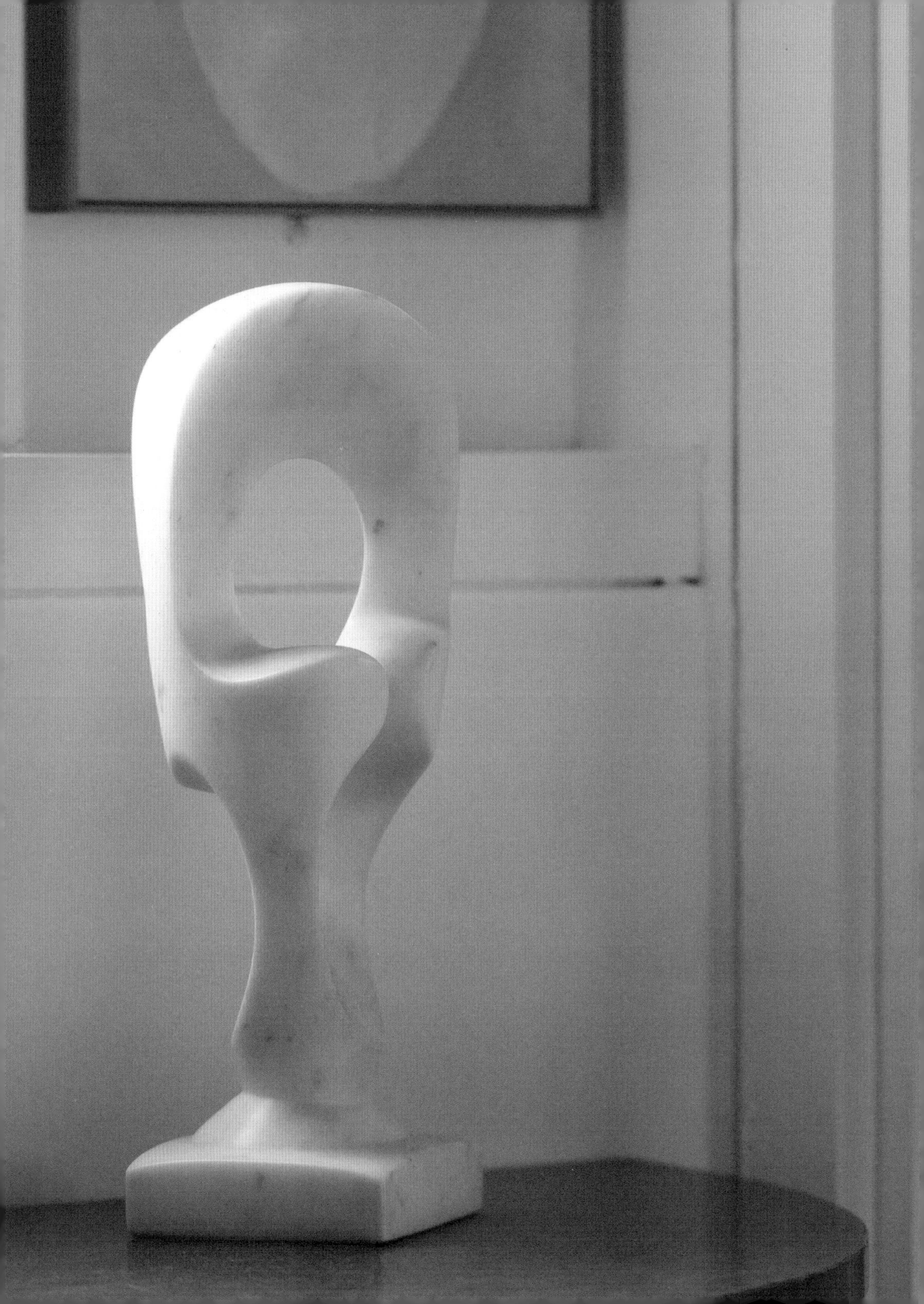

KENJI UMEDA

(1948–2019)

Kenji Umeda was born in born in Miyazaki, Japan. He came to Cambridge in the 1970s, and there discovered Kettle's Yard. Umeda befriended Jim Ede, who was by then almost seventy years old. Ede helped Umeda sell his paintings in Cambridge, and later Umeda began to help with the ongoing cleaning and maintenance of Kettle's Yard. Jim Ede found an almost spiritual pleasure in his daily tasks and shared this appreciation with Umeda. In caring for the house and collection, Umeda came to know the works on display well. He was especially drawn to the sculptures of Henri Gaudier-Brzeska. Umeda travelled to Carrara, Italy in 1973, where he studied sculpture at the Accademia Di Belle Arti and met his wife Jacqueline Benard, also an artist. The couple moved to the United States, settling in Phoenix, Arizona, where Umeda continued to practice sculpture, specialising in works sited outdoors. Umeda's work is included in collections such as the Scottsdale Civic Center and the Tucson Museum of Art in Arizona.

Kenji Umeda, letter to Jim Ede, 27 October 1973
Kettle's Yard Archive, Papers of Harold Stanley 'Jim' Ede. KY/EDE/1/1

Dearest Jim,
Suddenly weather is getting into cold air in Carrara, but
there are plenty of sunlights in Toscana every daytimes.
I have made a cup of tea just now for start of my working.
Holding a hammer and chisel in my hands go the marble
yard which is just in front of my room.
My friend's dog is looking and wagging his tail.
I will bring him to my place because he is quite gentle one.
I do not know that how long can I keep like this pleasant
time, one problem of my living expense.
Anyway I know my way what it is.
Tomorrow is my future always, must be.

Spirality, 1977
Marble, 35.5 × 14 × 11 cm
KY01111.EH

Kenji Umeda, letter to Jim Ede, c. 1973

Kettle's Yard Archive, Papers of Harold Stanley 'Jim' Ede. KY/EDE/1/1

Dear Jim,
It is very early morning now.
Sunlights are not coming yet.
All people are sleeping in their dreams.
Here, a kettle's boiling is beautiful
Jim - I love people
Dreamy rhythms are walking to us.
Let's open our windows and breath
Fresh air.
Your Kenji
from Carrara

Jim Ede, letter to Kenji Umeda, 3 March 1976

Kettle's Yard Archive, Papers of Harold Stanley 'Jim' Ede. KY/EDE/1/1

Here is a little extra for you - I'm sure you can do with it. Marble must be quite expensive. I hope your work is going well & that you are well & feel that your purpose in life is being achieved. We go along quietly and keep moderately week & the weather has turned to Spring and I have been clearing the garden.
Love from Jim.

Kenji Umeda, letter to Jim Ede 12 August 1981

Kettle's Yard Archive, Papers of Harold Stanley 'Jim' Ede. KY/EDE/1/1

'I am very pleased that *Spirality* is in Kettle's Yard [...] Kettle's Yard has always remained with me [...] I have been in many museums + art galleries and you are right in saying that Kettle's Yard is a unique place for showing and appreciating art.'

Jim Ede, *A way of life: Kettle's Yard*
(Cambridge University Press, 1984) pp. 123-124

[...] he called on me to show me some paintings he had done. They were strange but interesting. I found he was alone and in need, so I told him that I would show his work to undergraduates and sell them if I could – they were cheap, a few pounds each. They were soon sold. After a little I asked him if he would like to come in twice a week for an hour or so and help me with the cleaning of Kettle's Yard. He enjoyed his cup of coffee and a little talk but I had great difficulty in giving him anything else. He was very silent and may have been 22 at this time. While he cleaned he watched all the lovely things in the house and perhaps in particular those of Gaudier-Brzeska. In his secret heart he knew that he also was a sculptor, but he said nothing. This lasted for a year or more, when as silently as ever he got himself to Carrara, the home of marble. There he got scholarships and worked by day and by night for the next four years [...] One day the postman here staggered in with a large wooden box and inside, exquisitely packed was *Spirality* which I have greatly enjoyed here in Edinburgh. I kept wondering where I could put it in Kettle's Yard, and at last thought of a perfect position, and so sent it there; thus it finds its place [...] It is another conveyance of light and peace.

Yesterday i had got one of my small work in bronze.
This is my first one in bronze, i cannot forget the day of yesterday with thanks to people.
"a child in the wind"
4.5 inches
5 inches
Jim, i have started my new plan that is going to create 20 pieces at least and then i will back in England for my exhibition in the Kettle's Yard in one or two years.
i will send you some photos of my new work in next month.
i have done two sculptures in marble already.

Yours Kenji.

Kenji Umeda, letter to Jim Ede, 17 October 1973 Kettle's Yard Archive, Papers of Harold Stanley 'Jim' Ede. KY/EDE/1/1

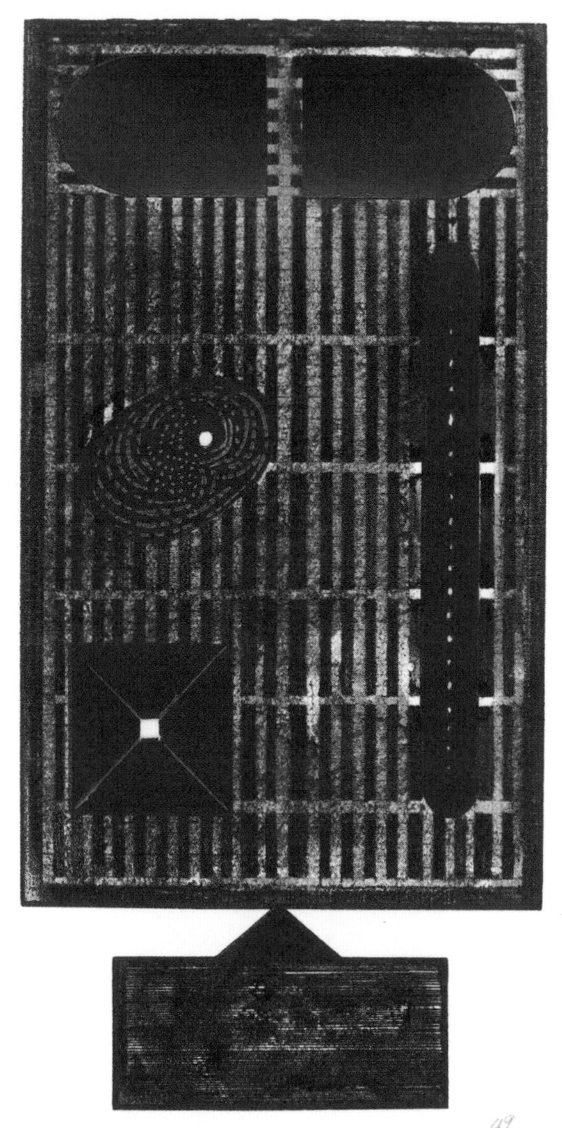

Cantos - 2, 1982
Serigraph print on paper, 34.29 × 25.4 cm
KY01437

Cantos - 3, 1982
Serigraph print on paper, 34.29 × 25.4 cm
KY01438

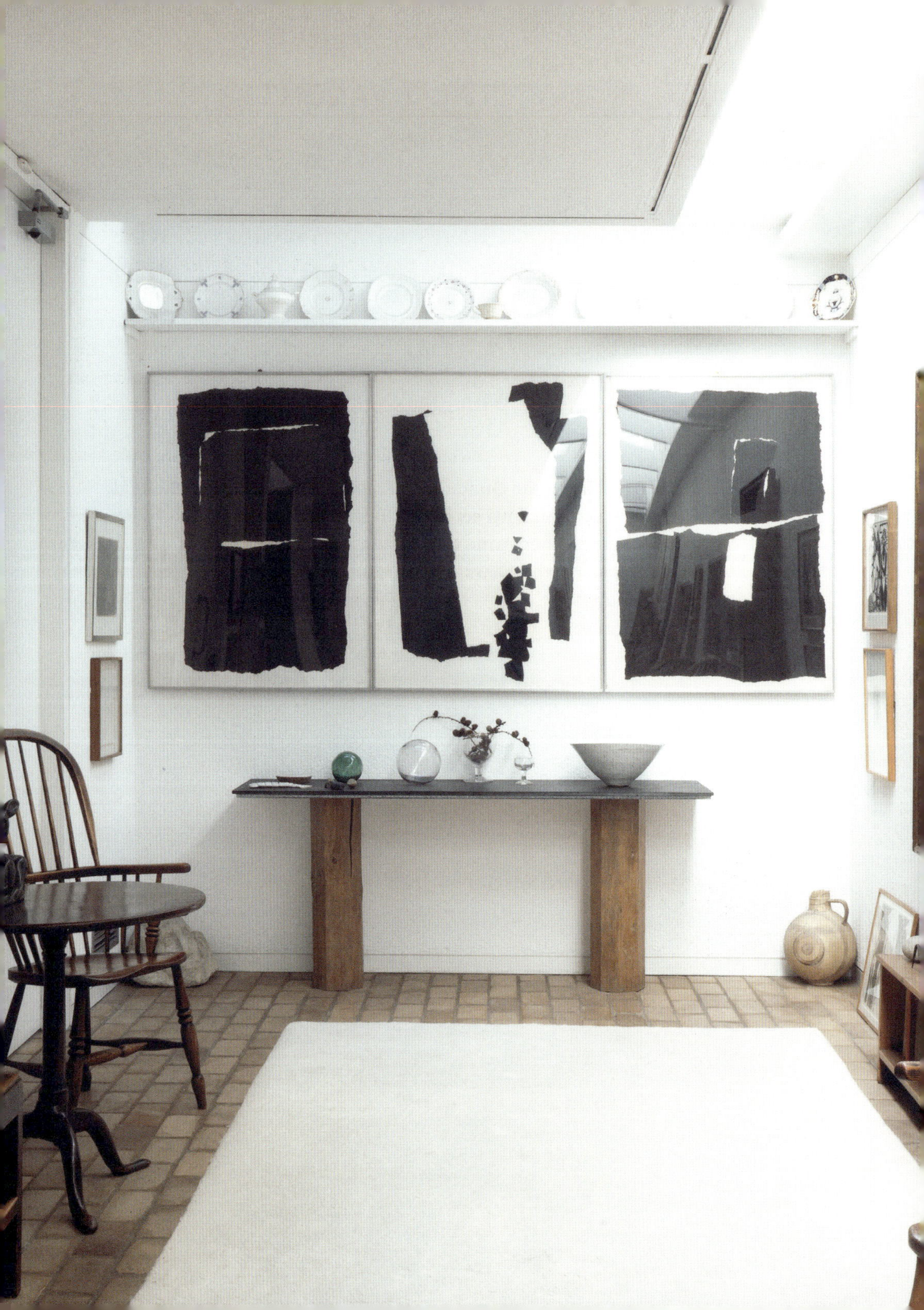

ITALO VALENTI

(1912–1995)

Italo Valenti was born in Milan. He studied drawing at the Accademia in Venice before returning to Milan to study at the Accademia di Brera 1932–37. Under the tutelage of Aldo Carpi, he initially adopted an expressionist style, depicting subjects concerned with society and morality. After completing his studies, Valenti travelled to Paris and Brussels. Upon his return to Italy, he joined the anti-fascist group of artists associated with the Milanese magazine *Corrente*. During the second world war, Valenti painted landscapes influenced by Paul Cézanne and taught life classes at the Milan Accademia. His work was exhibited at the Galleria La Bussola in Turin, the Rome Quadriennale and the 1948 Venice Biennale.

In 1952, Valenti settled in Ticino in Switzerland with the poet and photographer Anne de Montet, who he later married. Abstract collage became his primary medium from 1959, and Valenti's work was exhibited widely in Italy, Switzerland, the United States, Britain and Germany. He became friends with noted critics, including Manuel Gasser and Christian Zervos. It was Ben Nicholson who introduced Valenti to Jim Ede, resulting in Ede's purchase of three of Valenti's collages at the 1964 *Documenta* in Kassel. These were the first of many Valenti acquisitions for Kettle's Yard, and Jim Ede developed sympathetic friendships with both Valenti and de Montet. In 1980, the Scottish National Gallery of Modern Art staged an exhibition of Valenti's work in Jim Ede's honour.

Nr. 284; Etana, 1964
122 × 90.5 cm
KY00876.EH

Nr. 287; Giardino a mezzogiorno; Jardin à midi, 1964
123 × 91.5 cm
KY00877.EH

Nr. 286; Pietra; Pierre, 1964
122 × 90.5 cm
KY00878.EH

Paper on hardboard

Also pictured are works by Ben Nicholson, Bryan Illsley, Henri Gaudier-Brzeska, John Acland, Lucie Rie, John Lyons, Frank Auerbach and Christopher Wood.

Ben Nicholson, letter to Jim Ede, 12 October 1962

Kettle's Yard Archive, Papers of Harold Stanley 'Jim' Ede. KY/EDE/1/11

> Glad you like Valenti's work – (he's also a singularly likable chap (so is his wife)). Now about your buying one [...] Remember he is a man of 50, not a youngster of 25 just beginning, & has exhibitions in Germany, Switzerland, Italy, England etc. [...] He is a very generous chap by nature & I guess he'd always let you have more than the value you put down.

Anne de Montet, letter to Jim Ede, 29 July 1963

Kettle's Yard Archive, Papers of Harold Stanley 'Jim' Ede. KY/EDE/1/16

> [...] We were very happy to hear that the collage had finally arrived and that you like it. Italo [was] enchanted by your sensitivity: that you found perhaps superfluous the white mark at the right, [the] mark on which he continued to work, put[ting] it in and taking it out. In the end, he was won over by the number 3 of the superposed elements. (I deduce reason, nature and light). Today he would perhaps agree to remove it – but there is also another super-position to the reason: that of augmenting the light, which led him to leave this little space – so the problem continues! [...]

Anne de Montet, letter to Jim Ede, 21 July 1967

Kettle's Yard Archive, Papers of Harold Stanley 'Jim' Ede. KY/EDE/1/16

> Fond thanks for this beautiful book on Wallis. We are enchanted by his vision and we see that you chose the most beautiful of his paintings. We are touched by the correspondence which you managed to have with this withdrawn old man. It is typically Jim Ede, inclined towards friendship – not only for the work of an artist that he values – but for the man himself. This complete attention of your sensibility is a very remarkable way of living. So yes, we love you and we love the presence that you have left in our home, as if you had lent us your eyes to see in our company. [...]

Jim Ede, *A way of life: Kettle's Yard*
(Cambridge University Press, 1984) pp. 196-197

Great lovers are rare and Italo Valenti is amongst them in the genius of his love for the ineffable quality of Balance. His expression of this balance, this union of white, of black, is something not to be explained in words; it is entirely a visual creation, known by him as one would know the beauty of sunlight in a wood, or a pebble on the seashore. I obtained long ago one of his larger collage works, an area of white, but what a white, with a shaft of black, and what a black, falling across it; and somewhere as if by accident, and certainly by magic, a tiny edge of darkness, as of a fallen leaf. It was called 'The Shadow' [*Nr. 345; La Tua Ombra; Ton Ombre,* 1966]. It was for me the impulse of day and night [...] A few years later we were having an evening bathe, and the shadow of Italo Valenti's leg prolonged itself across the sunlit grass. 'There is your picture', he said.

Mesure, 1969
Lithograph print on paper, 37 × 27 cm
KY01012.E

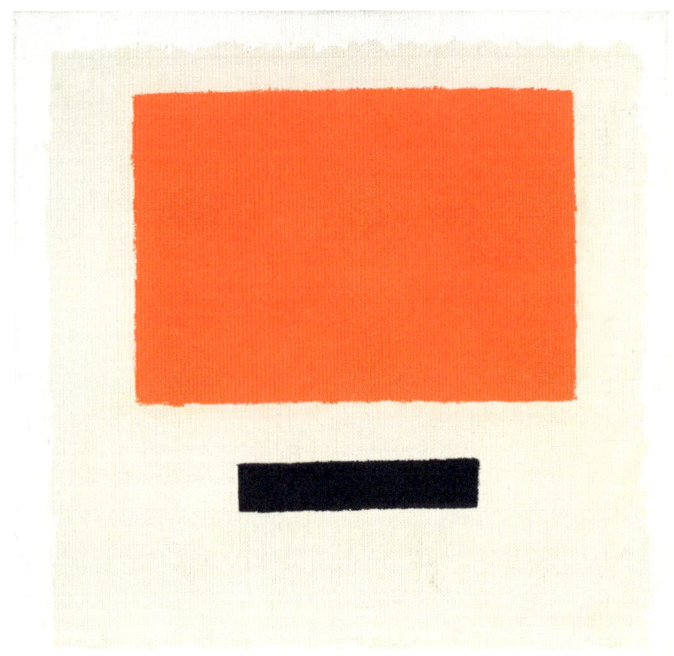

Nr. 121; Olanda, 1968
Oil paint on canvas,
32 × 33 cm
KY01004.EH

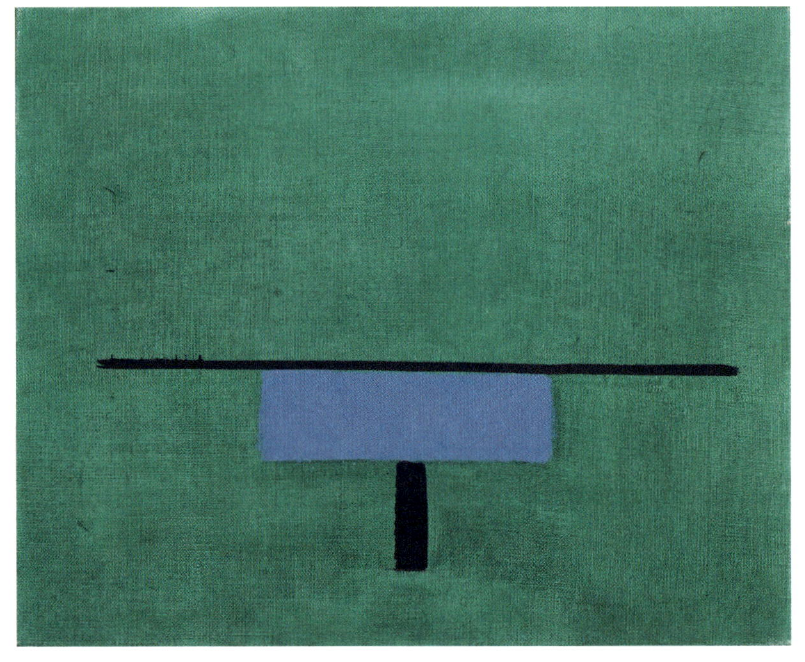

Nr. 145; Laguna; Lagune,
1968
Oil paint on canvas,
32.5 × 41 cm
KY01005.EH

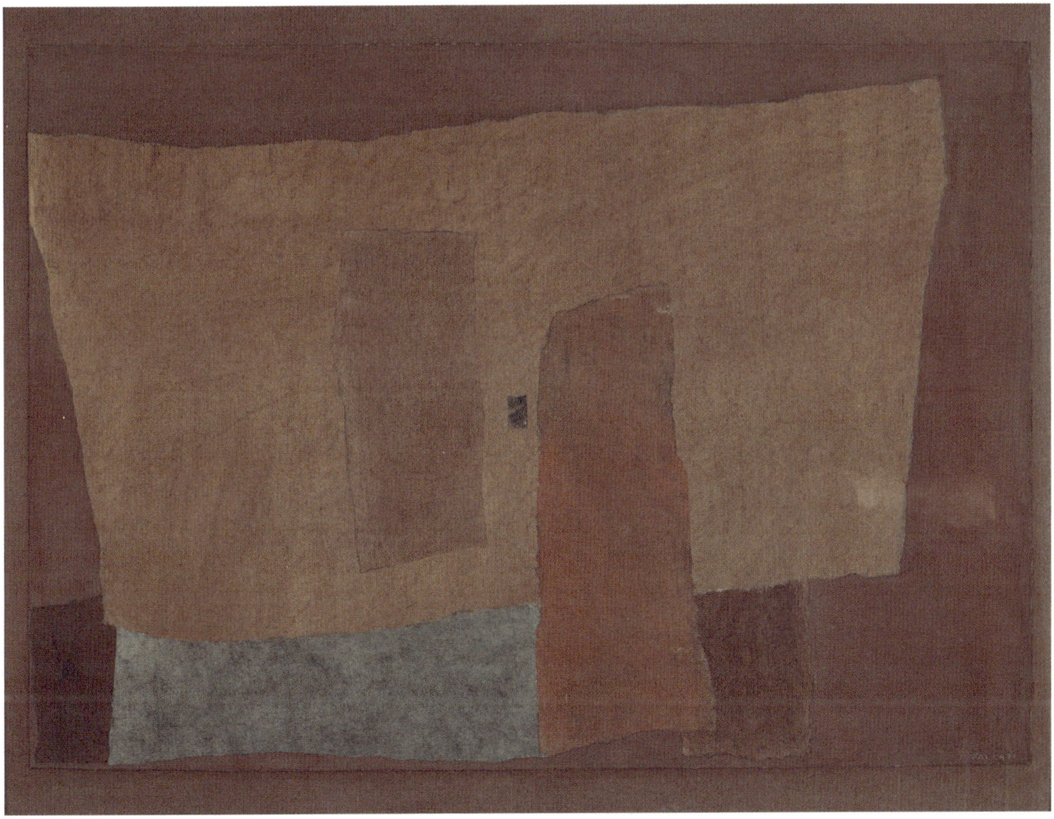

Veneti, 1962–64
Paper on composition board,
80 × 110 cm
KY00918.EH

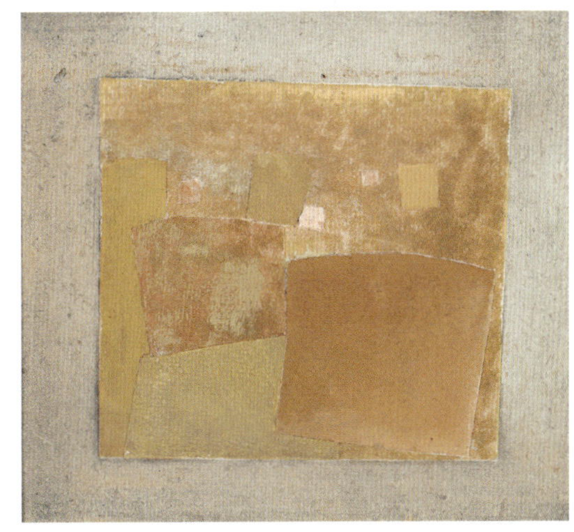

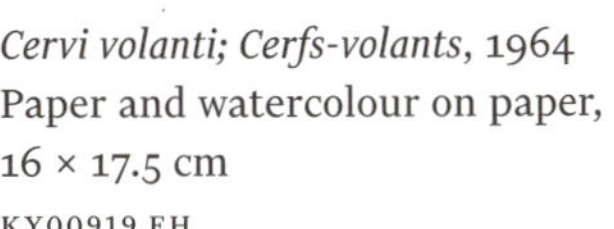

Cervi volanti; Cerfs-volants, 1964
Paper and watercolour on paper,
16 × 17.5 cm
KY00919.EH

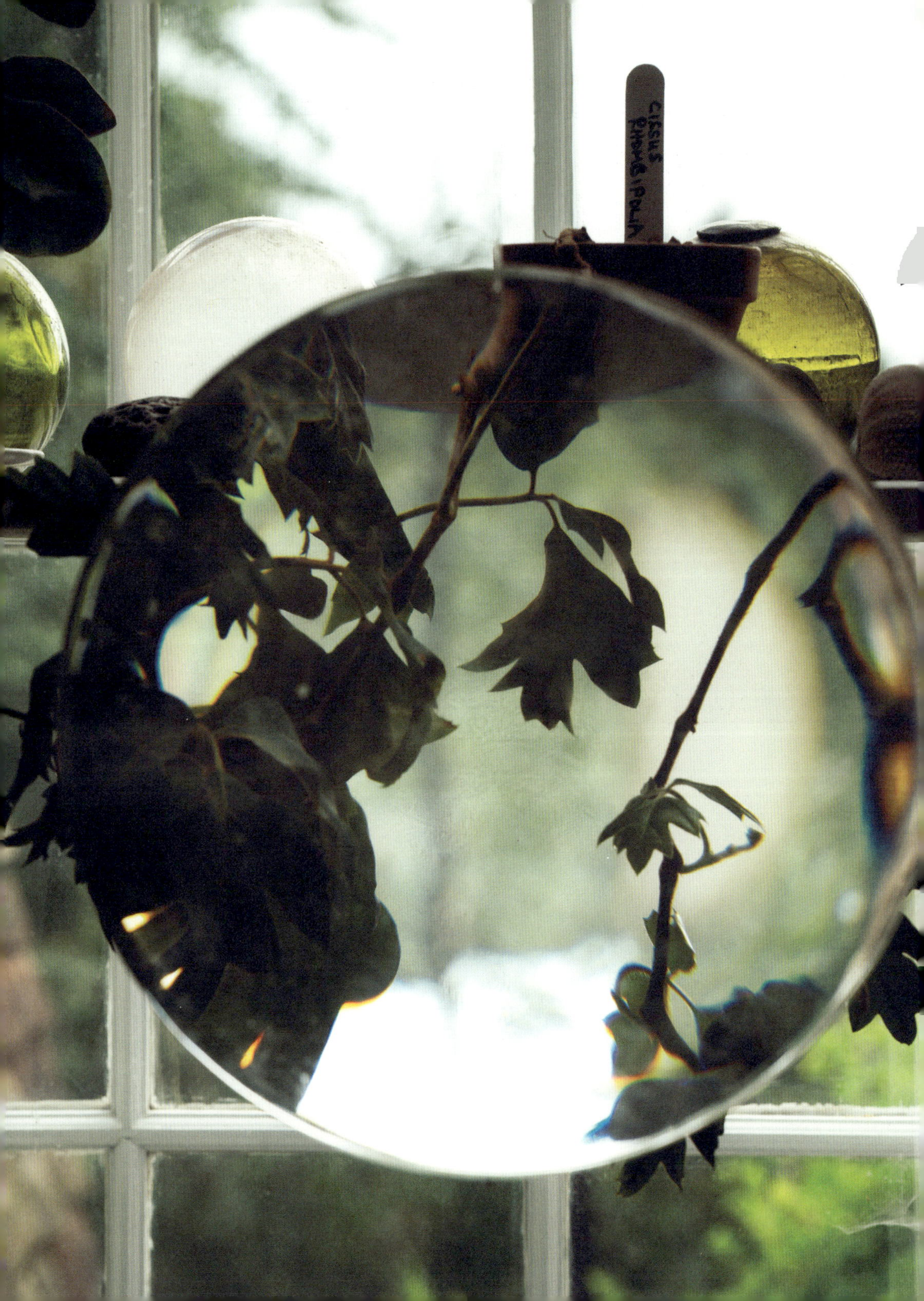
CISSUS
RHOMBIFOLIA

GREGORIO VARDANEGA

(1923–2007)

Gregorio Vardanega was born in 1923 in Passagno, Treviso, Italy and moved with his family to Buenos Aires, Argentina as a child. He studied at the Escuela de Bellas Artes from 1939, where he became a drawing professor from 1946. Early in his career, Vardanega exhibited with the Asociación Arte Concreto-Invención (AACI). He travelled to Europe in the late 1940s, and exhibited with the Salon d'Amérique Latine in Paris, France in 1949, where he met artists including Max Bill, Sonia Delaunay, Antoine Pevsner and Georges Vantongerloo. Upon returning to Buenos Aires in 1950, Vardanega began to make kinetic works, experimenting with metal bands and celluloid. He became a founding member of several groups devoted to abstract art including the Asociación Arte Nuevo in 1955 and the Agrupación de Arte no Figurativo Argentino in 1956.

In 1958, Vardanega received a gold medal in the Exposition Universelle et Internationale de Bruxelles in Belgium and his work was included in the fourth Bienal de São Paulo in Brazil. Vardanega and his wife, fellow artist Martha Boto (1925-2004), moved to Paris in 1959, where they collaborated on kinetic works that used Plexiglas spheres and light projections. Vardanega and Boto were the subject of a two-person exhibition titled *Chromocinétisme* at the Maison des Beaux-Arts in Paris in 1964, and during the 1960s, other exhibitions of Vardánega's work were staged in Zagreb, Venice, Zurich, Düsseldorf, Rome and Oslo. Jim Ede acquired three of Vardanega's works for Kettle's Yard just prior to his gift of the house and collection to the University of Cambridge.

Disc, c. 1960
Plexiglas, 31 × 4 cm
KY00894.EH

Gregorio Vardanega and Martha Boto, letter to Jim Ede, 25 April 1965

Kettle's Yard Archive, Papers of Harold Stanley 'Jim' Ede. KY/EDE/1/1

We received your charming and poetic letter. I am very pleased that the things arrived safely; I was worried about the fragility of the little circles. I also received the cheque you sent me. Thank you very much for your prompt attention. The beautiful and charming lady you brought to our home has not yet called upon us, but perhaps she will in future. In any case, I thank you very much for your good intentions. The people that you mention in your letter we are sure will be most welcome, especially if they are recommended by you. I tell you that it doesn't matter to me if people aren't rich; they'd be better off if they were spiritually rich. It's very pleasant to find people with noble sentiments, as I find you.

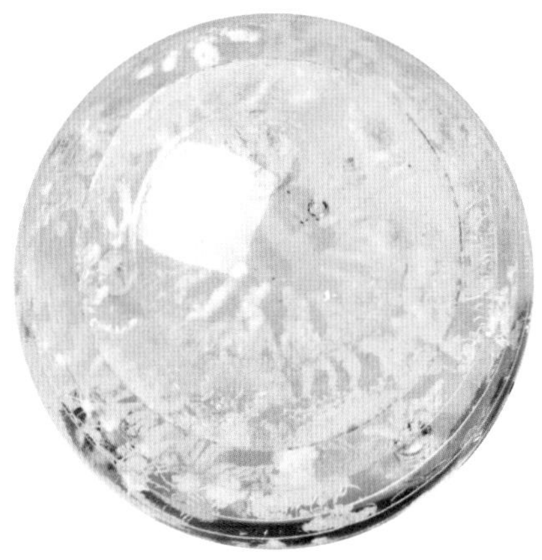

Left:
Small sphere, c. 1956
Plexiglas, 5 × 5 cm
KY00893.EH

Right:
Spherical Construction, c. 1963
Plexiglas, 18 × 10 cm
KY00895.EH

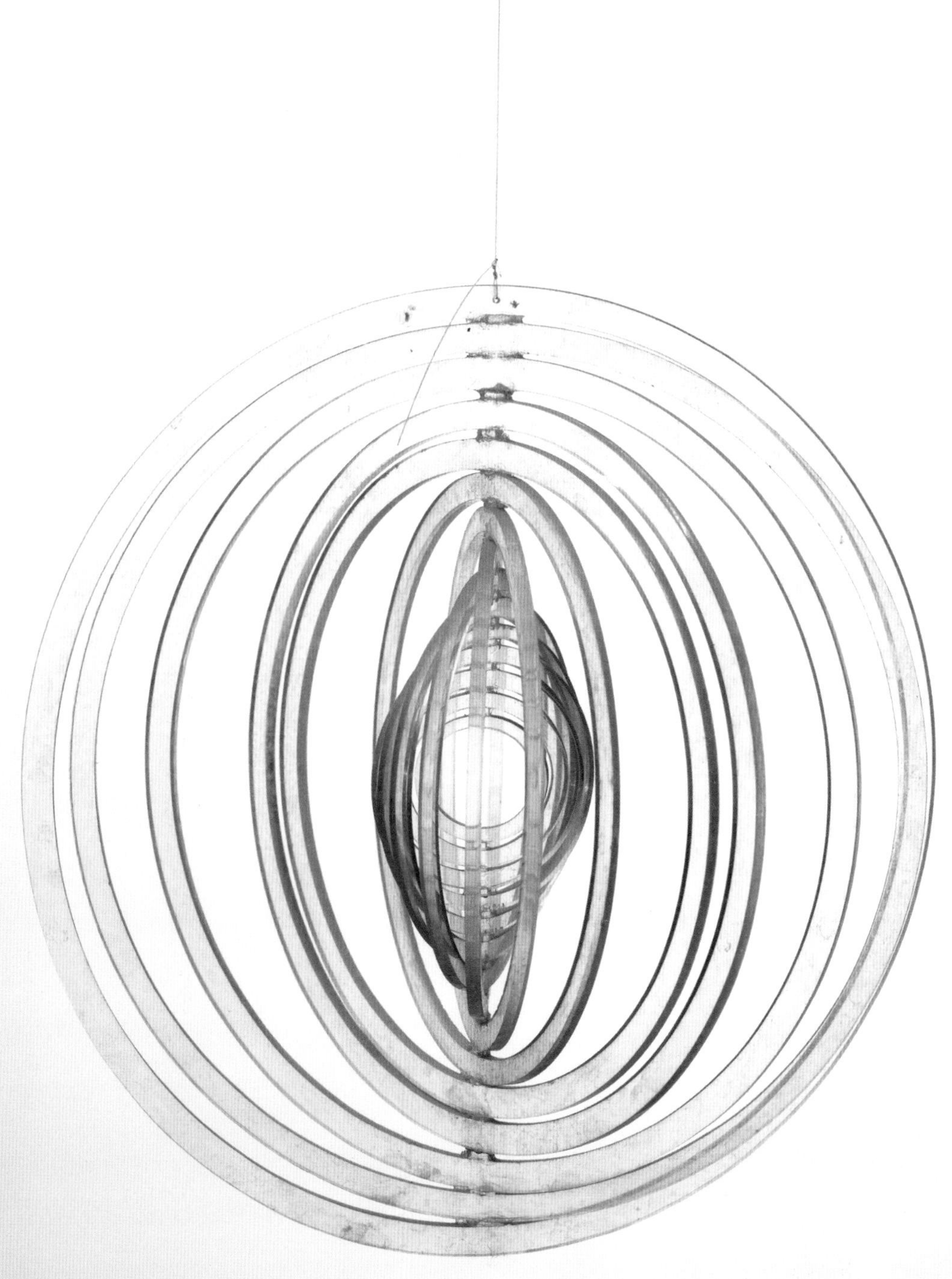

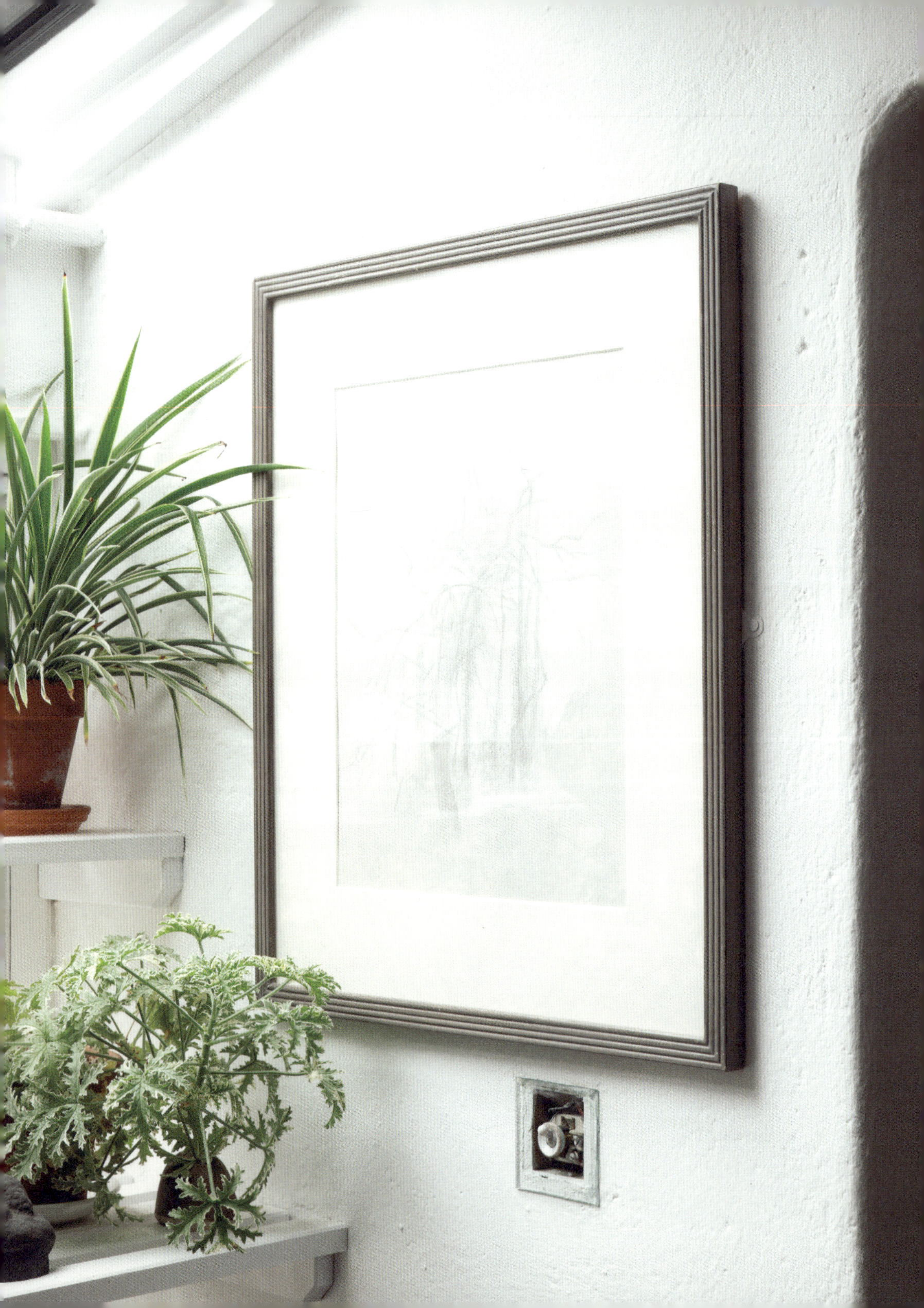

ELISABETH VELLACOTT

(1905–2002)

Elisabeth Vellacott was born in Grays, Essex and studied in London at the Willesden School of Art 1922-25 and at the Royal College of Art 1925-29. Vellacott worked in theatre and textile design in Cambridge, designing sets and costumes for the Cambridge University Music Society with her friend and fellow artist Gwen Raverat. In the 1930s, she also worked as an assistant scene painter at the Old Vic in London under Lillian Baylis. During the second world war, Vellacott stayed at the home of the writer Lucy Boston in Hemingford Grey, near Huntingdon in Cambridgeshire, and undertook agricultural work. During this time, she also produced fabrics and murals. Much of Vellacott's early work was lost when her studio was destroyed during an air raid in 1942, and after the war she earned a living through teaching at King's College School.

Vellacott was a founder of the Cambridge Society of Painters and Sculptors. She bought a small piece of land in Hemingford Grey and built a studio/ house on the tightest budget, designed by Peter Boston (the son of Lucy Boston). A solo exhibition of her work was staged in 1968 at The Minories in Colchester, Essex, followed by London shows at the New Art Centre on Sloane Street and the Warwick Arts Trust, Warwick Square. Bryan Robertson (later director of the Whitechapel Gallery) championed her work, and the Edes met Vellacott soon after they arrived in Cambridge. Jim Ede acquired several of her drawings and paintings for the collection, and a retrospective exhibition of her work was staged at Kettle's Yard in 1981.

Trees, c. 1970
Graphite on paper,
40 × 31 cm
KY01293

Jim Ede, letter to Elisabeth Vellacott, 22 March 1978

Kettle's Yard Archive, Papers of Elisabeth Vellacott

> I'd like to write you a most elegant letter on this beautiful bit of paper you have enclosed - but I see at once that the greatest elegance I could achieve would be to leave it blank - expressive of all beauty. (These chaps who leave their canvas blank are no doubt wise, but they don't know what they are up to - for their canvas already lacks beauty in itself & is RAW) [...] In a geological book I have just bought 'on the Rocks' I find that Anglesea is a Precambrian area & I look with renewed interest at the pebble you sent me [sketch of a pebble] with a dark base, a grey belt & a lighter top - not an egg in a cup.

Jim Ede, *A way of life: Kettle's Yard*

(Cambridge University Press, 1984) p. 94

> This Elisabeth Vellacott [*Bare Trees and Hills*, c. 1960] was the first of her works which I acquired, perhaps in 1960. It was a great joy to me to find an artist who could leave untouched a large area of paper and yet keep it full. Never in the drawing itself does her paper become empty, so subtly does she approach it with her pencil. No photograph could realise this.

Elisabeth Vellacott, [untitled manuscript], February 1995

Kettle's Yard Archive, House & Gallery Records

> When Jim first arrived in Cambridge, few people, except for the small group of artists living here, were aware that they lacked any place where they could see and enjoy any contemporary 20th Century Art. The Fitzwilliam were not concerned. Jim was a beam of light to us. He visited my studio, and as soon as Kettle's Yard was opened, I went often to see him - and Helen. To my astonishment, he thought well of my drawings, and bought them for his collection - I felt for the first time that they were acknowledged, and had a place. It was possible to go forward. Jim was always a very good friend.

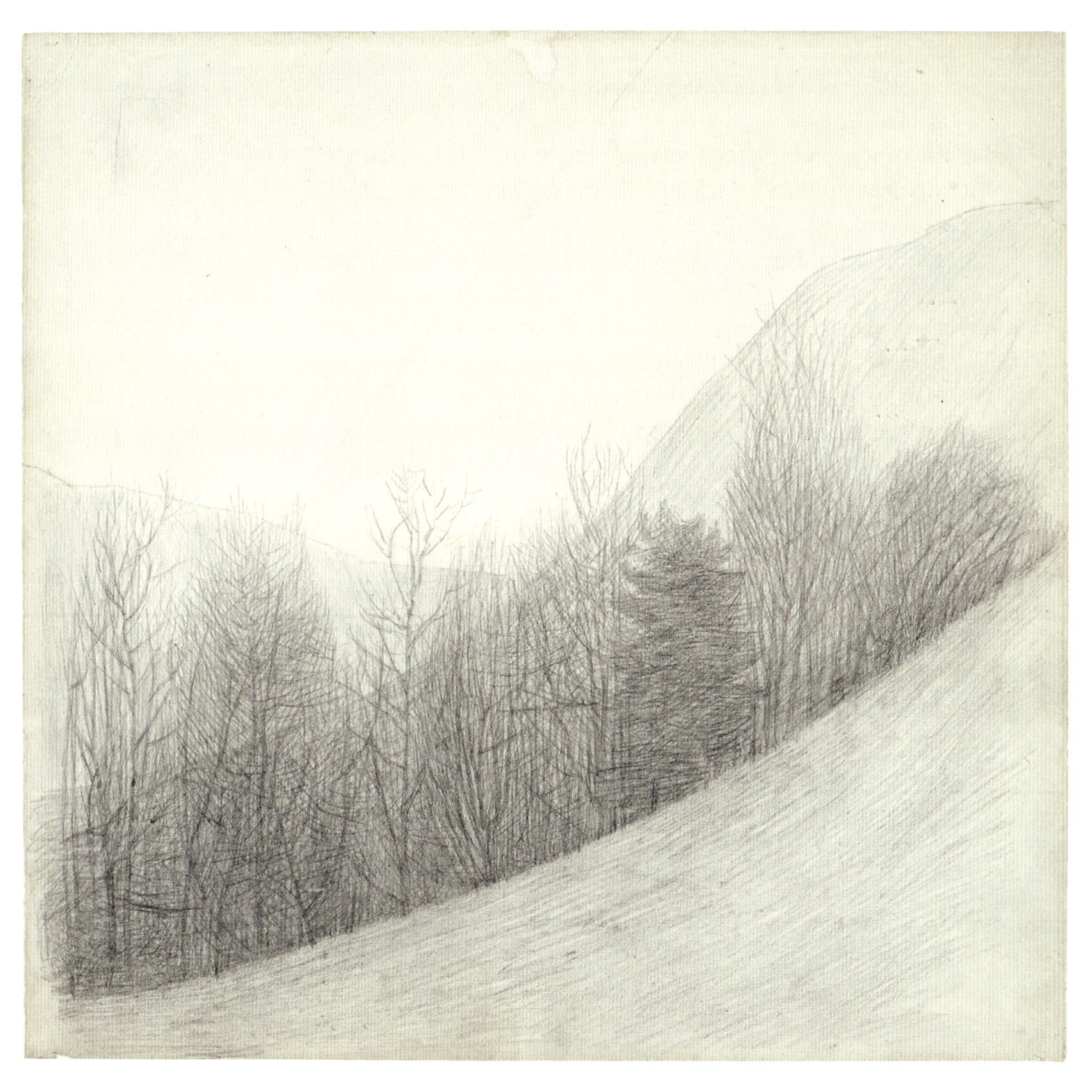

Bare Trees and Hills, c. 1960
Graphite on paper, 36.9 × 38.4 cm
KY00803.EH

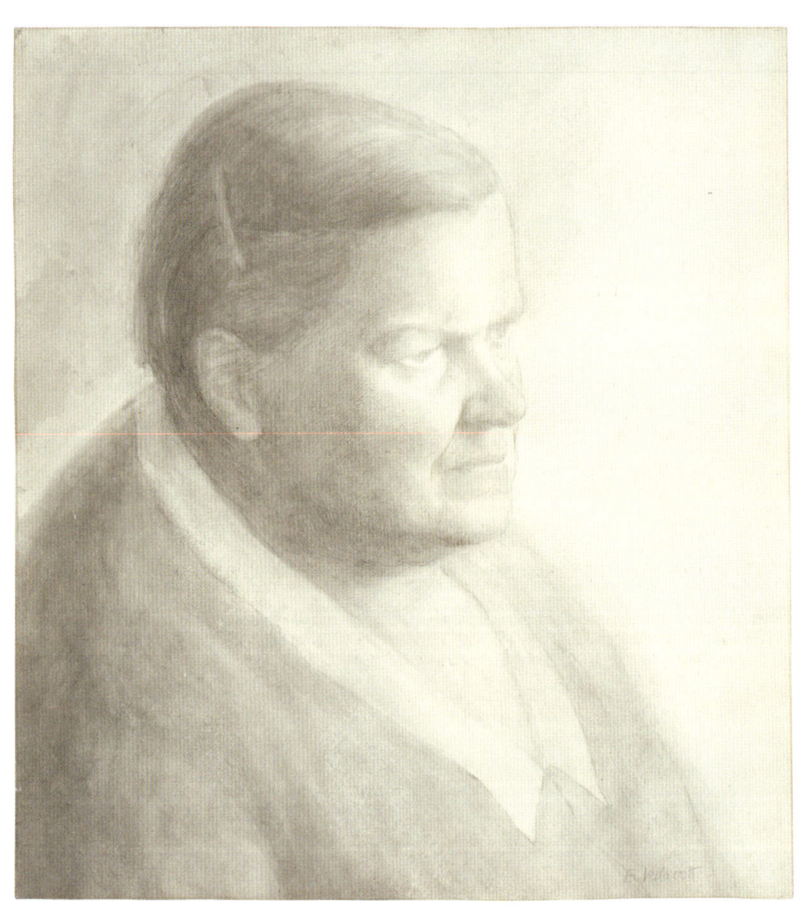

Portrait of Gwen Raverat, 1954
Graphite and ink wash on paper, 38 × 35 cm
KY00892.EH

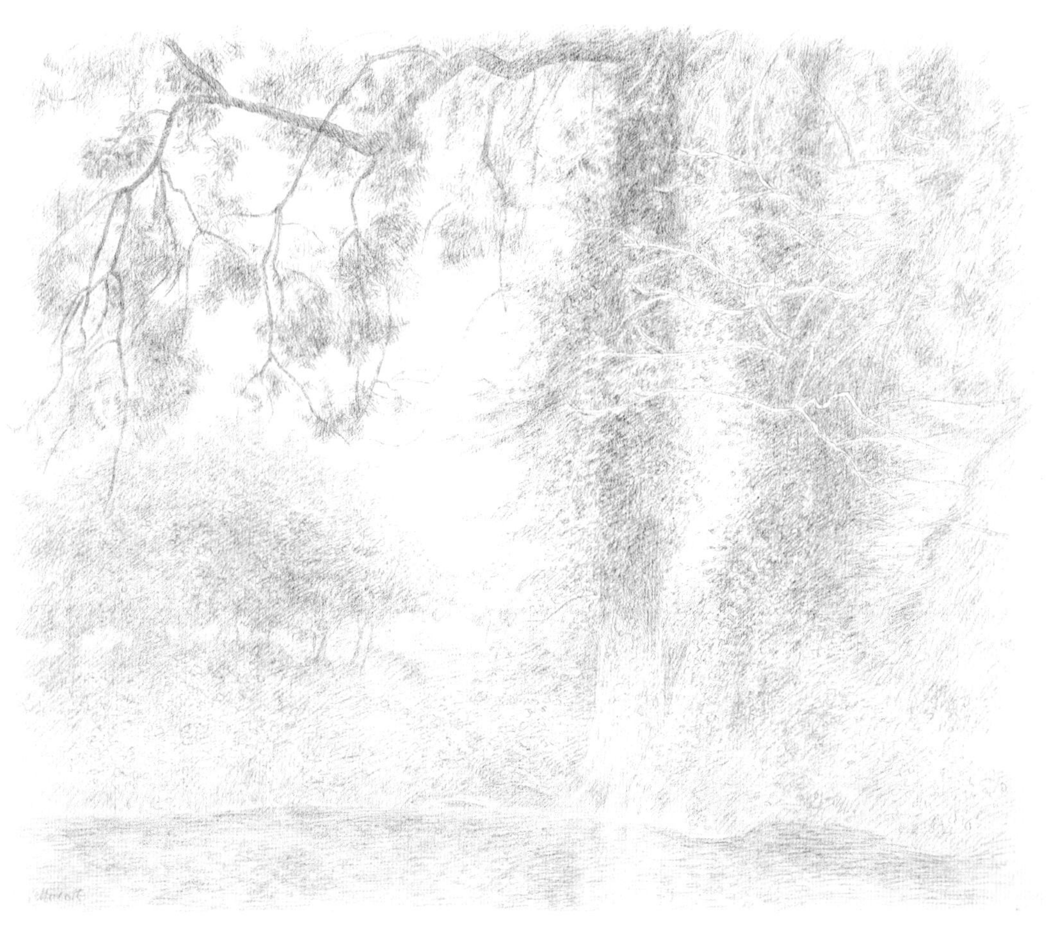

Entangled Trees, 1976
Graphite on paper, 43.8 × 53 cm
KY01107.EH

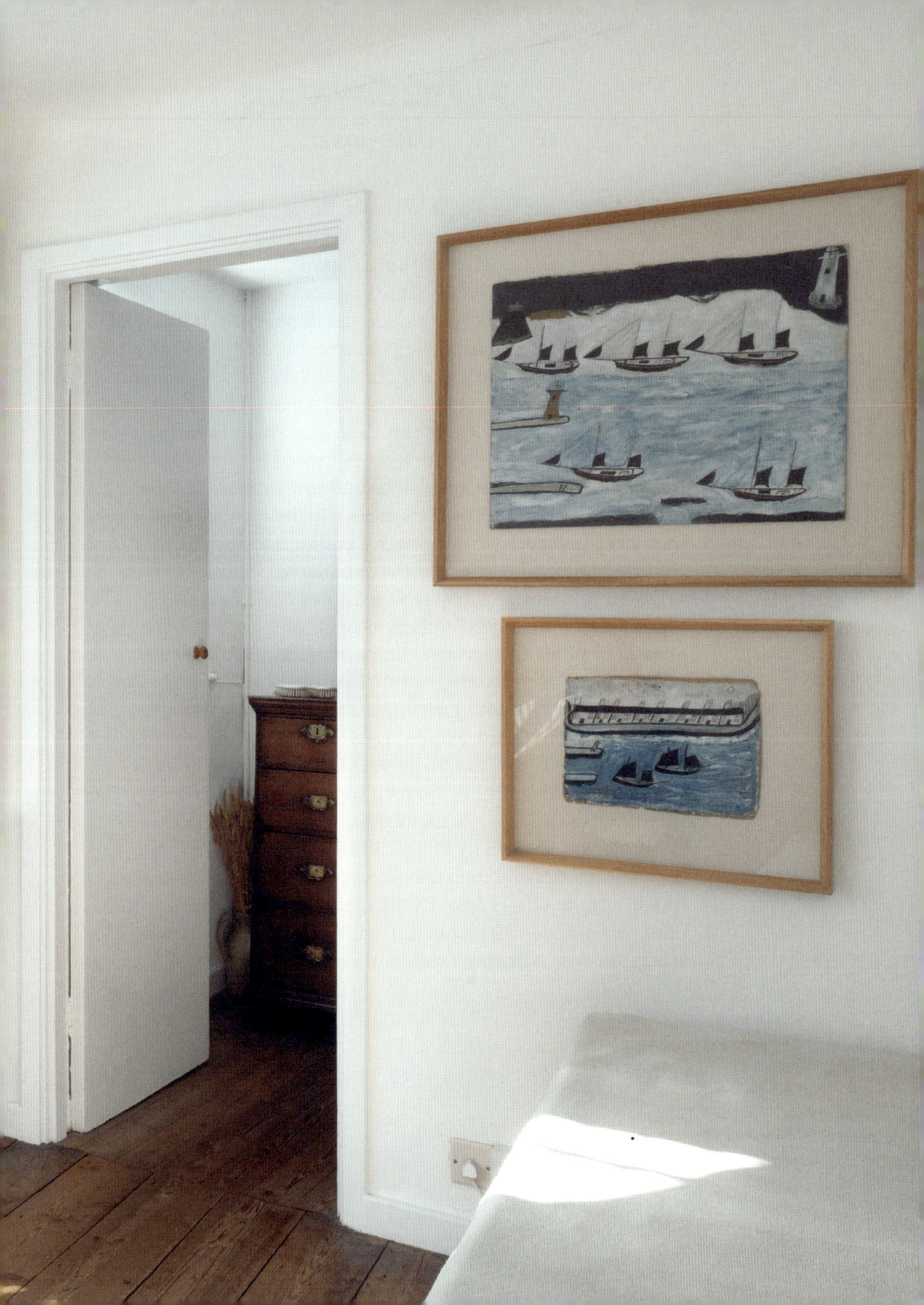

ALFRED WALLIS

(1855–1942)

Alfred Wallis was born in Devonport, Devon. He was apprenticed as a basket maker and employed as a sailor and a deep-sea fisherman off the coast of Newfoundland, Canada. In 1876, Wallis married Susan Ward (née Agland) and his family later moved to St Ives in Cornwall where they became members of the Salvation Army and set up a shop trading in second-hand goods and scrap materials. Susan's death in 1922 forced Wallis to sell their cottage and instead rent a single room, where he was largely reliant on charitable support. It was at this time that Wallis began painting, using household or boat paints on discarded cardboard packaging. His subjects were seascapes, ships and townscapes, and the paintings he produced over the next two decades are characterised by a steep perspective, imaginative scaling and specific palette of colours - blue, grey, green, white and black.

In 1928, on a daytrip to St Ives, Ben Nicholson and Christopher Wood met Wallis by chance, having passed the open door of his cottage and glimpsed paintings 'nailed up all over the wall'. Shortly afterwards, Ben and Winifred Nicholson returned to St Ives with Christopher Wood and developed a friendship with Wallis. Wood stayed on longer, and learned much from Wallis's vision. The Nicholsons introduced Wallis's work to friends, including Adrian Stokes and Jim Ede, who corresponded with Wallis over many years. Wallis's paintings were included in exhibitions organised by Ben Nicholson and Lucy Wertheim; and reproduced in the French magazine *Cahiers d'Art* and in Herbert Read's 1933 book *Art Now*. Wallis spent the last fourteen months of his life at the Madron Institution, a workhouse, near Penzance, where he was visited by Ben Nicholson.

Five Ships - Mount's Bay, c. 1928
Oil paint and graphite on card, 44 × 55.5 cm
KY00404.EH

Houses at the water's edge (Porthleven?), 1925-28
Oil paint and graphite on card, 22.8 × 30.4 cm
KY00405.EH

4

Ap 6 1935

Dear Sir i Receved
your letter with Thanks
and also The pantins wich you
Did not want
what i do mosley is what
use To Bee out of my own
memery what we may never
see again as Thing are altered
all To gether Ther is nothin
what Ever do not look like
what it was sence i can Kember
if i live Till The 8 of august
next i shall Be 78 years old
i was Born in Devenport
Born on The day of The fall
of Servesetpool Rushan war
so i cos from your
friend alfred wallis

Alfred Wallis, letter to Jim Ede, 12 February 1934

Kettle's Yard Archive, Papers of Harold Stanley 'Jim' Ede. KY/EDE/1/17

> sir i have sint on a parcle as they are dray i think they will do as they are what used [to] be most all i do is what use to be in ships and boats what you phrape what you will never see any more i like sailin craft best for looks so i must clos wishing you good speed From you friend alfred Wallis

Alfred Wallis, letter to Jim Ede, 30 November 1935

Kettle's Yard Archive, Papers of Harold Stanley 'Jim' Ede. KY/EDE/1/17

> sir i am glad you have receved the pantins all right and that you like som i do not to put collers what do not belong i think i spoils the picturs their have been a lot of paintins spoiled by putin collers where they do not blong good work it want pay to ad collers it spoiles ther work so i must clos wishin you all well from your friend alfred wallis

Alfred Wallis, letter to Jim Ede, 4 November 1936

Kettle's Yard Archive, Papers of Harold Stanley 'Jim' Ede. KY/EDE/1/17

> [...] i never see any thing i send you now it is what i have seen before i am self taught so you cannot me like thouse that have been taught both in school and paint i have had to learn myself i never go out to paint nor i never shaw them.

Alfred Wallis, letter to Jim Ede, 6 April 1935

Kettle's Yard Archive, Papers of Harold Stanley 'Jim' Ede. KY/EDE/1/17

Alfred Wallis, letter to Jim Ede, 27 July 1938

Kettle's Yard Archive, Papers of Harold Stanley 'Jim' Ede. KY/EDE/1/17

> i receved your letter i see by it you have arived home saf i am thinkin of givin up the paints all together i have nothin but percuitin and gelecy and if you can com down for a hour or 2 you can take them with you and give what they are worf to you afterwards these drawers and shopes are all gelles of me send or com you can have them all there is alot of them and at my age it is mor than i con stand i may do one now an then when i feel able send down anyone that is coming this way or com nothin but perecuitin i want to live to the schpter not mallace you can com or send and take them away and pay what ther worth afterwards so i clos wishin you well from your friend alfred wallis

Ben Nicholson, letter to Jim Ede, 29 August 1942
[the day of Wallis's death]

Kettle's Yard Archive, Papers of Harold Stanley 'Jim' Ede. KY/EDE/1/11

> Wallis got too old to look after himself alone about a year ago & went off to the Madron Institute near Penzance – we (Adrian [Stoke], Barbara [Hepworth] & me) were worried about this at first but could find no other solution owing to war conditions & in the end he settled in v. well & with an extremely nice Welsh 'Master' & charming Matron who I know have looked after him well & after a month or two his paintings were admired greatly by them & the nurses & the cooks & the inmates! But he has had to go to bed about 3 weeks ago & I went over shortly after & he seemed to me through with this life. Up till quite a short time ago he'd been drawing & painting but he seems so old now that there is not much of himself left. He asked after you once or twice sometime ago & I said you were in America which seemed to comfort him as otherwise I think he thought you had forgotten about him or his work. No, I don't think a good Wallis is representational, it is simply REAL? For the same reason I don't think a good 'non-figurative Picasso is photographic' – it simply is an immensely real experience &

since our visual experience has come from what we've seen it is necessarily representational in the sense that it's been experienced visually? People confuse 'representationalism' with 'reality'?

Jim Ede, 'Two Painters in Cornwall: Alfred Wallis and Christopher Wood'

World Review, March 1945, pp. 45-51

Though he is always drawing the same ships, the same houses, the same water, each of his pictures is a new experience, and this is natural in one so direct. His mood, the thing which made him want to paint, to tell himself as it were some past memory, dictates the composition. He does not set about to enclose his vision, his thought, into some preconceived scheme of colour or design. It is the immediate welling up of his vision, rich in actual experience. It is experience which enables us to do things rightly, and the use of experience which gives colour to our action. So with Wallis design comes, with its subtly variant lines and spaces, not through experience in the art of drawing or painting, but from closeness, almost identification with the thing he is drawing. I remember another painting expressive of this. It is of a high, many-arched bridge and several boats [*Boats before a great bridge*, c. 1935-37] [...] To each arch of the bridge, following from one to another, there is a change of shape, each one a new arch, for a new sensation is experienced in going through each, and yet each is entirely part of the same bridge. The fundamental character of things is never for a moment lost sight of, yet nothing is ever fixed into the frigid limitation of a particular moment. It is, I think, in this direction that art lives, and Alfred Wallis was here tremendously alive.

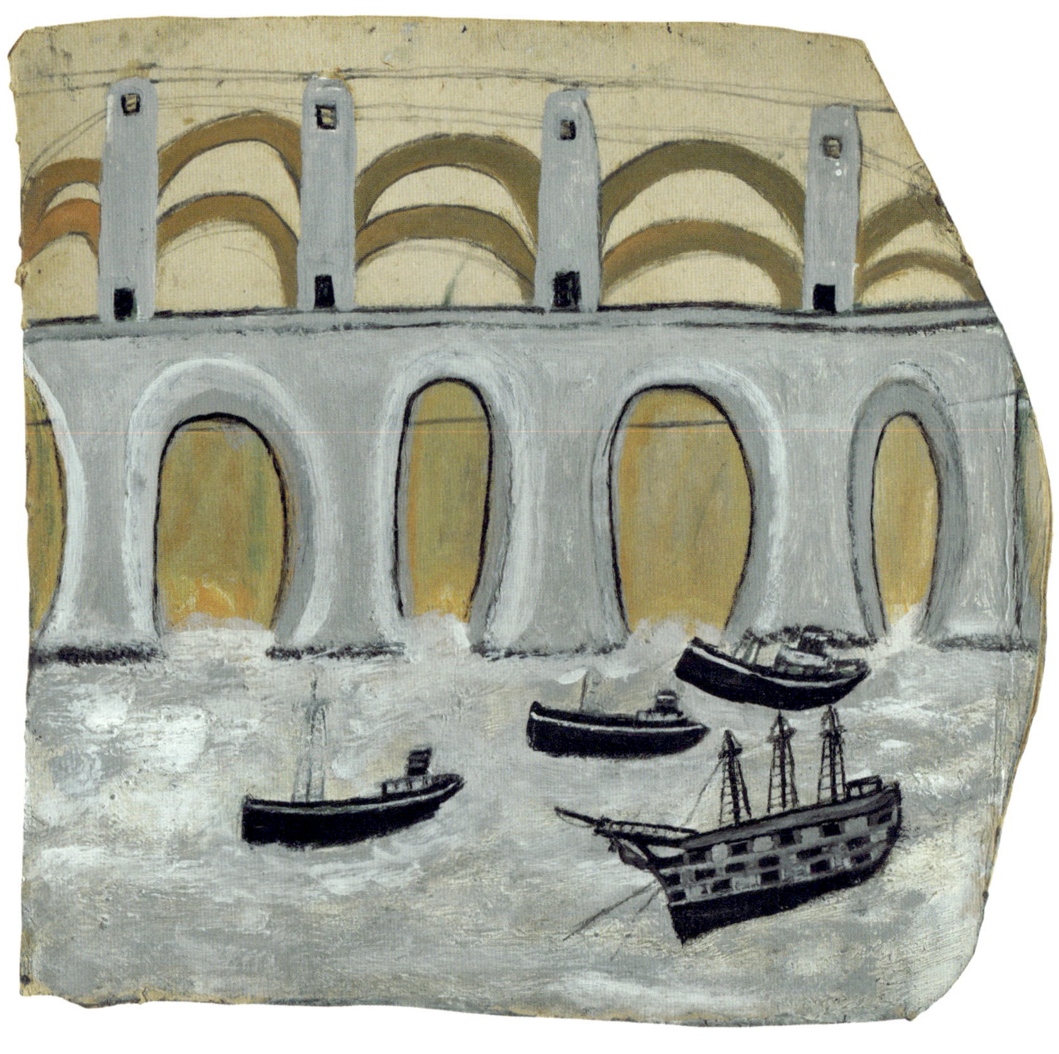

Boats before a great bridge (Royal Albert Bridge?), c. 1935-37
Oil paint on card, 36.7 × 39.2 cm
KY00680.EH

Saltash (or Devonport), 1928-30
Oil paint and watercolour on board, 74.7 × 53.2 cm
KY00402.EH

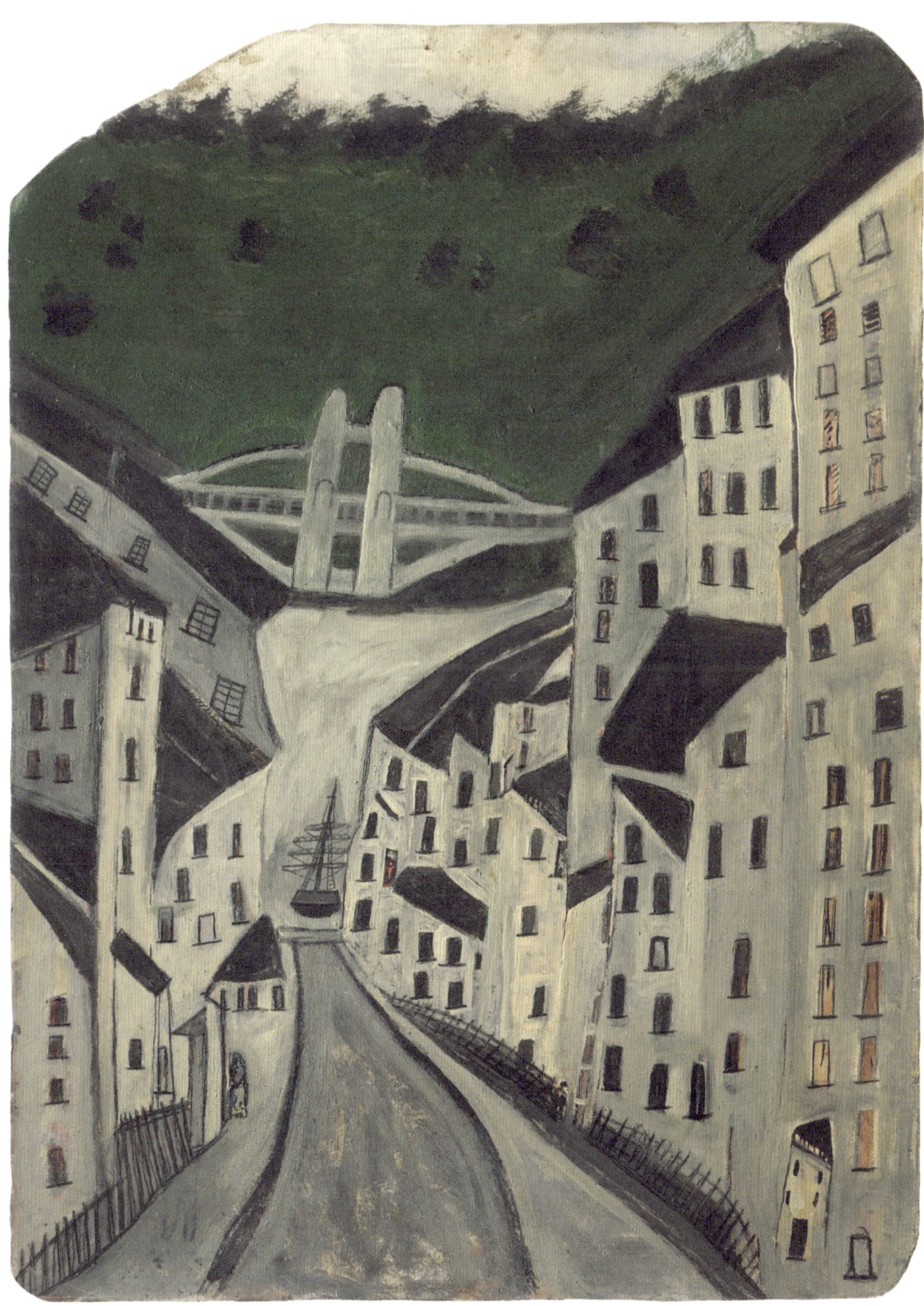

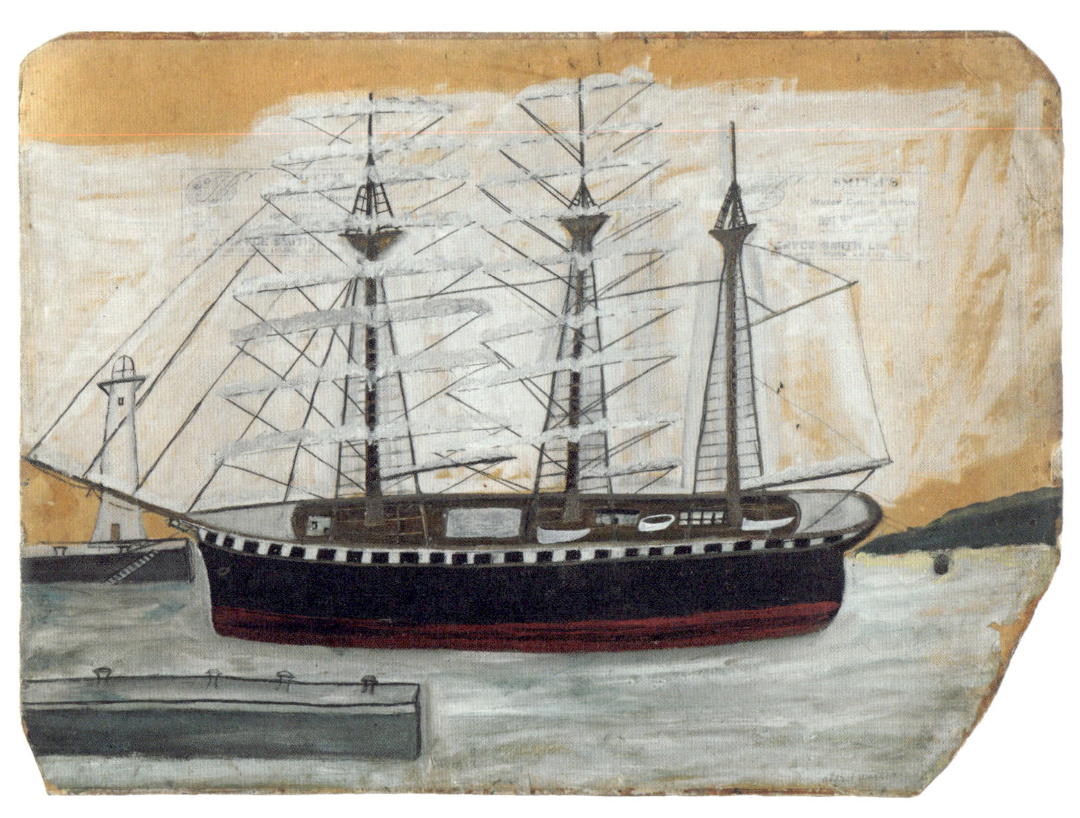

Three-masted ship near lighthouse, 1928-30
Oil paint on watercolour board, 53 × 74.7 cm
KY00450.EH

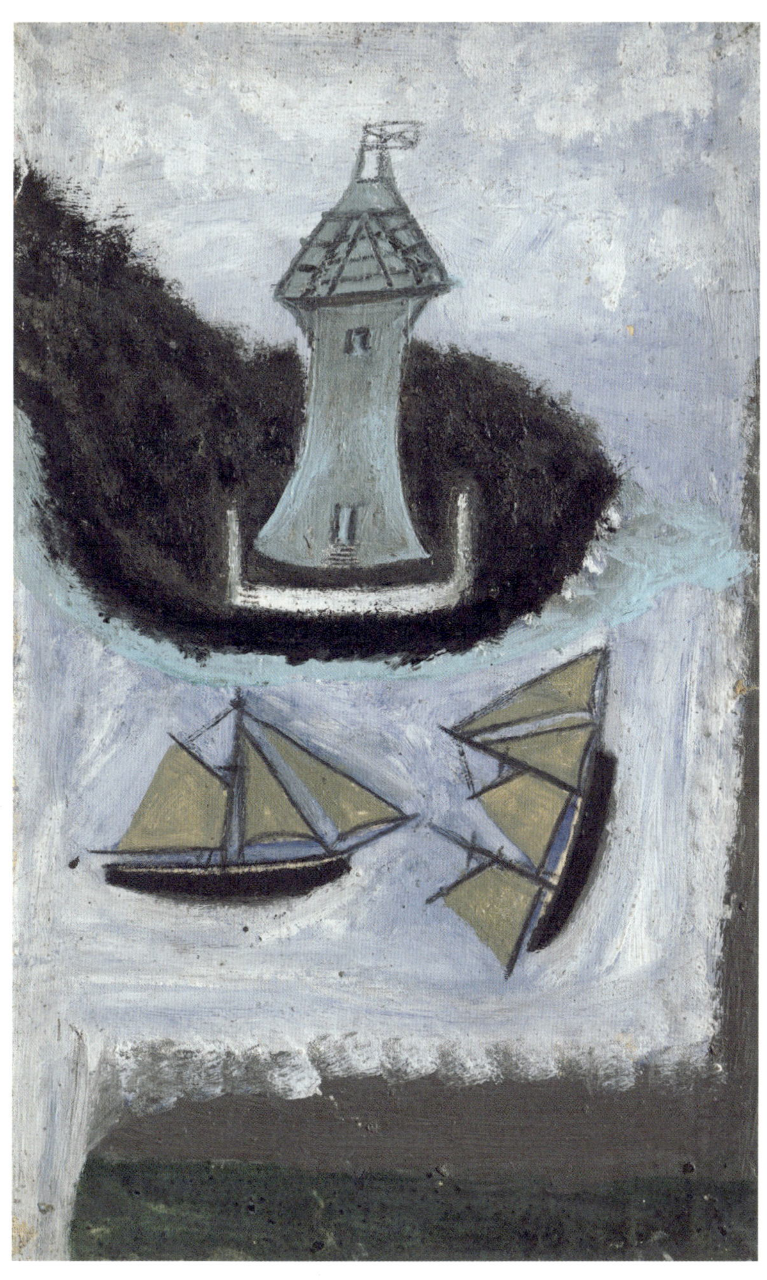

Lighthouse and two sailing ships, undated
Oil paint on card, 28 × 17 cm
KY00400.EH

Boats under Saltash Bridge (Royal Albert Bridge), c. 1935-37
Oil paint on card, 30 × 50 cm
KY00677.EH

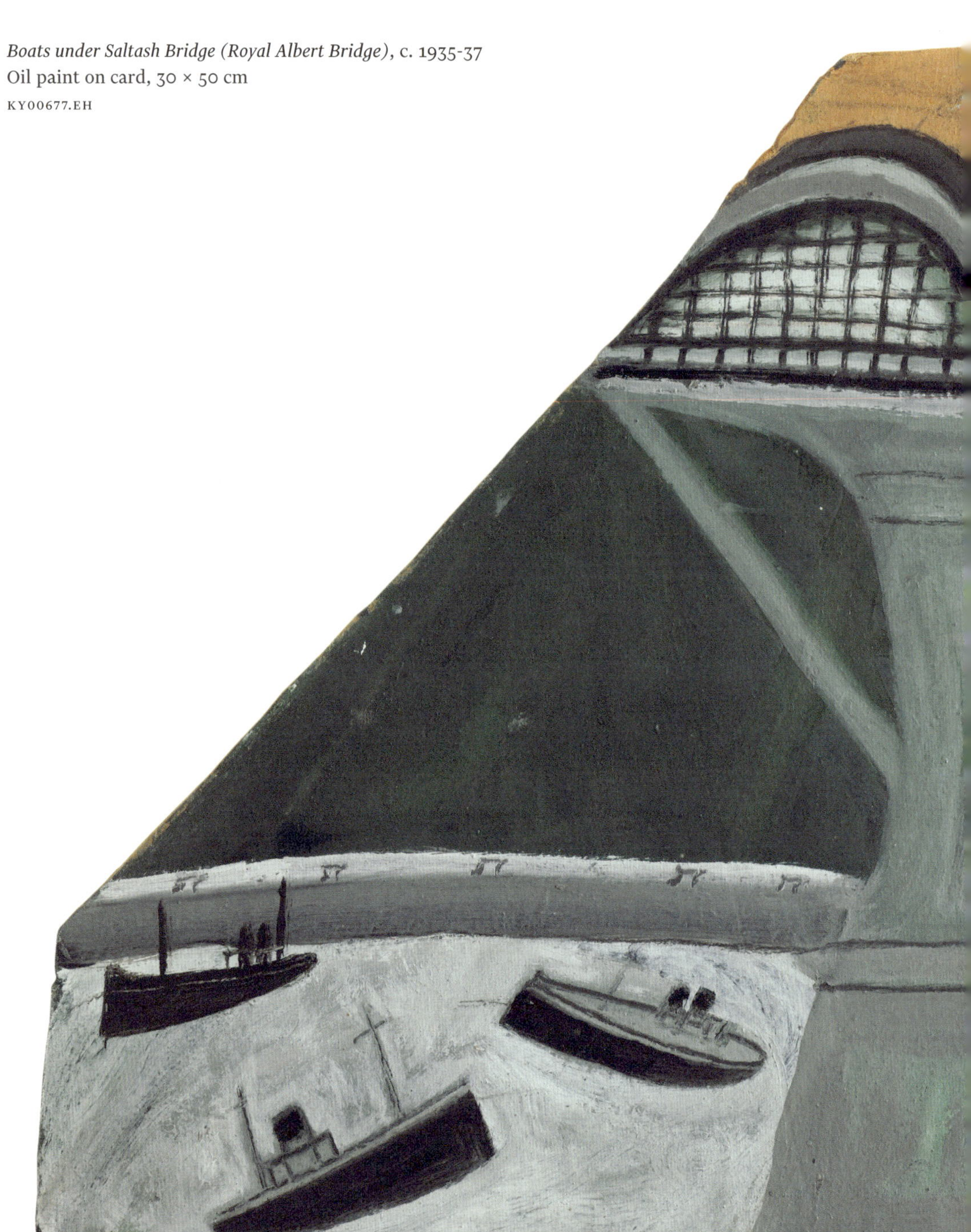

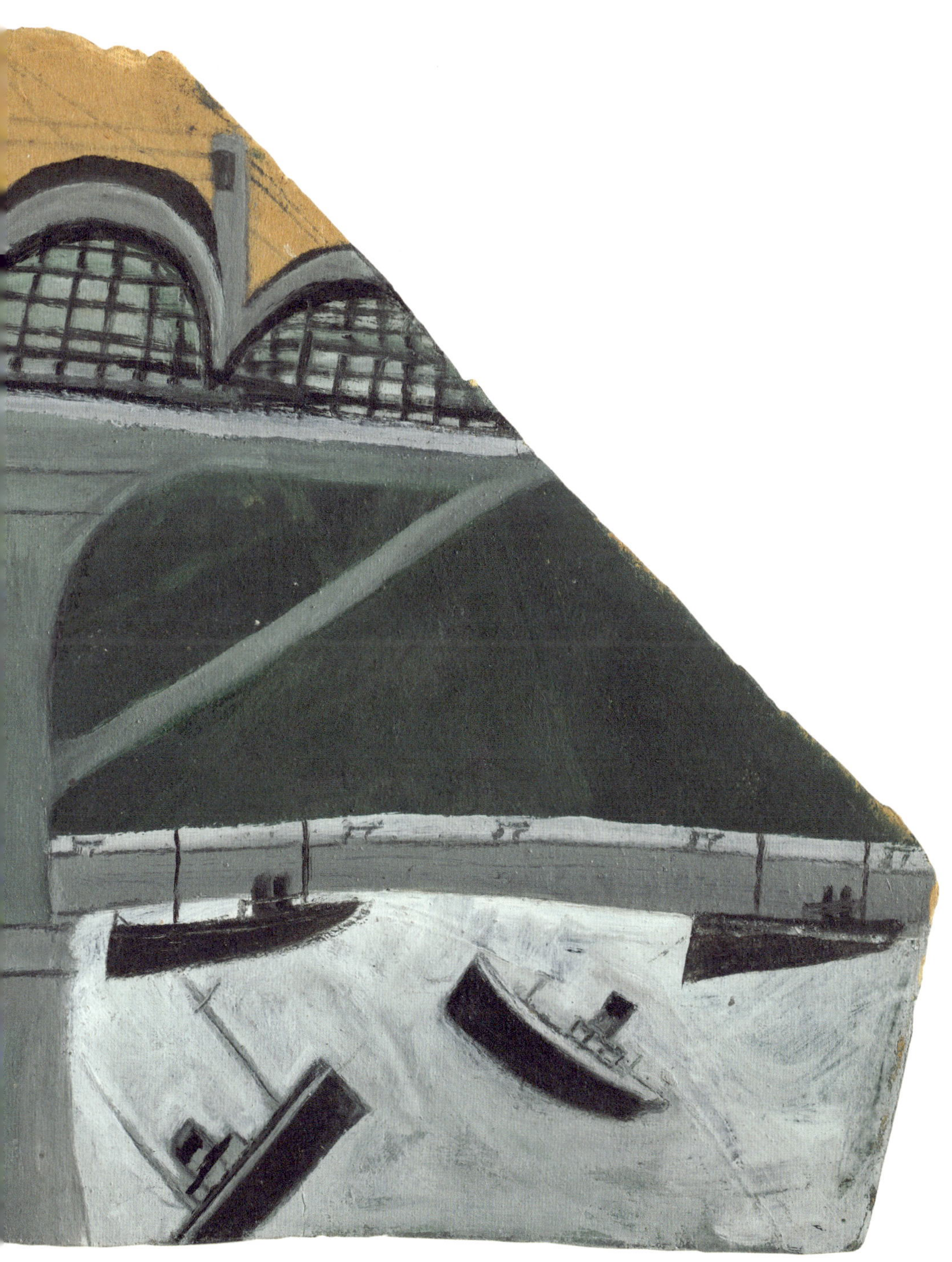

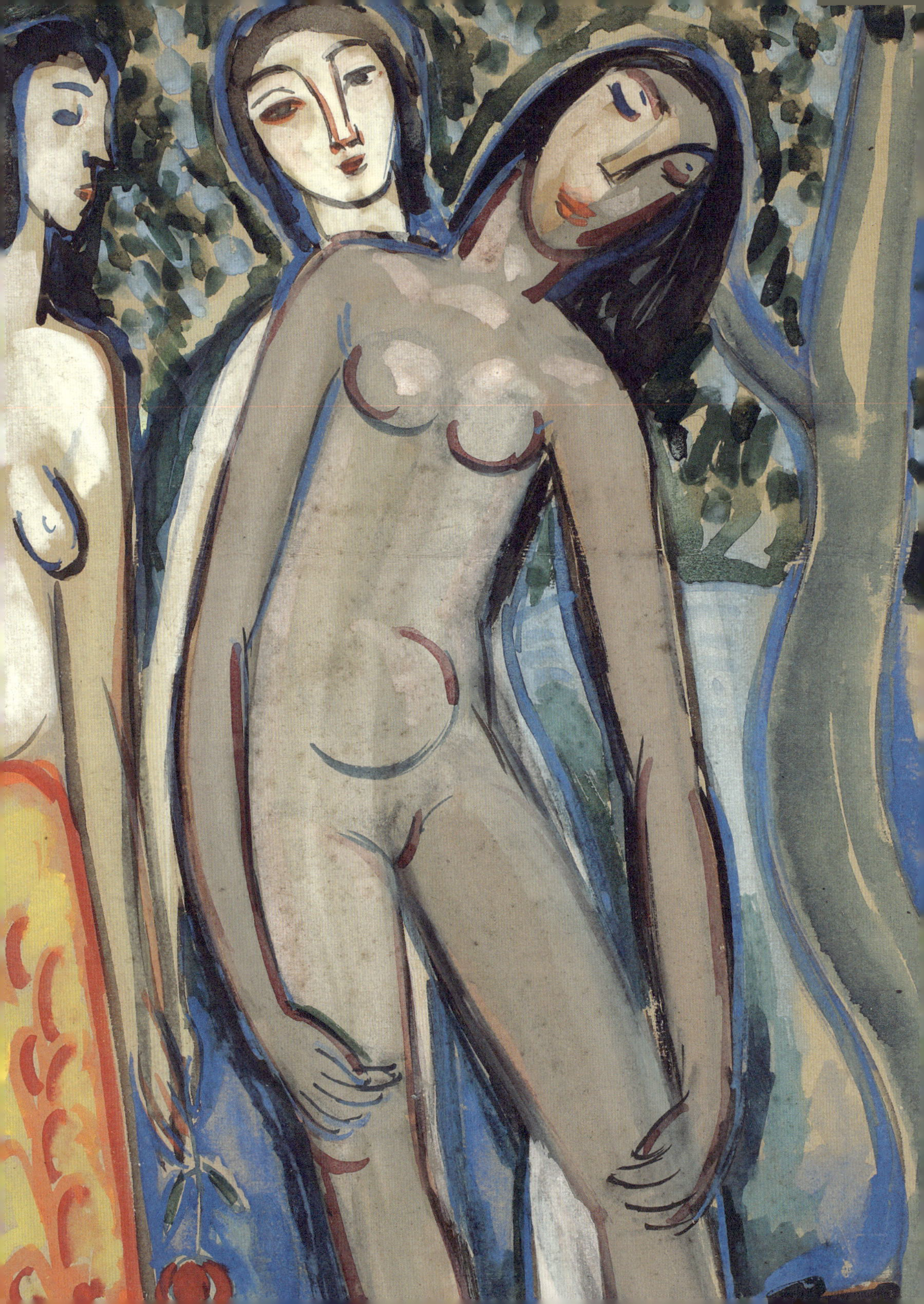

EDWARD WOLFE

(1897–1982)

Edward Wolfe was born in Johannesburg, South Africa. He spent two years in London as a child, and returned in 1916 to enrol at the Regent Street Polytechnic and then the Slade School of Art (1916–18). Artist and writer Nina Hamnett invited Wolfe to join Roger Fry's Omega Workshops. From 1918, he also exhibited with the London Group and the Friday Club, which had been founded by Vanessa Bell but came to welcome artists working in a range of painterly styles including David Bomberg, Paul Nash and Christopher Nevinson. Back in Johannesburg, Wolfe was given a solo show at Leon Levson's Gallery in 1920. In 1922, he rented a studio in Montparnasse in Paris, France, where he became friendly with artists including Natalia Goncharova and Ossip Zadkine. Wolfe spent periods in Florence, Italy between 1922 and 1925, and it was here he first met Jim Ede.

In London, exhibitions of Wolfe's work were held at the Mayor Gallery (1926) and the Warren Gallery (1929). Wolfe travelled to Morocco, Spain and Tunisia in the 1920s, painting portraits influenced by Henri Matisse. Jim and Helen Ede's first visit to Tangier in Morocco was at Wolfe's invitation, a stay that provided Jim Ede with the respite needed to finish his biography of Henri Gaudier-Brzeska. Wolfe's portrait of Jim Ede was painted at this time. Wolfe was supported by the London Artists' Association, backed by Samuel Courtauld and John Maynard Keynes, who staged exhibitions of his work on Bond Street in London in 1929 and 1931. In 1934, Wolfe spent six months in New York, USA, before moving to the city of Taxco in Mexico where he lived until the summer of 1936. Wolfe acted as a censor for the BBC in Bristol during the second world war, while continuing to exhibit widely. A retrospective exhibition was mounted by the Arts Council in 1967, and Wolfe was elected a Royal Academician in 1972.

Three Graces (detail), 1930
Watercolour and gouache on card, 50.1 × 30.4 cm
KY00633.E

Edward Wolfe, letter to Jim Ede, c. 1930

Kettle's Yard Archive, Papers of Harold Stanley 'Jim' Ede. KY/EDE/1/1

> My dearest Jim, How wonderfully nice it is to hear that your book is doing so well. I have a feeling that it is going to do even more than you had hoped for, you really deserve that it should get every success as it is a most lovely work dear Jim I am so glad. My own world is toppling down upon me and to be able to rejoyce [sic] in ones friends' success is the next best thing to having success oneself. I long to see you but you know what my life has been these last weeks. Have a good holiday and think of your Teddy sometimes. Give Helen my love [...]

Edward Wolfe, letter to Jim Ede, undated

Kettle's Yard Archive, Papers of Harold Stanley 'Jim' Ede. KY/EDE/1/1

> Jim my dear We all wish that you were here with us and no one more than I. It was great fun the other night and I simply adored Agatha [Walker?]. When she is at her best she is very heavenly I always think. David [Jones] is a lovely fellow and I am enjoying the odd talks we have together. It is strange how often your name comes up when we all talk together. You seem to stand for so much goodness in all our lives. Vera [Moore] you no doubt have seen and have heard all the news. Helen S[utherland] is in such a very sweet mind and she is an extremely rare bird like creature shy and lovely and oh so very nice. [...]

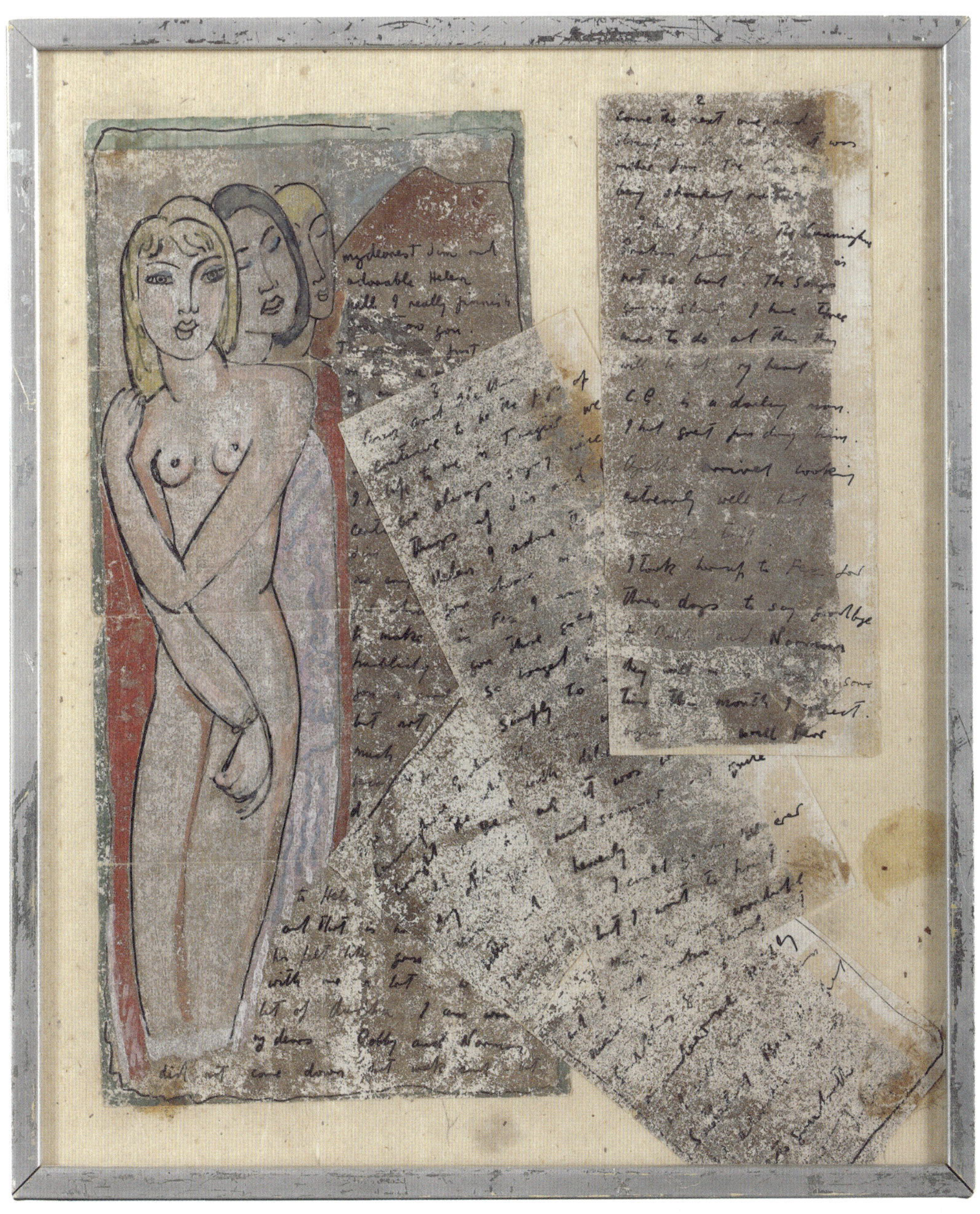

Letter with drawing, 1930
Ink on paper, 37 × 27 cm
KY00632.E

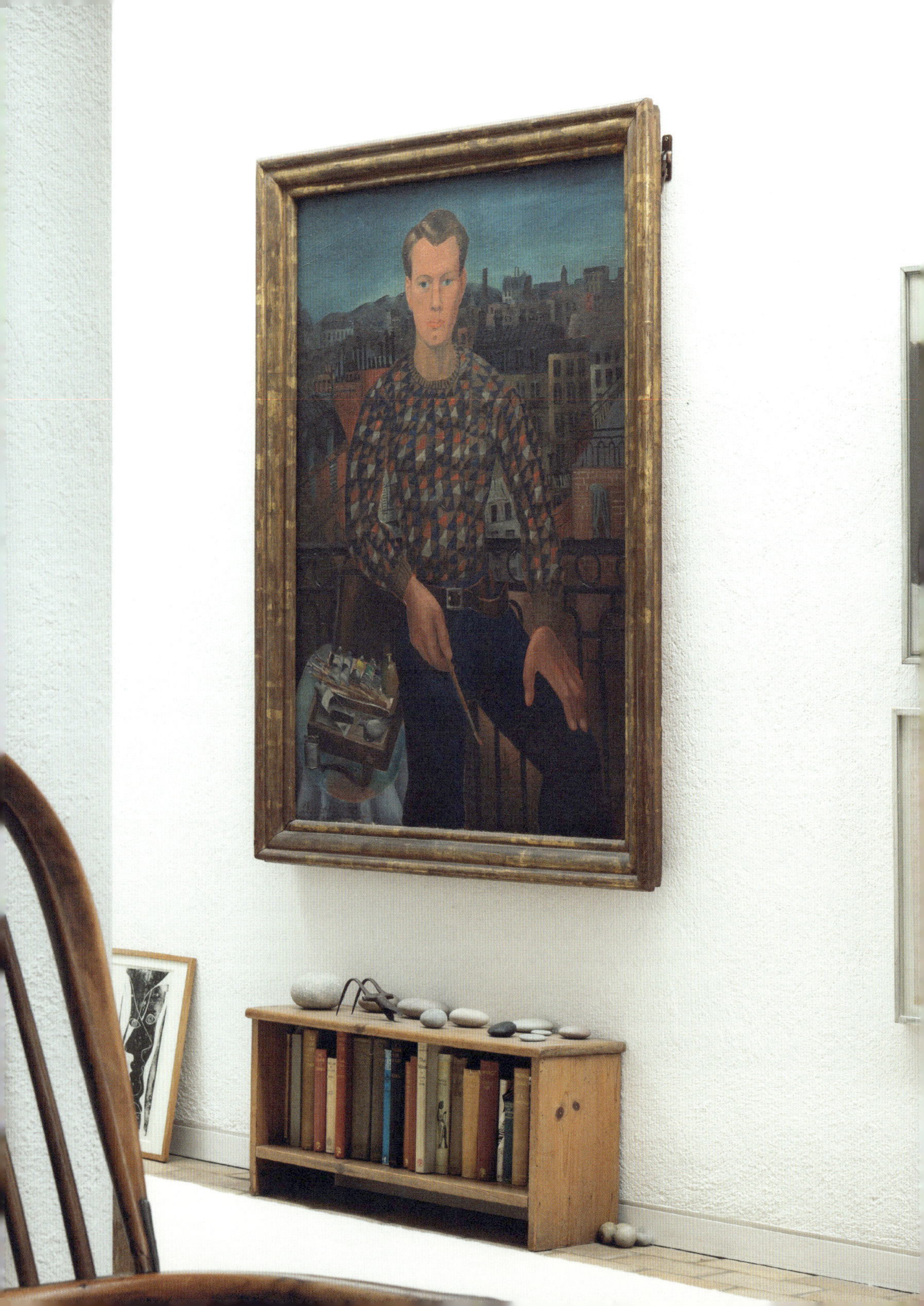

CHRISTOPHER WOOD

(1901–1930)

Christopher Wood (known as Kit) was born in Knowsley, Merseyside. He studied architecture at the University of Liverpool 1919–20, and was later apprenticed to an import company, Thornley and Felix in London. Wood aspired to be an artist, and in 1921, accepted an invitation from the wealthy art collector Alphonse Kahn to stay with him in Paris. This marked the beginning of a peripatetic decade, during which Wood would attempt to establish himself as 'the greatest painter that ever lived'. In Paris, Wood became popular in wealthy social circles but, through Kahn and others, was gradually introduced to the artists who lived and worked in the city at that time. Wood benefitted from the emotional and financial support of the Chilean diplomat José Antonio de Gandarillas, who became the artist's most consistent partner during these years. He was also encouraged by Pablo Picasso and Jean Cocteau, and was commissioned by Sergei Diaghilev to design sets for his Ballets Russes production of *Romeo and Juliet*.

Wood was one of very few British artists to have a solo exhibition in Paris in the 1920s, and also showed in London with the Seven and Five Society. He developed close and mutually inspiring relationships with Ben and Winifred Nicholson, staying with them in Cumbria and Cornwall. It was through the Nicholsons that he met Jim Ede, who purchased his landscapes of Vence in the South of France, a still life of flowers and a barely visible incised work on brown-washed board. In 1929 and 1930, Wood spent time in Brittany, which proved to be highly productive for his painting. In 1930, on his return to England from one such trip and likely suffering from the effects of opium withdrawal, Wood was killed by a train at Salisbury station. Devastated by the death of his friend, Jim Ede organised a memorial exhibition for Wood in 1932 and assisted the artist's parents Clare and Lucius in settling Wood's estate.

Self-Portrait, 1927
Oil paint on canvas, 129.5 × 96 cm
KY00338.EH

Christopher Wood, letter to Jim Ede, c. April 1927

Kettle's Yard Archive, Papers of Harold Stanley 'Jim' Ede. KY/EDE/1/18

I wish to thank you again for all the kind things you have done for me which I will never forget and I hope that I may repay you for them in some way one day. I will do anything I can in my power to help you if ever there was a possibility of doing so. If I don't see you again goodbye and all my thanks.

Ben Nicholson, letter to Jim Ede, 1930

Kettle's Yard Archive, Papers of Harold Stanley 'Jim' Ede. KY/EDE/1/11

I am so sad about Kit. I miss him more than I can say. I could have parted with almost anyone but him – & I realize that every single day up here I thought of him. No person has ever given me so much in the painting sense, & in every way. His generosity and his beautiful loving power how I loved it, the reality of his vision was amazing & he was the most beautiful creature. Well he will be all that & more now I feel, for he feels happier to me now, as if free from some frightful struggle. I had that same feeling of complete repose after he died that I've only had before after Mother died. They must both have wanted to go very much [...]

I don't think I shall ever feel the same about anyone as about Kit. He was like one's own most beautiful child, of one's own age. We did try to help him – tried & tried – & Winifred especially gave him one of the most beautiful affections I have ever seen. Well – she's giving him it still – but the change feels very sad. I would like you someday to read some of the letters, if they exist, that Winifred wrote – some of the most beautiful I have read, & thoughts that only went so freely to him [...]

He was so pleased when you liked that last batch of work of his, & was saying nice things about you when we were in Paris. I want so much to see this last work he did in Brittany. We must make a special show of his work in the 7&5 show in January. But we were counting on all that lovely work to come, he never really again got onto that lovely Italian design & big, simple, free conception which he had when we first saw him. I think our meeting him divided his life in some way. He longed to marry a painter – before that he thought marriage an outrageous thing.

One thinks too much of a future in this life. It's absurd that the continuity is only faith, one day we will see it all so easily.

Jim Ede, 'CW', unpublished manuscript, c. 1970s

Kettle's Yard Archive, Papers of Harold Stanley 'Jim' Ede. KY/EDE/4/2/4/21

Nothing is lost by simplification, everything is gained. By his remarkable sense of tone, a sense seldom at fault, he gives authority to his simplest statements … He does not clutter his idea with irrelevant furnishing, indeed so truly is he master of the situation that he can leave large restful spaces for the eye to dwell upon, spaces held by the force of his intention. 'I love ships' he said, 'they have such interesting lives'.

In 'Boat Building' [*Building the Boat, Tréboul*, 1930] we can see these spaces, but so clear is the bone structure of the picture, that we are unaware of them. The facts are so exactly stated that the whole story is before us at a glance. He was very impressed by the sadness of this scene, skeletons of ships in process of being built, which foreshadow the skeletons of the fishermen who would take them out to sea and not return. Mothers and wives, who had sent their sons – their husbands, helping a younger generation to build new ships of death. I see this in his thought since he wrote of it in a letter. How pictorially he has visualized it; without a shade of sentimentality. It is a clear straight statement, vigorous and human, which belongs to that very English world of such clear statements as Shakespeare's sonnets. This was painted two months before his death.

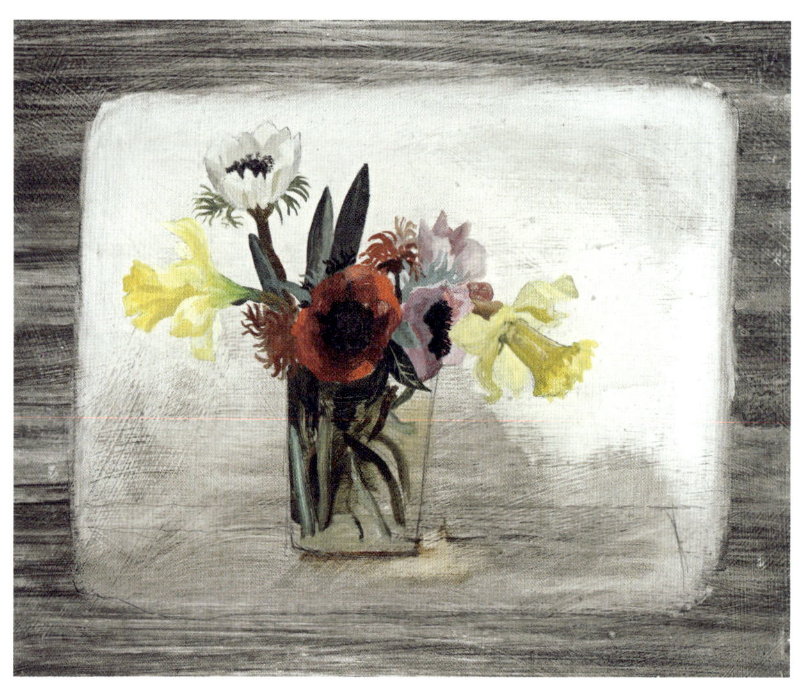

Flowers, 1930
Oil paint on board, 33 × 40 cm
KY00629.EH

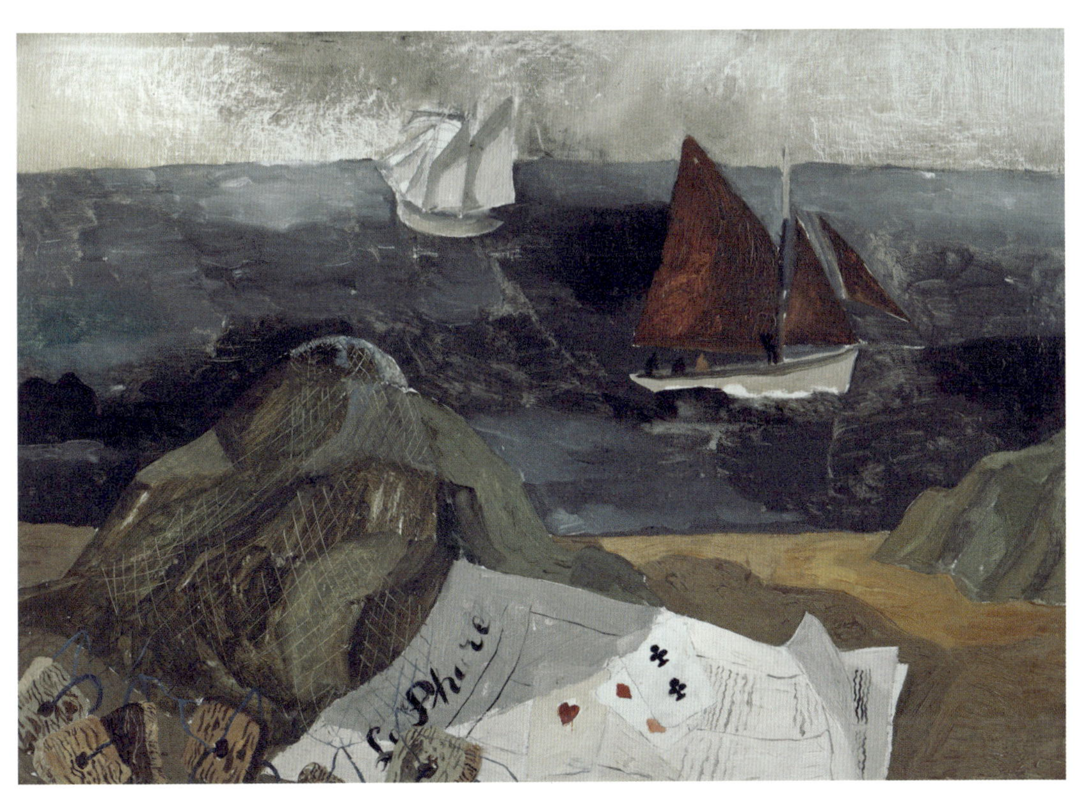

Le Phare, 1930
Oil paint on board, 53.5 × 79 cm
KY00342.EH

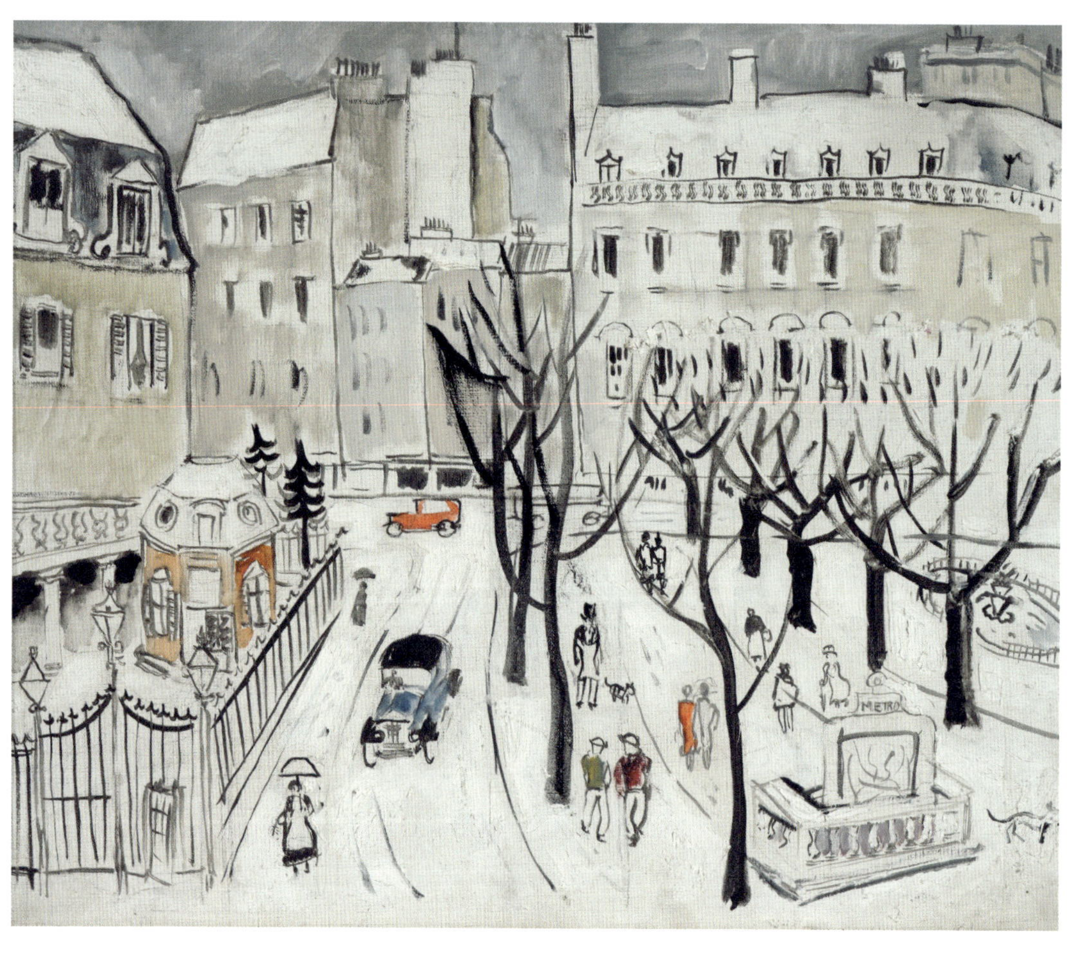

Paris Snow Scene, 1926
Oil paint on canvas, 45 × 54.5 cm
KY00343.EH

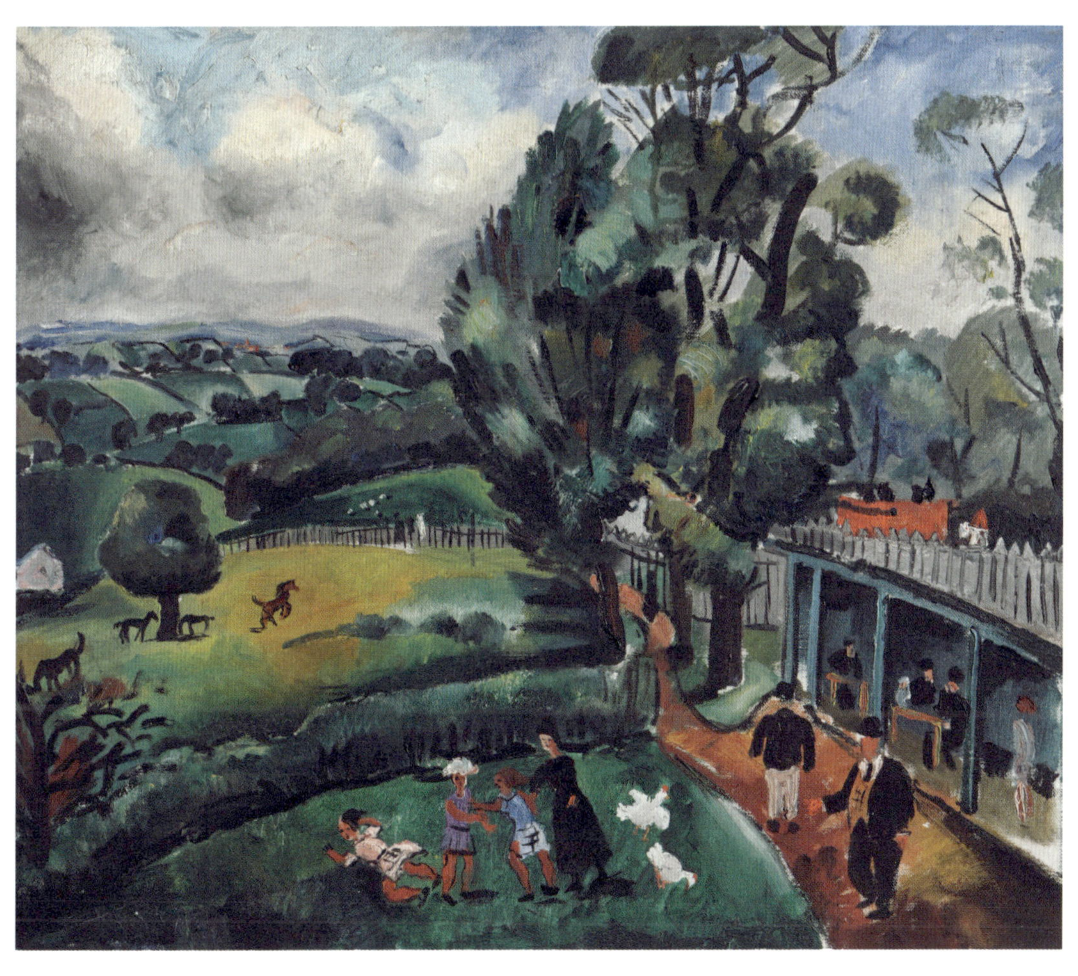

Landscape with Figures, c. 1926
Oil paint on canvas, 50 × 60 cm
KY00341.EH

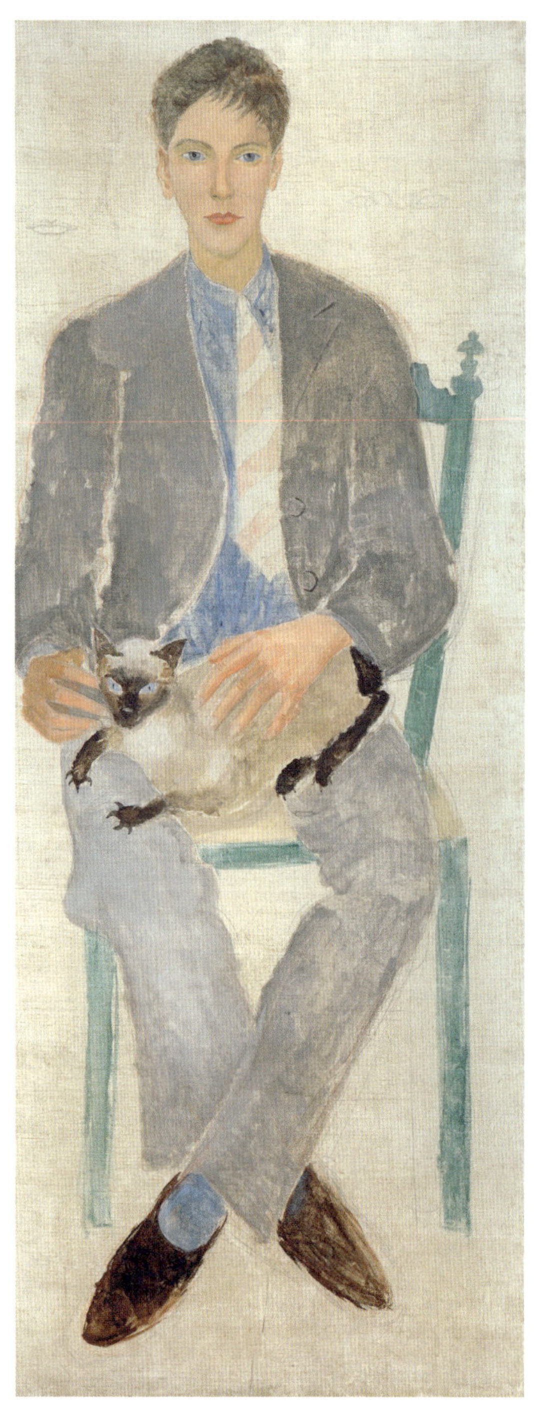

Boy with Cat (Jean Bourgoint), 1926
Oil and graphite on canvas, 148 × 58.5 cm
KY01161.EH

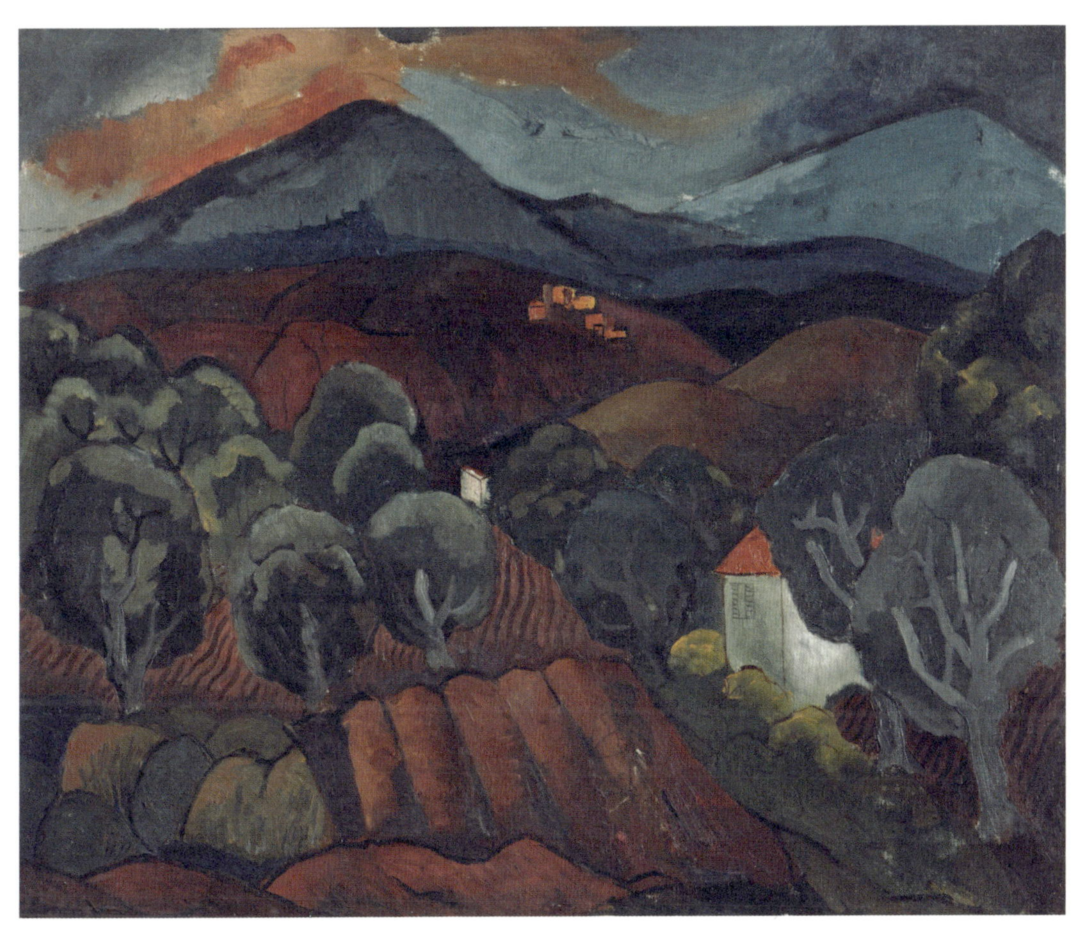

Landscape at Vence, 1927
Oil paint on canvas, 53 × 65 cm
KY00614.EH

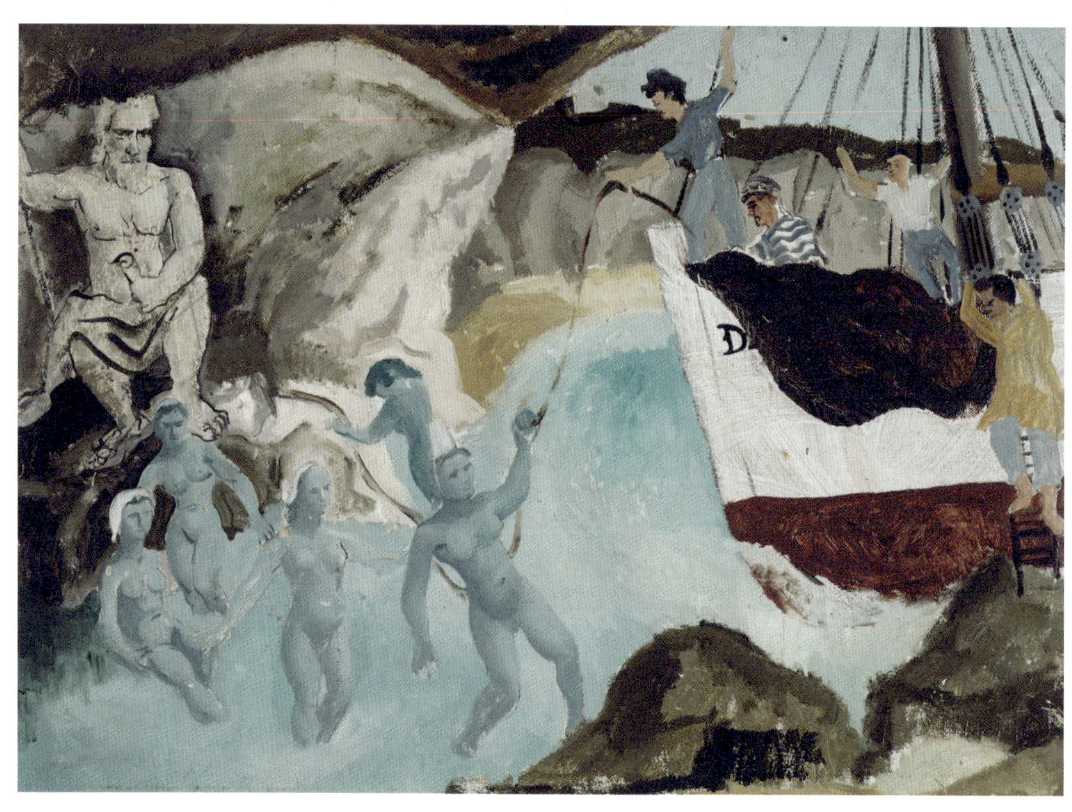

Ulysses and the Sirens (Mermaids), 1929
Oil paint on hardboard, 55 × 79 cm
KY00659.EH

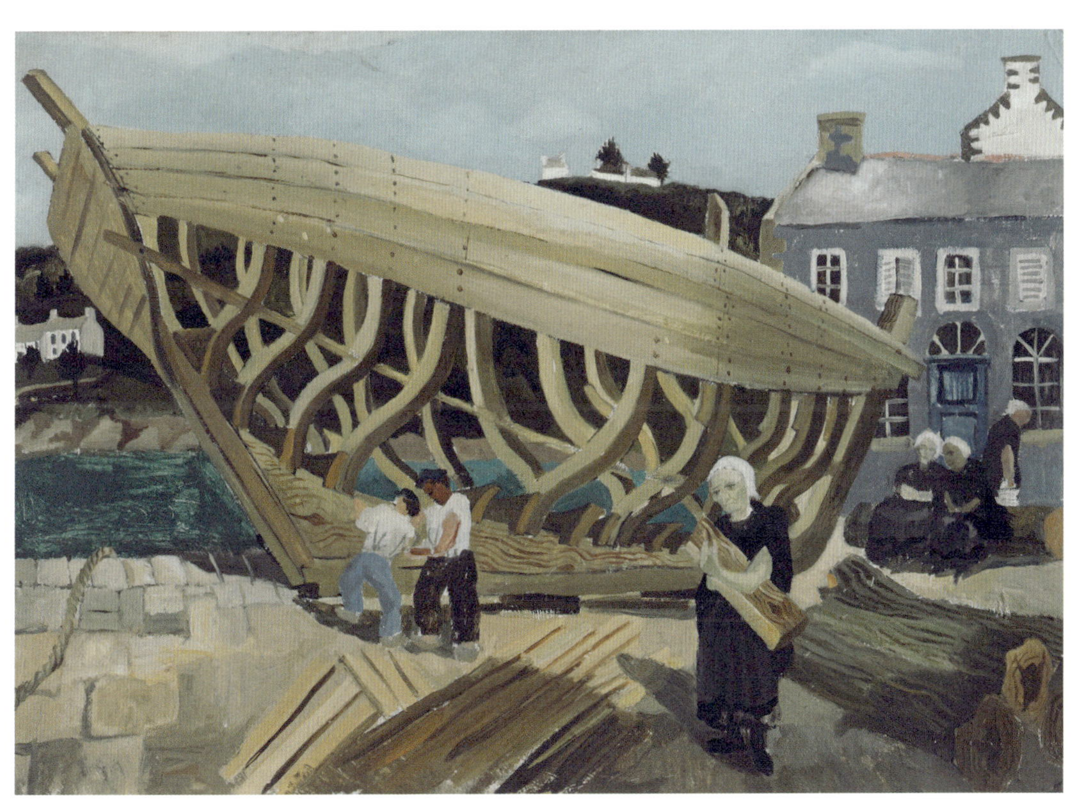

Building the Boat, Tréboul, 1930
Oil paint on board, 56 × 81 cm
KY00630.EH

CREDITS

p. 6 Photographer unknown. Photo courtesy of Mary Adams.
p. 9 © Estate of Elisabeth Vellacott.
p. 10 © Richard Pousette-Dart Foundation.
p. 12 Photographer unknown (possibly Helen Ede). Photo courtesy of Mary Adams.
p. 13 Photographer unknown. Kettle's Yard Archive, Papers of H.S. Ede. KY/EDE/1/11 © Kettle's Yard, University of Cambridge.
p. 14 Photographer unknown. Kettle's Yard Archive, Papers of Elisabeth Vellacott © Estate of Elisabeth Vellacott.
p. 15 Kettle's Yard Archive, Papers of H.S. Ede. KY/EDE/8/2 © Estate of Italo Valenti.
p. 16 (above) Photographer unknown. Kettle's Yard Archive, Papers of H.S. Ede. KY/EDE/1/1 © Estates of Jan and Zoë Ellison.
p. 16 (below) Photographer unknown. Kettle's Yard Archive, Papers of H.S. Ede © Estate of Ovidiu Maitec.
p. 17 Photographer unknown. Kettle's Yard Archive, Papers of H.S. Ede. KY/EDE/1/1 © Jacqueline Benard.
p. 18 © Kettle's Yard, University of Cambridge.
pp. 20, 24, 30, 36, 42, 46, 54, 66, 70, 78, 80, 88, 92, 96, 100, 104, 108, 122, 126, 130, 140, 144, 150, 156, 162, 168, 172, 178, 184, 188, 194, 210 © Gilbert McCarragher. All other images reproduced pp. 18-221 courtesy Kettle's Yard, University of Cambridge. All artworks depicted and texts cited are courtesy of the artists' estates as below. All rights reserved.
pp. 20-23 © Estate of John Blackburn.
pp. 24-29 © 2026 Succession Brâncuși - All rights reserved. ADAGP, Paris and DACS, London.
pp. 30-35 © Estate of Avinash Chandra.
pp. 36-41 © The William G. Congdon Foundation, Milano, Italy congdonfoundation.com.
pp. 42-45 © Estate of Zoë Ellison.
pp. 46-53 The Work of Naum Gabo © Nina & Graham Williams / Tate.
pp. 54-65 Courtesy of Kettle's Yard, University of Cambridge.
pp. 66-69 © Estate of Ian Hamilton Finlay.
pp. 70-77 Barbara Hepworth © Bowness.
pp. 78-79 © 2026 Estate of Roger Hilton. All rights reserved, DACS.
pp. 80-87 images © The Estate of David Jones. All Rights Reserved 2026 / Bridgeman Images; text courtesy of the Estate of David Jones and Faber & Faber Ltd.
pp. 88-91 © Estate of George Kennethson.
pp. 92-95 © Estate of Winston McQuoid.
pp. 96-99 © Estate of Ovidiu Maitec.
pp.100-103 © 2026 Successió Miró / ADAGP, Paris and DACS London.
pp. 104-107 images © 2026 The Henry Moore Foundation. All Rights Reserved, DACS / henry-moore.org; text reproduced courtesy of the Henry Moore Foundation.
pp. 108-121 © Kettle's Yard, University of Cambridge.
pp. 122-125 © Estate of Kate Nicholson.
pp. 126-129 © Estate of Simon Nicholson.
pp. 130-139 © Trustees of Winifred Nicholson.
pp. 140-143 © Estate of David Peace.
pp. 144-149 © Bryan Pearce. All rights reserved 2026.
pp. 150-155 © Richard Pousette-Dart Foundation.
pp. 156-159 © Estate of Lucie Rie.
pp. 160-161 © Estate of Abani Roy.
pp. 162-167 © Estate of William Scott.
pp. 168-171 © The Estate of William Staite Murray. All rights reserved, ACS 2026.
pp. 172-177 © Jacqueline Benard.
pp. 178-183 © Estate of Italo Valenti
pp. 184-187 © 2026 ADAGP, Paris and DACS, London.
pp. 188-193 © Estate of Elisabeth Vellacott
pp. 194-205 Courtesy of Kettle's Yard, University of Cambridge.
pp. 206-209 © Estate of Edward Wolfe
pp. 210-221 Courtesy of Kettle's Yard, University of Cambridge.

Writings throughout by H.S. 'Jim' Ede reproduced courtesy of Mary Adams.

ACKNOWLEDGEMENTS

This book is adapted from an earlier title which included research, transcriptions and translations undertaken by Sebastiano Barassi, Nicola Boden, Matthew Gale, Sarah Glennie and Michael Harrison - first published in 1995 and edited and reprinted with colour photographs in 2009. *Kettle's Yard Art & Artists* preserves most of the archive letters originally published in that book, to which are added additional sections on eleven artists not previously included. Artists' biographies have been newly written, extended and updated. *Kettle's Yard Art & Artists* also includes newly commissioned photographs of the works in our collection by Gilbert McCarragher, as well as recently digitised photographs held in the Kettle's Yard Archive. I express my wholehearted thanks to the artists' estates who have given permission for the texts and images to be reproduced in this book. Their ongoing support for Kettle's Yard is invaluable.

Kettle's Yard Art & Artists is accompanied by a sister publication, the revised *Kettle's Yard House Guidebook*. In the making of both books, we acknowledge the research and writing of previous curators and assistants at Kettle's Yard, without which the current publications could not have been made. For the 2026 *Kettle's Yard Art & Artists*, I am grateful for the patience and skill of the book's designer, Mark El-khatib, to our multi-talented retail and publications manager Laura Pryke for guiding the process, and to our insightful freelance editor Sam McGuire. I would also like to thank our archivist Beth Darbyshire and assistant curator Gabrielle Brasier for their research assistance. Administration & reporting assistant Shikha Dwivedi has been indispensable in picture research and securing image rights and permissions. Thanks also to publications assistants Florence Austin, Heather Boswell, Yasemin Gyford, Katie Maynard and Sid White-Jones.

— Inga Fraser, 2026

KETTLE'S YARD ART & ARTISTS
Published by Kettle's Yard
University of Cambridge, 2026

Kettle's Yard
Castle Street, Cambridge CB3 0AQ
kettlesyard.cam.ac.uk
Director: Andrew Nairne OBE
Assistant Director: Susie Biller
Chair: Sonita Alleyne OBE

Distributed in the UK, Europe and the rest of the world by ACC Art Books
Riverside House, Dock Lane, Melton, Woodbridge, Suffolk IP12 1PE
accartbooks.com

EU Authorised Representative:
Easy Access System Europe -
Mustamäe tee 50, 10621 Tallinn, Estonia
gpsr.requests@easproject.com

Written and edited by Inga Fraser
Copyedited by Sam McGuire
Publication managed by Laura Pryke
Photography by Gilbert McCarragher
Design by Mark El-khatib studio
Printed by Taylor Brothers, Bristol

ISBN 978-1-90456-162-0

Cover: Ben Nicholson,
1927 (apples and pears), 1927
Oil and graphite on canvas, 43.8 × 67.8 cm
© Kettle's Yard

SUPPORT US
Donate or become a member today and help us care for the house and collection, organise exhibitions and engage children, young people and community groups in our work.

Find out more about how you can help:
kettlesyard.cam.ac.uk/join-support/
development@kettlesyard.cam.ac.uk
01223 748100

KETTLE'S YARD

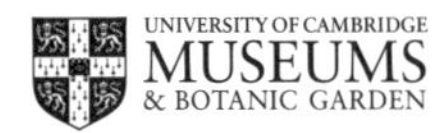

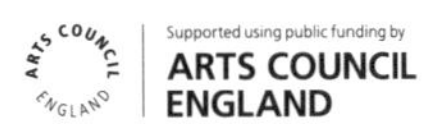

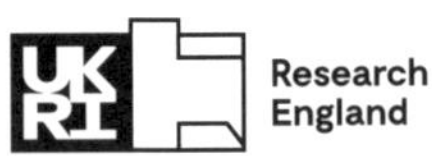